Archipelagoes

Archipelagoes

INSULAR FICTIONS *from*
CHIVALRIC ROMANCE
to the NOVEL

Simone Pinet

University of Minnesota Press
MINNEAPOLIS • LONDON

The University of Minnesota Press gratefully acknowledges financial assistance provided for the publication of this book from the Program for Cultural Cooperation between Spain's Ministry of Culture and United States Universities and from the Hull Memorial Publication Fund of Cornell University.

Portions of the Introduction and chapter 4 appeared previously as "On the Subject of Fiction: Islands and the Emergence of the Novel," in *New Coordinates: Spatial Mappings, National Trajectories*, ed. Robert A. Davidson and Joan Ramon Resina, special issue of *Diacritics* 33, no. 3–4 (2003): 173–87; copyright 2003 by The Johns Hopkins University Press. Portions of chapter 3 appeared previously as "El *Amadís* como arte de marear: La Insola No Fallada," *Medievalia* (2000): 25–34. Portions of chapter 4 appeared previously as "La traducción de lo visible: Un tapiz del *Amadís de Gaula*," in *Los bienes cuando no son comunicados no son bienes*, ed. Axayácatl Campos García Rojas, Mariana Masera, and María Teresa Miaja, 107–17 (Mexico City: Universidad Nacional Autónoma de México–Universidad Autónoma Metropolitana–El Colegio de México, 2006), and also as "The Knight, the Kings, and the Tapestries: The *Amadís* Series," *Revista Canadiense de Estudios Hispánicos* 30, no. 3 (2006): 537–54.

Copyright 2011 by the Regents of the University of Minnesota

All rights reserved. No part of this publication may be reproduced, stored in a retrieval system, or transmitted, in any form or by any means, electronic, mechanical, photocopying, recording, or otherwise, without the prior written permission of the publisher.

Published by the University of Minnesota Press
111 Third Avenue South, Suite 290
Minneapolis, MN 55401-2520
http://www.upress.umn.edu

Library of Congress Cataloging-in-Publication Data

Pinet, Simone.
Archipelagoes : insular fictions from chivalric romance to the novel / Simone Pinet.
p. cm.
Includes bibliographical references and index.
ISBN 978-0-8166-6671-3 (hc : alk. paper) — ISBN 978-0-8166-6672-0 (pbk. : alk. paper)
1. Spanish fiction—Classical period, 1500–1700—History and criticism.
2. Romances, Spanish—History and criticism. 3. Islands in literature.
4. Geography in literature. 5. Cartography in literature. I. Title.
PQ6142.P56 2011
863'.30932—dc22
2010032609

Printed in the United States of America on acid-free paper

The University of Minnesota is an equal-opportunity educator and employer.

17 16 15 14 13 12 11   10 9 8 7 6 5 4 3 2 1

For Bruno

Contents

Acknowledgments ix

INTRODUCTION
Spatial Concepts, Medieval Context xi

1
FOREST TO ISLAND
Sites of Adventure from Arthur to *Amadís* 1

2
ISLANDS AND MAPS
A Very Short History 29

3
ADVENTURE AND ARCHIPELAGO
Amadís de Gaula and the Insular Turn 75

4
SHORES OF FICTION
The Insular Image in *Amadís* and Cervantes 109

CONCLUSION
Archipelagic Possibilities 155

Notes 163
Bibliography 203
Index 223

Acknowledgments

In the process of writing this book I have benefited from institutions whose faculty and resources have made my work a challenge and a pleasure. This project has its roots in a seminar with Francisco Márquez-Villanueva at Harvard University. At home south of the border, as I wrote a seminar paper on *Amadís* over the summer, I wrote him a postcard mimicking chivalric prose, and he was kind enough not to mention it but generously offered his encyclopedic advice. Mary Gaylord prodigiously guided my scattered curiosity through the intricacies of English academic prose and of Cervantine complexity, as she advised me on my dissertation along with Tom Conley, who has since been a constant source of intellectual support, a marvel to read and dine with, and the single most generous academic mind I know. Funding from the Department of Romance Languages and the Real Colegio Complutense allowed me to spend months at the Biblioteca Nacional researching the first materials for my dissertation. Some years later, at Yale, Roberto González Echevarría found time to read a first version of the book, and María Rosa Menocal shared with me her dynamism and vision for the humanities; from their books I have learned humility, for I will never be able to write like them. At Cornell University, the President's Council of Cornell Women and the Humanities Council provided funds for research at the Newberry Library, the Princeton Art Museum, and Houghton Library. I have been fortunate enough to find friends in many colleagues, and I owe heaps of gratitude to Mitchell Greenberg, Jeannine Routier, Timothy Murray, Tim Campbell, Michela Baraldi, Piero Pucci, Renate Ferro, Richard Klein, Cynthia Robinson, Jonathan Culler, Marie-Claire Valois, Luz Horne, Edmundo Paz-Soldán, Brett de Bary, Joan Ramon Resina, and most recently David Cruz, Gerard Aching, and Miguel Balsa for their support.

Over the years I managed to collect accomplices with whom I shared incipient ideas and confusing papers, and who patiently and incisively pointed out gaps in argumentation and writing style, provided references or encouragement, and shared coffee or a beer after one of the many island movies I have seen over these years. I am indebted to their astonishing minds and kind advice: Elisabeth Hodges, Diane Brown, Maurice Samuels, Cristina Moreiras-Menor, Oscar Martín, Lourdes Casas, and Gareth Williams. Readers of the manuscript at different stages, both anonymous and well known, were generous with suggestions, and I am grateful to all; those whose names I know are Ricardo Padrón and Jesús Rodríguez-Velasco. Graduate students asked fundamental questions during seminar discussions; I particularly want to thank Henry Berlin and Sarah Pearce for their curiosity and insight. Finally, I would like to extend my gratitude to a discipline, Hispanomedievalism, which across continents, north to south and east to west, is open to other perspectives and to productive dialogue and is supportive of all of its members; among them, I especially thank Sol-Miguel Prendes, Isidro Rivera, and George Greenia. Across the Atlantic, I thank the brilliant Juan Manuel Cacho Blecua; south of the border, I am indebted to Aurelio González, Axa Campos, and, most recently, the members of the SENC. I thank my parents, Esmeralda Peralta and Mauricio Pinet, and my wonderful grandmother, María Esther Mendizábal, who instilled in me a taste for adventure and taught me how to spend afternoons with books. None are responsible for any errors in this book, which are all my own.

The staff of many libraries shared with me their treasures and expertise. I owe special thanks to the staff in the reserve room of the Biblioteca Nacional de España (which during renovations found me a computer spot at a table and brought me my first Buondelmonti), at the Newberry Library, and at Houghton Library. At the Princeton Art Museum, Maureen McCormick and Betsy Jean Rosasco made a special visit to examine their tapestry possible and productive. At Cornell, Cal Hile and Debra Kastenhuber have seen to it that I can print my long drafts and finance my trips. Finally, I would like to thank Douglas Armato and Richard Morrison at the University of Minnesota Press for believing in this project and Adam Brunner for his help through the editorial process.

This book has benefited from Bruno Bosteels's sharpness of mind and clarity of voice. This book is dedicated to him, and to Lucas and Manu, whom I isolated at times in writing it but never ceased to rely on as sources for wonder.

Introduction

Spatial Concepts, Medieval Context

From Antiquity onward, there exists an inaugural relation between geography and history. Confirmed by the modern era's most famous of cartographers, Abraham Ortelius, or the travel writer Samuel Purchas, who both made of geography the eye of history, however, this well-loved sisterhood often obscures that other intimate relative of geography, literature. Narrative, especially, was for the ancient geographer both a source and a medium of representation, much in the manner that developed again in the Renaissance in what we familiarly know as humanist geography, producing new and surprising overlaps and hybrids. These geographic engagements with literature have been studied extensively, often brilliantly.[1] In relation to Iberia, in particular, the literature of the age of discoveries has received much attention, although until very recently, developments in the discourse and study of the history of cartography had not been part of the discussion, and even less in direct relation to literary genres, aside from the articulations between history and fiction (whether in relation to politics, racism, colonialism, etc.), which have provoked a continuous critical discussion, pointedly in the genres of the chronicle and the *relación*.[2]

People in the Middle Ages were not unaware of these relations between geography, history, and literature, and they elaborated the correlation between these discourses through various established genres or by incorporating them into new formulations. This book seeks to investigate these relations through a particular geography, that of the island, by putting together two specific and well-defined genres of the late medieval period, one pertaining to literature and the other to cartography, in order to assess the import of spatial configuration in narrative fiction of the period. The book of chivalry and the *isolario* or book of islands are coeval: that is, they emerge, develop and fade into history at almost exactly the same time, and crucially, they cross over from manuscript into print culture, bridging and evincing the technological challenges posed to a genre in order to accommodate new media, exploit new features, and address new audiences all the while keeping to a certain tradition and format that made them immensely popular. These two genres, moreover, make a particular geography the focus of their structure: the island.

Islands have a very specific and long tradition in both cartography and literature. The period that I study here, however, is of special interest in this regard because specific genres emerge centering on islands. If island fictions have a continued and prolific tradition to our day, perhaps even more specialized than the book of chivalry itself in the genre of *robinsonnades*, for instance, or in fantastic literature, there is no comparable cartographic genre that emerged to substitute or take up the specific project of the *isolario*. Perhaps its only possible continuation may be traced within prose fiction itself in the numerous maps of imaginary islands that accompany literary works, from Thomas More's *Utopia* to Jules Verne's *L'Île mysterieuse* to Robert Louis Stevenson's *Treasure Island* and the myriad islet fictions that one can associate with them. There, however, the archipelago is lost from sight, and the emphasis on the single, often fantastic island is what prevails. By contrast, it is this fictional openness, fiction's very possibility but also its theory, that is particularly linked to insularity and systematically articulated in the late medieval period in the genres of the book of chivalry and the *isolario*.

In placing the two disciplines of literature and cartography side by side, I want to suggest that the overlaps are not mere coincidences, but historically specific strategies that can be traced to structural concerns. Moreover, their parallel study can be useful to distinguish solutions, problems, and theorizations common to both discourses that can lead to productive discussions in either discipline. Another striking parallel between these two genres, the book of chivalry and the *isolario*, is that they are the immediate forerunners of what can be called the major modern genres of each discipline: the modern novel and the atlas. In the spectrum of possibilities explored, in the many successful and failed attempts at structure or style that book of chivalry and *isolario* present, one might also find, I contend, new perspectives on the anchoring, lacks, and ambitions of both novel and atlas.

This book is thus one that will dwell on geography, understood in a vast sense, to inquire into how a period thought about a space through its writerly elaborations thereof. Focused on the specific space of the island in two parallel texts, the question on the geography of a genre, then, becomes both literal and symbolic, asking about both a structure and a metaphor, about genre and its dissolution. This is, ultimately, a study that aims to reveal something about the culture that produced late medieval and early modern Iberian prose fiction, so its conclusions will be mostly literary, but I hope that whatever connections might be brought out can also be rewarding for cartography.

If one is to consider the relation between islands and fiction, even though historical context alone should suffice to suggest the differences in articulation, one must address the *Odyssey* in some way, for there the entire repertoire for an insular fiction such as the book of chivalry is already present. Narrative, a hero, adventure, marvels, a voyage, islands, and the surrounding sea make up both book of chivalry and the Homeric epic. In the *Odyssey*, however, there is another space of crucial importance that structures the narrative from outside this seascape: the polis, whose historical specificity points to how the different genres elaborate new forms for fiction at different periods.

In the *Odyssey*, the sea implies a return because it is not the Mediterranean but the polis that centralizes space through its spatialization of community. The medieval romance, from which the book of chivalry takes its basic structure and fundamental content, articulates the notion of community and thus of the subject not through the polis but through the court and the possibility of inaugurating new courtly spaces and their corresponding codifications. Beyond the repertoire that romance and Homeric epic (and a host of other ancient and medieval genres) share in the first instance, there is in the *Odyssey* a poetics of fiction, an inaugural articulation of fiction as a necessary and inevitable truth—even separately, through the siren's voices—that links this inaugural insular fiction to my investigations, which have as their object texts and practices contemporary to the rereading and retranslating of Homer in Western Europe and in Spain in particular.[3] One could say that the *Odyssey*, structured in a pendular movement between the polis and the distancing from and eventual return to it, schematizes a basic thread of all narration, and one might even argue that this movement between community and the outside is the structure of fiction itself. What lies beyond (or betwixt), however, are the specific itineraries between those two spaces, marked by distinct historical, economic, and social changes that give shape to a literary genre, a style, a particular work. The emphasis on the space of community or on displacement from it in fact marks two extreme possibilities within this play of spaces. Between them lies the literary text, or, the possibility for fiction.

Texts are, obviously, a space in themselves, in their materiality: the space of the scripted or printed word, the page, the volume itself. But texts also articulate spaces through fabling, that is, in the manner they tell stories: "stories organize places through the displacements they 'describe,'" as in the actual narration of a voyage or a wandering, or in the use of topoi—narrative landscapes. They even do so within rhetoric itself, since metaphors, as Michel de Certeau emphasizes, are a way of "transporting" or displacing meaning.[4] (Henri Lefebvre, the most complex of theorists of space, writing about metaphors and spatiality, proposes textual criticism as a way of bridging the apparent disparity of levels between spaces within narration and narration itself as spatiality.)[5] Spatiality is organized by delimitation, whether related to genre, content, or rhetoric. Stories, according to Certeau, participate in the establishment and the rupture of such delimitations in parallel and intersecting movements that can be represented by the figures of the frontier and the bridge. This, a logic of aporia and overcoming, is labeled by Certeau as "ambiguity" by making the terms reversible, which is to say that the "frontier" can always become a "bridge" and vice versa. They make each other possible in their very opposition; their establishment, in a way, already contains their transgression.[6] The story, then, relies on the spatiality it produces in order to reflect upon itself, upon its own condition of possibility. As such, even if narration has content, "it also belongs to the art of making a *coup*.... Its discourse is characterized more by a way of *exercising itself* than by the thing it indicates. And one must grasp a sense other than what is said. It produces effects, not objects," Certeau insists.[7] This production is what makes the story and allows it to think itself, to become its own theory. It is also what will allow the close analysis of island fictions in this book to move from the representation of insularity in these texts to a theory of insularity in the late medieval and early modern periods, exercising that literary criticism that Lefebvre proposed.

But what is this space where metaphors as means of transposing meaning move about? What use is there in affirming, "every story is a travel story—a spatial practice"? Can this statement be inverted? Are all spatial practices stories? How is one to differentiate among them? Is the analysis of space always an analysis of a story?[8]

This is where a working distinction between space and place becomes necessary for what will follow. "A place (lieu)," writes Certeau, "is the order (of whatever kind) in accord with which elements are distributed in relationships of coexistence. It thus excludes the possibility of two things being in the same location (place).... Place is thus an instantaneous configuration of positions. It implies an indication of stability." Space is something that comes into existence "when one takes into consideration vectors of direction, velocities, and time variables. Thus space is composed of intersections of mobile elements.... Space occurs as the effect produced by the operations that orient it, situate it, temporalize it, and make it function.... In short, space is a practiced place."[9] For the moment, what I wish to retain from Certeau's analysis is that he sees space in an inevitable relationship with a practice that one can take as a synonym for production: the production of space.[10] Such a practice Certeau reads as "rhetoric," a sort of unraveling of the practices of everyday life, such as walking, cooking, narrating. Narrations themselves, "stories," as he calls them, are always a spatial practice by dint of their use of metaphor, a "transposition of meaning."

The classic work on space, Lefebvre's *The Production of Space,* gives a much more detailed and complex historical account of the concept of space. Lefebvre analyzes the expression that titles his book very closely in his second chapter by reworking, from a Marxist perspective, concepts such as labor, product, object, and subject in order to arrive at a definition of social relations of production that sheds new light on the concept of space. He does so by establishing, first, a dividing line between nature and society. However, Lefebvre insists on the presence of "intermediate" spaces that are, at the same time, natural and cultural, immediate and mediate, given and artificial. All such spaces, having nature as a starting point, a "raw material," are produced by the activities that crisscross them, that effect them but that also extend beyond those spaces into other realms, interconnecting human activity—political, economic, technical—and or as the production of space itself.[11]

A produced space, Lefebvre argues, connotes a task of signification, a process that produces space and meaning concurrently, a meaning that must be negotiated by the subjects or members of the particular society that move in and through that space and denotation, and thus "comprehend" them.[12] A critic's task would then be to elucidate the appearance, role, and permanence of spatial codes characteristic of particular practices produced alongside the spaces that correspond to them. Thus, not only the history of space should be studied, but also the history of the representations of space and especially their interconnections, distortions, displacements, and relation with the society or mode of production that gives place to them.

This book will move between these terms, not with an eye on studying a particular verifiable group of islands of the Mediterranean, but so as to assess how "real" insularity is perceived, transformed, and refigured in two disciplines, in order to see how these representations in turn have an effect on any discourse on insularity, whether in science, philosophy, or literature, all the while remembering that spaces and the relations that produce them are continuous and overlapping.

The theory of space, borrowed from Certeau and Lefebvre, provides us with a set of terms and lines of discussion that will be developed in situ in the following chapters. Thus, we shall consider that places, common to all narratives, exist only as abstractions, uncharacterized and unindividualized (or overcharacterized in their refusal to admit difference within them), much like the "community" and the "outside" with which I began this introduction. These places become spaces when they become individualized, when they are practiced, when they are demarcated through history and economy, when they become a genre, a style, a work of fiction. As such, these spaces become essential to the story and how it constructs itself; that is, these spaces are a privileged site for the study of a poetics. Finally, these spaces function in constellations or clusters, in webs of relationships that are both diachronic—as elaborated in literary histories—and synchronic, relations that become visible when one studies the spaces of the text in dialogue with other disciplines or in relationship to itself, to its own constellation of spaces. Before embarking on an overview of the spaces that in romance and cartography lead to the production of insularity in the book of chivalry and the *isolario*, I shall sketch out the basic plot of relations that, for the medieval period, link geography and fiction, thus establishing some general paradigms for medieval space. Then, a swift review of the spatial typologies of medieval fiction provides a diachronic analysis that will lay the ground for a comparative study of insular space in cartography and in the Spanish book of chivalry in ensuing chapters.

HERE AND THERE

Interrogating one of those changes that at a certain point mark a stage, Paul Zumthor asks if the word "modern," coined in 1100, can be in fact sutured to the change or reduction of perspectives to horizontality.[13] A slow displacement of emphasis from the vertical to the horizontal had taken place during the early Middle Ages. Not that this change canceled in any way the vertical—nor had it existed by itself before—but that which structured interpretation was, by the fifteenth century, a series of discourses that had horizontality as their point of departure. From literature to cartography, allegorical interpretations by the late Middle Ages became contested through new, dialectical forms of interpretation.[14]

The discourse on space is perceived as one illustrating the move from verticality to horizontality. To express the idea of space, Romance languages took from Latin the word *locus* and its derivatives for words meaning the emplacement of a determined object: *lugar, lieu, luogho*. *Spatium*, on the other hand, made a late entry into Romanic languages, signifying a topographic or chronologic interval between two determined points. Sebastián de Cobarruvias arranged all of these ideas in his entry on *espacio* in his *Tesoro de la lengua castellana o española* of 1611:

> From the Latin name *spatium, capedo, intervallum;* that is, place. A lot of space, little space. It also means interval of time and we say for the space of so many hours, etc. Space, among musicians, is the interval between one line and another where the figures are placed, some in line, others in space. For something to go slowly or fast. To walk slowly/spacedly. Talk slowly/spacedly, etc. There is no space, there is no time.[15]

Space was, in fact, lived in unison with time: to convey the abstract notion of a limit of time, Isidore of Seville illustrates it with a spatial limit: "Tempora autem momentis, horis, diebus, mensibus, annis, lustris, saeculis, aetatibus dividuntur. Momentum est minimum atque angustissimum tempus, a motu siderum dictum. . . . Hora enim finis est temporis, sicut et ora sunt finis maris, fluviorum, vestimentorum."[16] The emphasis, however, is on a subordination of time to spatial formulations; that is, chronological concepts often find expression in spatial terms. Even today, expressions such as "forward" mean "future" *(más adelante)*, "to leave behind" is to leave in the past *(dejar atrás)*, and in Spanish, the very word *espacio* translates a time *(por espacio de dos años . . .)*. To move *despacio* means to move "slowly," to take more *space* doing it: "Spacious, as movement, one who walks slowly. Spacious time is time that takes long," explains Cobarruvias (s.v. *espacioso*). It was not until the thirteenth century, with the *temps des marchands* (time of merchants), as Jacques Le Goff terms it, that time began to be unsutured from space.[17] These separations, however, took a long time to become pervasive or dominant. Sudden ruptures would not be the rule, perhaps not even until the sixteenth or seventeenth centuries, when the subject as individual took her place as a center. Miguel de Cervantes's *Don Quixote* (1605–15), whose insular geography will be the focus of the last chapter, is a case in point: of the seventy-two times the word *espacio* is used, only seven specifically denote a space. All other occurrences are meant to express a chronology.

Space is, then, in medieval times, an emptiness that must be filled, practiced, given meaning. As such, the concept contrasts with that of place *(lugar)*, which has the richness and stability of a historical given. The place is a characteristic of the object or the one who occupies it. The opposition between space and place entails numerous differences in all aspects of medieval culture, which can be articulated in parallel to the opposition of the same terms argued by Certeau. While a varied mythology corresponded to open spaces, places were so closed and rich in themselves that they could support universal archetypal images, they are literally *commonplaces*. All of these are ultimately, in one way or the other, related to movement, stopping it or urging it on. In between these two possibilities is the idea of limits and their transgression. The concept of the limit, however, is not continuous, but rather reversible: frontier and bridge may designate one and the same thing, as discussed above via Certeau. On the topic of reversibility of limits, Zumthor observes that twelfth- and thirteenth-century writers emphasize such ambiguity through the frequent tracing of frontiers over unstable mediums such as water, making of the risky element an isolating limit but also the possibility of a passage.[18]

The first dividing line is the limit of the body. All grand images of the Middle Ages—man as a microcosm, the mirror, the mystical body of the Church, the social body, the idea itself of a corpus of images of the Middle Ages—point us in the direction of an opposition between the soul—that which escapes representation—and its material container, the ground for all these images. The body was the primary reference for any idea of space. The consciousness of self that makes *I* a microcosm of the world is the expanded formulation of the *hic et nunc,* all the way to a phrase such as "to be beside oneself," *estar fuera de sí,* and others of the sort. The body is an instrument for measuring, as Lefebvre reminded us: cubits, inches, feet; in Spanish *palmos, codos, brazadas,* in common use to this day. The body is thus the source of a language; externalizing the invisible and objectifying experience, it becomes a model for conceptualizing space.[19] Around it and in relation to it, extension, measure, and distance are organized as a system, originating oppositions that entail their own rules and taboos: inside/outside, leading to metaphors of content and container; full/empty, the couple enter/exit, which can also turn into the trio enter/traverse/exit; here/there, which rapidly transforms into close/far and which establishes distinctions going from the private to the public; high/low, which engendered the couple ascent/descent; and left/right. Antiquity preferred laterality, the high Middle Ages, verticality: the high and the low, profundity, elevation. Modernity privileged movement exemplified in behind/in front—a horizontality—a spatialized *progress* that in the idea of development resutures space to time.[20]

The most valued spatial orientations for the Middle Ages, in particular relation with the body, were the high and the inside, ascent and interiorization. With the high were associated life, love, euphoria, the superhuman—the good; height semanticized the idea of rise and fall (Icarus, Babel). Ascension was equated with a will to light, an aspiration of not only physical, but also moral elevation related to sanctity and heroism. With the low were associated demons, death, immorality (*ha caído muy bajo* [he has fallen to low depths]), evil emblematized in sexuality, defecation, and filthiness. Fall, or descent, received its own name, original sin, and signified the temptation of the putrid and the extremely painful.[21] Even though the human body was a measure of the world, it was an ambiguous one. Partially or fully naked, it could trigger different symbolic meanings according to the circumstances. Christianity would favor an emphasis on a negative sign of carnal pleasure, giving a transcendental justification for this condemnation founded both in theology and in the interpretations of Genesis and the first Fathers; and at the same time providing the dominant classes with corresponding behaviors, and vocabulary, definitions that control the body and its signification.[22]

Different examples can be quoted to illustrate this distancing from the body, particularly from the thirteenth century on; for example, variations on dismemberment as criminal punishment, spiritual penance marked in the obligation to perform an auricular confession at least once a year (imposed after the Fourth Lateran Council in 1215), the invention of the fork as a way of distancing the body from the flesh it consumes, the equation between sin and sickness, the use of nightgowns and robes, or the closing down of public baths across Western Europe.[23] This rejection of the flesh had its own spatial consequences visible in the geographic search for purity, the grand symbolic migration to the "desert" that comprehended many "victories" over the body: sexual, nutritional, and so forth. Paradoxically, as we anticipated, the body remained a privileged site for the contact between the spiritual and the material world. Martyrs received the stigmata on their bodies, and sainthood became concrete in the smell of the body of the saint, the *olor a santo*. Visions, though, whether demonic or mystical, would manifest themselves in dreams: that is, in a curious *absence* of the body.

As a translation into Christian terms of Aristotelian categories explained in the *Politics*, man also became, from the material reality of the body, a symbolic reference. Metaphors of the body extended from figures of authority to the idea of community, of collectivity, from the "body of the church" to the "social body," concepts dependent on the reciprocal necessity of their members, on the idea of a publicity of behaviors viewed as performances, and of the strict balance within the community making everyone responsible for all others. As such, the concept of the body is the place where the biological and the social, in fact, meet. This change, in turn, structured "social space," articulating not only geography, but also morality, according to which hierarchies were assigned. Crime would be conceived thus in terms of social space, as a diversion or distortion of it (*yerro, tort*) and even law would be referred to in similar terms, as in the French *droit* or Spanish *derecho*.

In a society that codified everything in the binomes here/there, high/low, it was inevitable that a center/margin opposition would appear. Isidore, in book 5 of his *Etymologies*, defines *exilium*, a form of punishment described by law, as meaning *extra solum* for, indeed, exile is to live outside one's "land," a geographic notion. He further emphasizes the notion of limit by writing that "Vnde postliminium redeuntibus, hoc est de exilio reducendis, qui sunt eiecti in iniuria, id est extra limen patriae" and by distinguishing between deportation, relegation, and proscription.[24] Already in Roman law, different forms of banishment were pointed out, among them the prohibition to live in a given territory, exile assigned in a specific place, or even deportation to an island (*insulae vinculum*), legally ascribing the geography that will occupy us throughout this book to the margins.[25]

Closer, at the limit or *in* the "margin" were outlaws, dissenters, and heretics. Different *mesteres* or tasks were also pushed to live there, such as those specified by the Church Fathers (first of all usurers, then prostitutes and entertainment professionals) or by canon law (performers, prostitutes, procurers; all those having to do with blood, animal meat, or dead bodies; sometimes enchanters, sorcerers, or trash collectors).[26] This thrust to the margins is revealed not only at the level of common practices of law, but in the image itself of a Christian *oikoumenē*. The depiction of this *oikoumenē*, as expressed in the cartography of the period, shows the "civilized or known world" and, in its permeable, flexible margins, monsters, savages, pagans, and infidels, often upon islands.

The space of everyday existence was lived as an intimate system of functions and meanings. But the idea itself of the limit of the "near" or the "here" was unclear: it separated the ego, the body, from the Others, but it served as well as a way of communication with them, and community offers the only idea of coherent identity for medieval culture. The effects of this contradiction of the limit are a general and constant desire to leave or flee the community and to communicate with and appropriate the Other, all in a society that, after the great migrations, placed a high value on its sedentary character.

The "beyond" would eventually stop beckoning as the opposition between the here and there; for, between the fifteenth and the seventeenth centuries, the polarity became one of near and far, highlighting the impact of travel in the production of space. For centuries, however, the beyond was the equivalent of the unknown, a neutral and pure space, undifferentiated, as impermeable to meaning as to the eye. From the thirteenth century on and well into the sixteenth, the beyond begins to be seen less as a static place or time outside and more as the space where something might take place. The *vague* idea of limit is crucial to this conceptual development, as the path, the trail, the way is invested from then on with the meaning of a place in itself. And once a beyond and a trail become existent, a voyage is possible. Traveling becomes a fundamental activity.

The medieval traveler conceived the desire to travel, for the most part, as a desire for knowledge. Tourism is not a word that describes any part of the attitude of the medieval traveler, who saw the journey in terms of a destiny, most of the time related to or aimed at a form of eternity. The concept of the *homo viator* made anyone a potential if not always already a symbolic pilgrim of life.[27] Thus, travel was regarded as a form of the marvelous, responding to an elaboration of the (changing) concept of curiosity.

Specific forms of travel developed after 900, when the large population movements that characterized the first part of the Middle Ages under the name of "barbaric invasions" ceased and pilgrims and crusaders came into being. Similar to the pilgrim, the merchant was, by the thirteenth century, a typical traveler. As images of travelers merged, the merchant's activity was equated by the fifteenth century with that of the conqueror, as in some versions of the figure of Marco Polo. Within pilgrimage, one of the new models that emerged, inspired by Saint Columban, was that of the eternal pilgrim, emulating the life of Jesus in his wandering. This was a pilgrimage inspired by devotion; another kind of pilgrimage was that done for penance, usually taking the pilgrim to the Holy Land, Rome, or Santiago de Compostela. What this penance sought, even if secretly, was a miracle, an instance of the marvelous—a revelation, a vision; but what it most often obtained was a sort of "space therapy."[28] Monks turned pilgrimage into the image of Christian life, and through the complex cultural and religious practices that developed along these roads, space itself became produced in a way by the sacred.

"Christianity" itself would name a space, and not only a community or a set of beliefs, as the expression "leaving Christianity" would denote a form of traveling outside a certain limit, usually that of the Western sea, an image inherited from the Greeks who marked the passage into the alien Ocean with the Pillars or Columns of Hercules, their figuration for the twin rocks that make up the Strait of Gibraltar.[29] The idea of travel itself entailed a sort of marginalization, or at least the risk of marginalization, as the traveler abandoned the community to engage in a reality plagued with the new, another word for the different. The traveler left that limit behind, initiating a movement sutured to spatiality: "That is one of the meanings of errancy: everything that happens has a spatial nature."[30] Those who engaged in travel were suspicious, for they would willingly expose themselves to the dangers inherent therein. Sea travel represented the worst of dangers, as neither the security of a path nor that of a secure ground to walk on was possible. The folklore made up of tales of terror at sea constitute a corpus in the Middle Ages that finds cohesion in later genres such as the *historias trágico-marítimas*, or shipwreck narratives, which were still being recast in eighteenth-century Portugal.[31] André Thevet and especially Jean de Léry in the late sixteenth century record the experience of horror when faced with sea travel, even when they had traveled the seas many times before. Such horror was a literary topos, for sure, but it was also a technical reality. Usually destined to travel within the *mare nostrum*, technology, as is well known, was rudimentary up to the fourteenth century and would not be adequate until the fifteenth century for transatlantic navigation.

Travel had, of course, different signs across the periods, but a constant impulse behind travelers was to encounter the extraordinary: places, beings, phenomena recorded from Antiquity—that is, the traveler wished to find what he in a way already knew about, making of discovery a secondary or even unintentional effect. Among those to be found were all whom medieval society had expelled or at least marginalized from social space, and among the travelers were *clerici vagi*, troubadours, students, members of the new orders, and travelers of all sorts, statuses, origins, and dreams; and all of them produced narrations as individuals or in groups, from first-person accounts to complex collections of stories; travels imaginary and real, mostly both at the same time. For travelogues, in particular, reality remained a flexible term, producing thus a space for fiction paradoxically within and outside the real, supplementing it to give it a meaning—truth—that by itself it cannot provide: "the real has its soft zones, difficult to integrate; truth is less a natural given than the product of discursive rules, in some measure aleatory and subject to the irregularities of history. The discourse of the travelogue is never corroborated—nor can it be—in an immediate way: this is its unique trait, an undeniable kinship with fiction."[32] The travelogue would gradually incorporate a "scientific" methodology, along with a stronger presence of the subject as guarantor of the veracity of its data, but fantasy would keep a hold on the travelogue for all of the Middle Ages. As an example, John Mandeville, for a long time believed to be a real traveler, signed in the beginning of the fourteenth century his well-known imagined journey *Voyage d'outre-mer*. Two centuries later, the anonymous Spanish *Libro del conoscimiento de todos los reinos* incorporates enough verifiable data to have confounded many modern critics. And Marco Polo's *Milione* was taken to be a sack of hilarious lies, being, to modern eyes, the most "realistic" of the lot.

These connections between space and narration through a variety of genres that seem to speak directly to fiction are also present in Arabic literature, which also established a link between the travelogue and the concept of fiction. It identified, at least from the tenth century on, books of travel as an independent genre related to romance: "The word *riḥla* refers to both a journey and to its description. Such descriptions constitute a genre that flourished more than any and served scholarship—geography and cartography—as well as literature. It was capacious enough to include almanacs, calendars, grammars, zodiacs, horoscopes, the occasional map, and all sorts of accounts connected with peregrinations through the Mediterranean and beyond."[33] The *riḥla* is both the journey and its narration, and it had, as did its Christian parallels, a primary impulse in pilgrimage, and welcomed both the everyday and the extraordinary, geography and history and marvels. The medieval imagination would blend those two possibilities, spatiality and literary composition, in a complex generic experimentation that led to various forms of prose fiction. These hybrid genres bear out the varying degrees of the suture of time to space, of history to geography, and to narration as central to that articulation. Perhaps the most famous medieval texts to convey such experimentation in their coupling of traveling and narrating are the fourteenth-century *Riḥla* by Ibn Baṭṭūṭa and Polo's *Devisement du monde* or *Milione*, better known as the book of Marco Polo, which was translated by Rusticiano de Pisa, compiler of the well-known chivalric romance *Meliadus*.

The supernatural, the miraculous, the magical, the verisimilar, the fabulous, the boundless, the strange, and the imaginary that inhabit these narrations coincide in the Middle Ages in one term that encompasses them all: *mirabilia*. The Latin term, meaning "wondrous things or happenings," comes into Spanish as *maraviella*, as in French *marveille*, Old Provençal *meravelha*, or Italian *miraviglia*, "through a—culturally justifiable—semi-learned channel, namely as the folk-religious term of early Christianity par excellence"; however, notes Malkiel, some elements remain unaccounted for, such as "the local products of MIRABILIA cut loose from the core of the MIRARI family, as the meaning of the verb, i.e., of the entire family, drifted more and more in the direction of 'looking' rather than 'wondering,'" with paradigmatic examples in Spanish *maravilla* and *mirar* (linked through *admirar*) and French *merveille* versus *miroir*, a split that increased the distance between the miraculous (*milagro*, orig. *miraglo*) and the marvelous.[34] That distance is emphasized in medieval peninsular texts, separating the Christian supernatural from the magical pagan elements; both sharing procedures but prescribing specific expectations and reactions that ultimately distinguish them from each other.

The main differences between the marvel and the miracle can be said to be differences of (1) origin, (2) hierarchy, and (3) flexibility. That is, marvelous things or happenings have a multiplicity of forces at their origin, while miracles have only one author, God; while etymologically all miracles are marvels, within Christian ideology miracles have a higher power than marvels, which are, of course, subordinated to God—as we will see in the Christianized marvels in *Amadís*.[35] What these two extremes of the term "marvelous" share, in their "irrationality," is that they do not call for an interrogation of their "reality," but rather of their meaning. And, if the marvelous is the literary representation of the supernatural, and the supernatural is at the core of the medieval representation of the world, the interrogation of the meaning of the marvelous constitutes both its reason for eluding Christianization and its necessary gradual absorption into ideology.[36] Ultimately, the Christianized marvelous became assimilated to the miraculous, and the miraculous was not—except *in doubt* of the power of God—to provoke wonder: it is proof, visible proof of God's power. In other words, God's manifestations of power were meant to be *admirable* but not *marvels* in themselves.

Such ambiguity or reversibility of meaning was not limited to content, but could also be seen as an effect of the development of new genres and the production of novel textual spaces in the movements between the oral and the written. In written texts—to which the different materials considered in this study belong historically—the space of writing slowly encroaches on that of the voice, and illumination that of performance or gesture. However, "voice" would be kept in the way of performance, as not only epics but also romances were read out loud in small groups and then discussed.[37] The codex, as opposed to the scroll (papyrus), generates an order, to which the text of the prose romance of the thirteenth and fourteenth centuries refers constantly through adverbs of place: *plus, avant, delante, atrás*; and the space surrounding the text becomes more and more abstract as it becomes more independent of a performer, a reader, or an interpreter. In this process, Zumthor distinguishes two new kinds of stories not destined to be sung. The first generally produces a moral meaning and is constructed on an action progressing in a linear fashion, according to a predictable causality, sometimes even making the whole story depend on the last link in a narrative concatenation. In the second variety, meaning is above all historical. Here action is developed from within, sometimes in bifurcations and alternations that contrast with the linearity of language. A sense of ambiguity is present, and the unpredictable dominates. This structural chance, this hazard that is built into narration produces the space of the marvelous in chivalric romance that will, in Spain, produce a geography of its own: the island.

In these brief reflections, the insular has come up in the context of margins, of limits, of cartography and juridical discourse, as a space produced in reality and in fiction. The location of islands at these limits of the imagination or representation makes them especially prone to links with the marvelous as a specific development in the medieval period, as will be detailed in later chapters. It is time to define precisely, though, what we mean here by "island." In his *Etymologies*, Isidore confirms the commonly accepted suggestion of Latin authors, who "suggested that *insula* evolved from the preposition *in-* plus 'salt,' as if it referred to the sea water," even if river islands were commonly accepted as following this denomination as well. In Latin, moreover, *insula* "was used, according to Paulus Festus, to indicate a 'block,' a group of buildings, given the similarity between this and those lands *quae in fluminibus ac mari eminent suntque in salo*."[38] We know that in late Antiquity the Latin *insula* could also be used to designate the "temple," underlining the architectural element along with a religious or at least ritual one.[39] The *Diccionario de la Real Academia Española* defines island in purely geographical terms as a "portion of land surrounded by water on all sides." The recurrent problem of the *size* of that portion of land is, however, not resolved. While I study here only literary *geographical* islands, in reading the primary texts I consider all of the connotations given to *insula* in Latin, that is, a fragment of land surrounded by water, the idea of architecture implied in *insula* as a block of buildings, and the connection to a religious practice or to a divinity in the meaning of *insula* as temple.[40]

Medieval and Modern

In the preceding introductory remarks I have argued for the study of space as produced space, closely following Lefebvre's seminal study and grounding it specifically in a series of practices in late medieval and early modern literature. Lefebvre's theory undergirds this book, complemented by Certeau's concept of practiced or lived space, and especially by his insights into the spatial poetics of movement, of the relations between linguistic operations and the traversing of space as it is produced. Thus, Lefebvre and Certeau offer the medievalist complementary concepts to analyze discursive practices of space. This conceptual articulation structures my argument, with the important addition of Zumthor, whose notions of medieval poetics are historicized in spatial terms in *La Mesure du monde*. This conceptual frame is necessary to understand the particular focus of the book. This book means to study space by itself, as separate from a temporality that often occludes it through concepts such as Bertrand Russell's chronogeography or the much hailed Bakhtinian chronotope, concepts that curiously impose a temporal component to the topos, a traditional spatial concept in poetics, and, more insidiously, invest the temporal with a hierarchy through notions of progress or development. While their functionality may be out of the question for other types of analysis, this book, in part, seeks to turn on their heads the many assessments and conclusions that are derived from such subordinations of space to time. That is why the book will return to questions of the relation between space and time, but space will be shown to be the determining feature of the different genres that will be discussed here, in the terms that have been presented: space as produced and practiced, therefore specific to a society or community, and open to historicization in its transformation. As the book argues for a close link between the production of insularity in literary and cartographic discourses, and in turn between these and the development of a new way of interrogating the real through fiction, this study is also a reflection on the cultural relations between fiction and space.

Taking as a starting point Jacques Lacan's statement that "fiction presents itself in/as a structure of truth,"[41] this book ultimately seeks to present these late medieval and early modern texts to the reader as uncommonly "modern." That is, the texts studied here will be analyzed to show how their fictive qualities—especially through the spatiality they articulate—produce meaning or truth at the level of politics, ethics, poetics, and so forth. This function of fiction, theorized in a way in *Amadís* through its archipelago, is not exclusive to books of chivalry, but sits at the origins of Castilian prose fiction itself, intimately tied to translation (in a sense, translation as political practice, as exercised by Alfonso X), and to the developments of historiography. These often coincide, as in the rewriting of Trojan materials, but techniques and contents also originate in works that deal with changing mentalities, such as the crusading idea emphasized in the court of Sancho IV. Such transformations are visible in texts that evolve through the expectations of different periods, monarchs, and courts, as the compilation known as *Gran Conquista de Ultramar* (a pilgrimage account), whose last textual evolution, following the death of Sancho IV, focused on the section called the *Estoria del Cavallero del Çisne*, highlighting chivalric fiction.

Fiction, defined simply by Fernando Gómez Redondo as the process of invention and construction of reality in a way that is similar to that of the receptor, bears the mark of the particular courtly setting that produced it and its evolving goals; it thus is similar to the way Barbara Fuchs defines romance as strategy in *Romance*. Medieval literature has many terms to address fiction of various lengths and structures—*cuento, fabliella, exemplo, fazaña, estoria,* and, of course, *romance,* which can denominate both prose and verse texts of diverse content, as well as the ballad. Literary historians and critics have more or less generally of late coincided in adopting, with some caution, the term "romance" as a classificatory label, both due to its medieval self-referentiality and its general connotation of fiction. Chivalric fiction thus encompasses a variety of genres, particularly short fiction, Arthurian romances and their relatives, and books of chivalry. *Amadís,* as the first book of chivalry—which is the term the genre was known by—is also a "romance," even if the term "book of chivalry" will be used in this book to denote Spanish chivalric prose fiction specifically.[42] Fiction, as a general marker of medieval Spanish literature—widely used in hispanomedievalism, especially to refer to sentimental and chivalric texts—will, in a sense, be used here in the same transgeneric way that Barbara Fuchs uses romance.[43]

Prose fiction in general, however, is further linked to the construction of certain behaviors, apt for particular social situations. For Gómez Redondo, this is the reason why the translations of the *Kalila,* the *Sendebar,* or the *Escala de Mahoma* were necessary; that is, they were key to the formation of a courtly ideology while constituting *at the same time* the origins of Castilian prose fiction. Gómez Redondo in fact argues that the translation of these texts "under the guise of fiction" allowed Alfonso X to disseminate knowledge about Islamic culture, knowledge used as political instrument."[44] As a working definition of the book of chivalry in this book, I would like to bring together Fuchs's definition of romance as strategy, that is, a definition that comes from a structure related to narrative delay and digression as form, and so forth, with Gómez Redondo's emphasis on prose fiction as the construction of behaviors, where the links with politics and ethics are visible.[45] Thus, the implications of finding a theory of fiction in the production of archipelagoes seem clearer.

While the arguments for opposing fiction, and especially chivalric fiction, to truth are contemporary to the book of chivalry, this book will seek to displace this often-repeated opposition by working with the truth of the book of chivalry itself. In a way, the "modernity" of the book of chivalry that will be argued here will not be one based on content, but one that will suggest that the insular structure of *Amadís* offers a theory of fiction in relation to truth that can be paralleled to contemporary thought. Reconsiderations of fiction in relation to truth are not openly stated for the most part in contemporary thought, though in theory, of course, someone from the position of psychoanalysis will always consider fiction in relation to truth, in the form of fantasy at least. As fantasy, fiction is not only a way of having access to the real (as in the analytical process), but also a way of living or dealing with, as a means of protecting, or of harboring, oneself from the onslaught of the real. Slavoj Žižek, in *The Plague of Fantasies,* wavers between these two positions: a commonplace negative one and a glittering positive one, presenting fiction as a condition for the real that, however, almost inevitably retreats to the idea of fantasy as a shelter from the truth, thus once again opposing the two terms.

Lacan's phrase, cited above, can serve as paradigm of such alternating positions. His phrase is ambiguous, supporting at least two immediate interpretations. The first is the popular pejorative connotation of fiction. Alain Badiou, in his *Peut-on penser la politique?* discusses fiction, in terms of politics, as something that constitutes a sort of frame in which truth makes a hole. Fiction here, following Lacan, is for Badiou a fixed object, with clear delimitations and a consistency that allows one to see where fiction is and where it has ceased to be. Badiou plays with the term *fixion* to mean not only fiction but also its rigidity, and one can further read into the word game an allusion to fiction as fixation, to its obsessive traits. In terms of politics, his immediate interest in that book, Badiou terms the social as that fiction in which politics irrupts, literally breaking the fiction of the social bond.[46]

Later in his work, in pivotal arguments on truth in *L'Etre et l'événement,* Badiou will revise his stance on the relation between fiction and truth. Here he presents two variations: hypothetical reasoning and reasoning through the absurd. The first of these operations works as follows: one can "make the hypothesis" from a statement A, which could very well be false, in order to draw a conclusion B and then conclude on the truth of the implication A—B (which does not, nonetheless, confirm in any way the hypothetical truth of A). Badiou will call this a "fictive" or "fictional" situation. It is on the passage through non-being, across an assertion that could very well be false, that truth is found.[47]

The second variation, reasoning through the absurd, follows apparently the same steps, but here, reason does not know where it wants to go, it does not know B. It is a stake, a leap that does not know where it will fall, or how the situation might be changed. Here, fiction works as a *supplement* that acts as mediation to truth. To refer to fiction, the vocabulary Badiou employs is that of spatiality.[48] Fiction is characterized as a space that allows movement: "One of the most powerful resources of ontological fidelity is found thus to be the capacity to move in adjacent fictive situations, obtained through axiomatic supplementation." This movement into the fictional is described as particularly attractive because of its *adventurous* character, its freedom, and its *uncertainty*.[49] Central to Badiou's argument here are not only the invocation of the absurd, which I will suggest is related to Alonso López Pinciano's characterization of the chivalric as nonsense *(disparates)* in chapter 3, along with Félix Lope de Vega's characterization of cartographic imagination in *El Nuevo Mundo descubierto por Cristóbal Colón*, but also the emphasis on the portrayal of fiction as a space. The relations between contemporary theory's elaborations on fiction also coincide with the book of chivalry's nuancing of the movement into fiction as being something tied to adventure and to chance. The production of truths, then, in the thought of Badiou, is tied to a space of fiction that has adventure and uncertainty at its core, much as the book of chivalry's structural production of insularity.

Further developing this idea of fiction as a supplementary space allowing for hypotheses from which to draw conclusions on truth, Badiou contrasts this type of reasoning (both *hypothetical* and *reasoning through the absurd*), which he calls apagogic reasoning, to constructive reasoning. While constructive reasoning goes from statement to statement toward another statement it has deemed its objective to establish, without retreating from the law of presentation, apagogic reasoning

> installs from the start the fiction of a situation, which it supposes incoherent, just to the point that such incoherence is manifest, in the hazard of a statement that contradicts an already established result. This difference is less close to the employment of a double negation than to a strategic quality made up on one side of assurance and internal wisdom to the order, and on the other of adventurous peregrination into disorder. . . . This combination of

zealous fidelity and of the hazardousness of the encounter, of the precision of the rule and the consciousness of the nullity of its place of exercise is the most striking trait of the procedure. Reasoning through the absurd is that which is most militant in the conceptual strategies of the science of being as being.[50]

As truth is something that always completely transforms the situation, this truth exists outside of the initial situation in its entirety, thus seeming absurd. Reasoning through the absurd requires considering this fiction *as if it were already part* of the situation. Badiou calls this a *generic extension of the situation*, which goes against the historical as the objectively given. Truth is that which is supernumerary with respect to the situation, which exceeds it. That excess, that outside space, such absurdity is, clearly, the realm of fiction. A generic extension of the situation is the consideration of such space, that of fiction (or the indiscernible), as already a part of the situation, as internal to it. Badiou is aware that he is calling here for a language to name the unnamable, a language that shall name without doing so; suggest something's existence without stating what *it* is.[51] In considering this fiction as intrinsic to the situation, thus in fact *changing* the situation, truth will be forced onto it in a procedure that Badiou calls torsion, or *forçage*, transforming the knowledge itself of that situation.

This type of reasoning, whether in its hypothetical or in its version as a reasoning through the absurd, is present at the core itself of chivalric romance in the conjugation between insularity and the chivalric concept of adventure. In fact, I believe it is precisely this philosophical (and conversely political and obviously literary) element that Miguel de Cervantes points to in his metaphorization of the space of the chivalric island in the *Ínsula Barataria* episode. Insularity, I claim, functions as a hinge between these two variations of reasoning, hypothesis and the absurd as elaborated by Badiou in his thought on the event, that enable truths.

The analysis of the spatialization of adventure, forged in the romances of Chrétien de Troyes and refunctionalized in the Spanish book of chivalry as insularity, conveys a series of elements that overlap with apagogic reasoning as explained by Badiou. In both, the element of uncertainty is key, and notions such as peregrination, an implied militancy, the incorporation of a "beyond" into the situation as if it were already part of it, play a fundamental role.[52] Even the idea of a future past of the event, conjugated into the etymology of adventure seems to mirror Badiou's concept of generic extension. As concept and as structure, adventure builds itself in its own action, its "happening," in its projecting itself not only in a future past but also onto a space and a conscience, ordered to the beat of what Zumthor in his *Essai de poétique médiévale* calls "lieux rythmiques" ("rhythmic places"). These places, which are crucial to the development of the Spanish book of chivalry, were islands. In the diatribe against the genre, islands summed up the elements of the marvelous adventure and came to signify fiction itself. As fiction, in its philosophical connotations as elaborated in the philosophy of Badiou, a study of insular episodes puts into perspective not only the literary solutions that work out the distancing between fiction and reality, but the political implications of spatiality in literature.

Through the increasing process of metaphorization, Cervantes, I will argue in the last chapter, seeks to emphasize not (or not merely) geography, not even politics, perhaps not the story itself. What is underscored, from the separation of protagonists to Sancho's arguable failure to govern, is precisely the subject that has been in the works: Sancho himself. In the reformulation of the insular model, provided by *Amadís de Gaula*, Barataria is the place for a change in linguistic register as a characterizing trait of Sancho. It is his language, his capacity for naming that stands out. Such language, in Badiou's terms, is what allows a subject to approach truth by making hypotheses on it that, in the end, are hypotheses on the subject itself:

> that which makes use of names to hypothesize on truth. But, as the subject itself is a finished configuration of the generic procedure from which results a truth, we can well say that a subject makes use of name to make hypotheses on itself, "itself" meaning the infinite where it is the end [*fini*]. Language is here the fixed order where a finitude turns to suppose, under the condition of the infinite it effects, a referent to come. It is the being itself of truth, in the combination of finished inquiries and the future past of a generic infinity.[53]

Within the Cervantine text itself this *ínsula* is already a metaphor; it has already been displaced from geography to a space in discourse, a function. As both a thematic island and an "island of style," the island serves as a figure for a new kind of structure, and for a complex kind of *amplificatio* that suggests a new form for the novel. In the displacement, what is revealed is the subject making hypotheses on truth, which are hypotheses on the subject itself: Sancho has been forced to consider himself.

This book will thus assess the production of insularity in two disciplines that are closely related and that share operations that illuminate the ways each other works, and how a specific period sought through the production of insular spaces to solve different problems of poetics and politics, of ethics and the articulation of fiction and truth. These two disciplines are cartography and chivalric romance, which from the second half of the thirteenth century undergo tremendous changes and a continued process of recreation. Islands figure in both disciplines as particularly malleable, but by the fifteenth century they will acquire specific meanings and thus configure specific genres in both disciplines in what I call an "insular turn," *isolarii* in cartography and books of chivalry in romance. The life of these genres is also parallel, as they come to a peak in the sixteenth century only to dwindle by the seventeenth century and disappear as a new genre takes center stage. The emergence of these new genres, the atlas and the novel, is intimately tied to the production of insularity in the *isolario* and the book of chivalry, for it is precisely the poetic extension of such an "insular turn" that makes these new totalizing mirror genres, atlas and novel, possible.

The conceptual framework anticipated here is used throughout the book to analyze space to first survey the production of insular spaces in medieval literature, progressively focusing on romance and specifically on Spanish medieval literature. The second chapter of the book is devoted to islands in medieval cartography and the emergence of the genre of the *isolario*. A series of theses on islands follow a close analysis of Christophoro Buondelmonti's text, which draws parallels with developments in narrative and shows how useful a comparable discipline such as cartography might be for the study of literature. Following the case study of Buondelmonti's *isolario*, the third chapter exercises close readings of three insular cases in the *Amadís de Gaula*, the first and most important of books of chivalry, where archipelagic narrative structure is presented as a model for Iberian prose fiction. The episodic structure of the archipelago in *Amadís* is studied in the last chapter through visual representations of the book's insularity, both through woodcuts and engravings and tapestries, showing how the concept of insularity is transformed, and metaphorized. This process, reworked by Cervantes in the *Ínsula Barataria* episode in the second part of the *Quixote*, is the focus of the last part of this chapter, looking at how the space of the island, a *topos* of the book of chivalry, is driven in *Don Quixote* back again into language from geography in a doubling of its commonplace status, parading self-consciousness, the independence of linguistic creation, and voiding the archipelagic structure of the book of chivalry from any geography to keep only its skeleton, its framing capabilities, laying bare fiction's thrust to truth.

The conclusions go back to the potential of the archipelagic in *Amadís* to emphasize the theoretical possibilities that the insular provides and that can perhaps be recovered through literary criticism. Badiou's reflections on fiction are here recalled to elicit and exemplify at the same time the productive notions of truth and fiction that can be drawn out of the insular model in the book of chivalry.

1

FOREST TO ISLAND
Sites of Adventure from Arthur to *Amadís*

> It also occurred to him that the generations of men, throughout recorded time, have always told and retold two stories—that of a lost ship which searches the Mediterranean seas for a dearly loved island, and that of a god who is crucified on Golgotha.
>
> —JORGE LUIS BORGES, *The Gospel According to Mark*

Medieval romance stems out from the articulation of two traditions, that of *chanson de geste* and that of historiography, the latter not at all new, as its origins are much more ancient and scholarly, but which gained renewed importance due to the series of developments that characterize the confluence of phenomena we have come to know as the Renaissance of the twelfth century.[1] The coexistence of epic and romance established a difference between the genres based on the social function they represented: collective versus individual; a complex set of situations versus the singular event; society versus one man.[2] Both participated in truth but for different reasons: epic drew its truth from the collective memory it articulated, while romance drew it from fiction to codify present behaviors and relations, for no romance dating before the fifteenth century was built on "lived experience," its threads derived from poetry itself and were anchored in tradition, even in the composition of historical subjects.

"Types" or styles of romance, those narrating themes from Antiquity *(roman d'Antiquité)* and Arthurian romance, shared a confrontation with epic. Within romance itself, the matter of Britain developed a prestige and popularity that came to dominate the *roman d'Antiquité* until the novel came into being. Arthurian romance managed to do this because it fulfilled three tasks: in relation to history, it anchored the meaning of a past and made an allegorical interpretation possible; it created narrative unity by designating a place of origin and destiny, allowing for the development of stories according to the structure of the voyage or the quest; and it created the frame not only for Arthurian romance but for virtually every romance that came after it. The story was not built on a traditional formula or a character but was due, as Erich Auerbach pointed out, to a "dynamic syntax," in the projection into the future of a present in order to contrast, to compare, and, thus, to extract meaning from this overlap.[3] This projection bears the name of adventure.

Adventure takes us back, first of all, to the two-fold nature of romance as it is determined by the tension between love and war. The text is simultaneously built in relation to these two levels, linked spatially through alternation: that is, love and war have a metonymic link, not a metaphoric one, thus the action is a series not of developments but of mirrored situations. In the words of Erich Köhler, adventure—in this specular form—is the means by which the contradiction between the ideal of life and real life is overcome: "Romance idealizes adventure and thereby gives it a moral value, dissociates it from its concrete origin and situates it in the center of an imaginary feudal world in which the community of interests between the different layers of nobility, which belong already to the past, seems still achievable."[4] In a more recent overview of the category of romance, Fuchs, following Cesare Segre, substitutes war for adventure, making the opposition one between eros and chivalry.[5] Adventure, however, is always implicit in the love encounters that may occur inside or outside the court, and the chivalric includes a skillful handling of eros as part of the knight's social identity, as it is indeed part of his heroism. A much larger structuring function, adventure works both at the level of narrative construction, and as the conceptual thrust of romance.

The rise of romance partook of a certain "atmosphere" in which monastic practices, new approaches to historiography, and a certain taste for popular culture, already mentioned, all became part of a movement of which the advent of prose would be one of the last effects.[6] The rapid spread of prose can be related to the different tendencies—didactic, moralizing, allegorizing—that, from the thirteenth century on, prevailed on the European continent and, remarkably early on in Spain, aimed at the constitution of a notion of "belonging," citizenship, or community through vernacular languages, as espoused by Alfonso X.[7] But by the second half of the thirteenth century, common procedures of the romance, such as interlacing, began to be abandoned in these circles in favor of others more appropriate to new needs of expression, whether it be causality, interiority, development, or other procedures. A change in form such as this had a radical effect on romance, in particular on the notion of adventure. Adventure became the sign either of a stage completed or of a moral quality. In any case, it became the sign of something else. As a sign for *another* thing, allegory became its natural companion, and the development of other generic forms, related to romance, such as sentimental fiction, bear witness to this. The metonymic became metaphorical in the most radical sense: it was driven into the long metaphor of allegory. In allegory, characters, actions, and interpretations were systematized and then formalized in such a tight structure that the unpredictable—the marvelous—could no longer take place in it.

Arthurian romance entered Iberia before the advent of prose, by way of Occitan troubadour poetry in the late twelfth century that introduced names and themes that permeated historiography. Geoffrey of Monmouth constituted an important historical source, but it would not be until a century later that the first translations, now in prose, of the Post-Vulgate trilogy, also known as the Pseudo-Boron, would circulate. Translated by Juan Vivas, a cleric, probably first into Portuguese at the end of the thirteenth century, from here on the fragments and versions multiply into the many Iberian romance languages.[8]

Of the later extant fragments and manuscripts, most from the fifteenth century, those based on the Post-Vulgate seem to prefer the second and third branches both in Portuguese and Castilian, summarizing and interpreting the first branch—the *Estoire*, translated as the *Libro de Josep de Abarimatia*—in terms almost exclusively limited to conversion, and articulating the structure of chivalric adventure from the other two—*Merlin* and the *Queste*, translated as *Demanda do Santo Graal* in Portuguese and as *Lançarote* in Castilian. By the fourteenth century, as Gómez Redondo notes, not only the vernacular languages of Iberia, but courtly communities themselves were able not only to interpret and appropriate the complex codifications of culture within chivalric fiction, but also capable of producing their own, as the *Çifar*, or more expertly, *Amadís*.[9]

Chivalric romance founded its action in the enterprise of its hero and was frequently framed in the quest, a type of journey that, by the testimony of extant manuscripts, interested Iberian audiences in particular.[10] The story begins in a community from which the hero is suddenly summoned to leave by an unforeseen situation, a situation that reveals the absence of an object or person that must be recuperated. Upon the completion of this quest, the reentry into the community reinstates the lost order. In his quest, the knight—on horseback, armored, and ready—travels the world from combat to combat, a task marked by chance and characterized by unpredictability. This unpredictability is the definition of adventure, which, in turn, effects a sort of causality, as the adventure provokes the quest and the quest is the guarantor of the existence of an adventure. Chrétien de Troyes and other writers of romances after him gave adventure the specific meaning of a *trial* inscribed in a series of trials, which produces the sense of a progress, not only spatial but also spiritual and moral, toward a stage of perfection that will allow the knight to restore order in society.[11] Duration is inevitably linked to this contrived unpredictability. Instability constitutes in this sense an essential order of the romance, founding its structure.[12] This precariousness was to be intimately associated, even made synonymous with the marvelous. All variations of the marvelous are present in the romance, from the fantasies of the Orient to Celtic folklore, bestiary traditions, tales of travelers, and popular stories. Erich Auerbach called these elements a "magical atmosphere," an "enchanted world" that the critic saw as having no function beyond signaling the distance the romance has with its social, economic, and political reality, and finds its origins in folklore.[13] These marvelous or fictional elements were alternately, according to Auerbach, a result of a feudal *ethos* that did not make sense anymore, an interiorization of knightly ideals and the substitution of *vassalage* for *courtesy*, thus preventing the entire courtly romance from representing historical reality in its depth and complexity; for Fredric Jameson, these elements are associated with evil, if he emphasizes the changing ideologies that take romance and adapt it to their own political and literary needs.[14]

In a chapter devoted to the concept of adventure within a study of the Grail cycles, Joan Ramon Resina remarks upon the same episode in *Yvain* as Auerbach, picking up on the spatial and moral dimensions of the concept of adventure. In regard to marvelous elements, Resina remarks instead that their function is quite practical, in the sense that these motifs point to their existence in the world as experienced by the author, and remarks that such marvels have a particular relation to language, that of namelessness. As interstices of the natural world, language fails to capture their meaning in description. For Resina, language comes into play only *after* the event, succumbing to its temporal limitations, while adventure must leave its meaning to an "act in the future, ignored; a sort of creative potential that nothingness possesses,"[15] leaving all of the determinations up to the subject undertaking the adventure and (un)naming the event that will have taken place. If, as Resina notes, the Grail cycles suffocated the unpredictability of adventure, this was not the case for all chivalric fiction. The productivity of a notion of adventure linked to hazardousness, to unpredictability, to an event that can transform a given situation to render it anew is enacted in Iberian chivalric romances such as *Amadís* where adventure, in terms of a subject, signals a work of self-transformation.[16]

By the thirteenth century the chivalric was an institution, the knight's lifestyle considered prestigious, and his prestige anchored in the mythical court of Arthur. The character entered the popular imagination as a mediator between the chaos of social life and an ideal order, and the space traveled by the knight, even if not completely interiorized, became symbolic of a domination, which can be related to cartographic procedures, made possible through its traversing.[17] Adventure, as the core component of chivalric romance, and as the defining action of the knight, imbricated with the marvelous, built itself within the romance in its own action, its "happening," in its projecting itself not only in a future but also onto a space and a conscience, articulating the figure of a subject.

Marvels

Discussions of the marvelous in romance often return to questions of verisimilitude. This preoccupation with levels of "truth value" in the romance is linked at the onset to the parallel development of historiography. Both romance and history develop new strengths in the expression of temporality, of the role of the past and the future in the articulation of a narrative, and their common origin results in many contacts, contaminations, and confusions. Historiography does not differentiate itself from romance except in the composition of the whole, whereas techniques, rules, procedures, and even the means are the same.[18] Spatiality, however, is differentiated within the genres, especially in its associations with the marvelous. While historiography concerned itself mainly with the production of spaces of sovereignty, the concerns of romance, while not excluding questions of nobility, genealogy, and courtesy, all related to sovereignty, were more diverse and included institutions, communities, and polities, figured through different instances of the marvelous.

Reflection on the marvelous had been intrinsic to juridical thought for a long time, especially in its relation to the miraculous. Alfonso X, the Learned King, in his ambitious legal project *Las siete partidas*, defined miracle as follows:

> A miracle, that is to say a marvelous work of God, surpasses what is done by Nature every day, and for this reason it does not often occur. That it may be accepted as true it must possess four things in itself: first, it must come through the power of God, and not through craft; second, the miracle must be contrary to the laws of Nature, for under other circumstances men would not marvel at it; third, it must be produced by reason of the merits of the sanctity and excellence of him by whose instrumentality God performs it; fourth, the miracle must relate to something which may tend to the confirmation of the Faith.[19]

While in the previous law he clarifies that

> This power is peculiarly that of God, and when it is manifested by Him the act is called a miracle, because when it happens it is a marvelous thing both to men and nations; and this is the case because nations see every day the acts of Nature and therefore when anything is done contrary to her laws, they wonder from whence it is derived, and especially when it takes place rarely; for then they marvel at it as something new and strange; and of this the wise man spoke, and with reason said: "A miracle is something which we see but do not know whence it comes."[20]

As we can see in Alfonso's definition, everything wonderful that had to do with the body, with physical materiality, particularly that of human beings and especially that which expressed bodily desires or fears, was usually interpreted as a marvel of nature. From the classification of deformations in Isidore's *Etymologies*, all the way to Hieronymus Bosch's corporeal composites, medieval representations attest to the intimacy of the marvelous and humanity. For there is humanity in cynocephali, cyclopes, hermaphrodites, and Amazons: their difference is primarily explained by the space—far away, different—they occupy.[21] Continuously rewriting the classical tradition of the marvel-collection,[22] the monstrous was to be catalogued incessantly from the third century on, in treatises such as the *Liber monstruorum de diversis generibus* (sixth century), or Thomas de Cantimpré's *De natura rerum* (1240), to name two of the most successful. From Ramon Llull's *Felix* or *Llibre de meravelles* (ca. 1310) to ordinary travelogues, no work with an encyclopedic pretense failed to address such matters.[23] Definitions of these beings tended toward moralization, as the body, as we have seen, was perceived to have a correspondence with the cosmos. Although the belief in monstrous races diminishes with knowledge from travels and the critical spirit of the thirteenth century, the fascination they provoked did not disappear, and would return, if transformed, in the sixteenth century, where the most eloquent testimony is provided by Ambroise Paré's *Des monstres et prodiges* of 1573.[24]

The relationship between monstrosity and the marvelous, as well as that between the admirable and the marvelous, points directly to the question of wonder. Wonder in the medieval and the early modern world has been recently studied from the perspective of the history of science, in particular, by Mary B. Campbell in *Wonder and Science,* and by Katharine Park and Lorraine Daston in their account spanning from medieval times to the eighteenth century, *Wonder and the Order of Nature.* The latter especially is quite critical of Le Goff's ideas on the marvelous due to their focus on literature, so I will detail now what this book will refer to as marvel. Daston and Park's emphasis on wonder as a recurrent sensibility, a "powerfully felt emotion" with a history in specific reference to the history of science as one of "wonders as objects of natural inquiry," is inadequate for a number of the questions this study will ask.[25] First, their definition of wonder (a Germanic word that does not contain the visual elements of the romance words) as a passion cannot be documented in any of the texts considered here, unless one uses a different term, "curiosity," from the Latin *curiositas,* documented in its modern sense in the *Diccionario de Autoridades,* but which can also be found in its sense of "care" (a sense which the modern *curiosidad* kept alongside "the desire, taste, want to see, know and find things, how they are, happen or have happened," *Aut.*), as *cura* from the thirteenth century onward, in Gonzalo de Berceo, Juan Ruiz, and so forth.[26] Secondly, the separation of verbs and nouns (to wonder versus wonders) as if the "passion" were not an effect of the "object" is problematic in relation to our primary texts, as is the equation between the popular and the vulgar.[27] Finally, the scope of Daston and Park's volume, even when accomplishing the task of documenting reflections on prodigies and portent for "much of the medieval West," rarely includes Iberian texts. One exception is the consideration of Llull's presentation of "wonder" in his *Llibre de meravelles,* which "attempted to combine all three types of wonder." Characterized as a "valiant effort to bridge the gap between university natural philosophy, Augustinian and monastic values, and the literary tastes of courtly and urban elites," it is carefully set aside by dint of its "very limited influence" and the characterization of its author as "idiosyncratic."[28] Llull's articulation of different narrative strategies, from the romance-travelogue frame narrative to the conceptual intellectual core of adventure is especially eloquent of the literary definition of the marvelous I shall here use to refer to specific elements of the texts I study. Precisely because of its direct consideration of literature I have chosen Le Goff's perspective to illuminate the role of the marvelous, and elected to interpret the medieval monstrous in the same way Felix, Llull's hero, views it: as part of God's creation that will, ultimately and strikingly in the books of chivalry of Spain, bear more relation to the political than to the causal inquiry of natural philosophers.

In the period when romance emerged and took shape as a genre, the marvelous took over the medieval imaginary with great force. In Iberia it invaded particularly the literature and social practices of that lesser aristocracy, the *caballeros,* or knights. The Church, influential enough by this time not only to not oppose the marvelous, as it had done before, but even to include it, appropriated it, particularly under the rubric of the miraculous. Not only within properly religious texts, but also at all levels of culture, the marvelous also was aestheticized, sublimated, and turned into ornament, literary procedure, and visual topos.

As the marvelous was incorporated into romance in Iberia, its difference from the miraculous was clearly defined, following strict rules like those by Alfonso X.[29] Even though the miracle is more a rejection of the marvelous than a force behind it, it constitutes one of the forms of recuperation of the marvelous in the later Middle Ages, present in hagiography of course, but particularly interesting in the development of Marian devotion, which in Spain has two spectacular examples in the thirteenth century, the *Milagros de Nuestra Señora* by Gonzalo de Berceo and the *Cantigas de Santa María*, compiled by the Learned King himself in Galician Portuguese and lavishly illustrated for a courtly audience. Scientific and historical recuperation would also take place from the thirteenth century on, and literature closely documents this transformation of the marvelous in Spanish romance. As scientific recuperation, Gervasius of Tilbury—a thirteenth-century English noble living in Arles who dedicated his work to the Holy Roman Emperor—provides in his widely influential *Otia Imperialia* (ca. 1210) evidence of a tendency to make of *mirabilia* not things outside nature but within it, even if exceptional, thus objects of science. One can also see in this a transformation of monsters into "freaks." Hand in hand with the scientific, historical recuperation inventoried, catalogued, and, most importantly, dated marvelous events, which Daston and Park relate to the emergence and development of the spirit of natural philosophy.[30]

Mirabilia, partaking of the root *mir* from which the French *miror, mirari* developed, also corresponds to a modern English *mirror* and to Spanish *mirar,* "to look," where the visual character of the marvelous is emphasized, a kinship that appeals directly to one of the senses, once again, to the body and its measures. Le Goff puts forth the question of the possible links between *admirabilis* and *mirabilis,* where the ambiguity of the marvelous is once again conveyed,[31] and if one is to believe the mid-sixteenth-century cosmographer Sebastian Münster, the king of Spain would have (mockingly) referred to Columbus's title of Almirante as more adequately translating his capacity for marveling as Admirans.[32] In Spanish literature these semantic links are immediately discernible, as in Alfonso's definition of the miracle or in any text where a marvelous thing or event is experienced: the effect on the spectator and, for that matter, the reader, is one of admiration, and explains the way for its evolution into the magical and the spectacular of sixteenth-century courts. But a more subtle link should be underlined, that of the marvelous and space, present to a secondary degree in the Columbus reference, and in the topographical organization of wonders in Tilbury. Iberian literatures, sometimes in ways more explicit than others, present this link in various genres, from Marian collections to encyclopedias, travelogues, and romance. Peter Linehan has made explicit this relation of the marvelous and land policy, for instance, by suggesting that the *Cantigas'* recounting of wonders were meant to promote the population of newly conquered territories, as the pictorial program of the manuscripts represent a sort of policy for the possession of new lands. In a different context, Jerrilyn Dodds sees in a dialogue between narrative painting programs and hunting manuals a series of intercultural territorial claims, sometimes allegorized through "marvelous" motifs, such as the fountain, the lion, or the wild man.[33]

As for the role of the marvelous in medieval society, especially in relation to geography, E. R. Curtius documented a supplementary function through the motif of the "reversed world" from Cockaigne to Jauja, from the Carnival to the late medieval motif of Utopia, all of them variations on the themes of abundance, nudity, sexuality, and idleness. In this motif are mixed the ideas of Genesis and Eden, of a Golden Age and Arcadia, which are seen as a source, as an origin and not as a future, a distant initial past ambiguously perceived as happening before Christianity.[34] Within chivalric fiction, the marvelous, tied to adventure, produced new hybrid variations from all of these possibilities that work at different narrative levels.

The quest for individual identity—the contact with the strange in chivalric romance—is at the same time a test that brings the knight to a new spiritual level but also something that is determined directly by the space in which the knight rides. It is in this sense that adventure, space, and marvel become tightly knit together, to the point that Köhler has written that adventure *is itself* a marvel.[35] In relation to truth, marvelous passages dot the romance landscape without affecting the truth-value of the narratives. The marvelous and its spaces have an everyday existence, but it is one that lies in the past and one that chivalric romance suggests can be recovered through fiction. Every space in a romance has a meaning in such terms. Thus, motifs are recast for their power of allusion, their symbolic force. Among them, as the result of the exploration of other spaces and the accumulations of meaning, the space of the island emerges in the late medieval period as a privileged setting for the marvelous as the stand-in for fiction.

LANDSCAPES

In *fabliaux* or *exempla*, and in the romance, events are not exactly said or told: to put it in spatial terms, they are staged. Throughout the twelfth century, a number of descriptive "types" were created to fulfill one or another well-defined function, among them the Unknown Land, the castle, the closed garden, the spring, the storm, to serve as "props" or to compose the set where events will take place. I refer to these spatial configurations as types, or commonplaces, because they do not enter the narrative by description but rather by figuration. Description in romance is cumulative, displayed on a surface rather than in depth; it is not there to present a "reality" or to "imitate" anything, but to suggest meaning. This is particularly relevant to the relation between literary and cartographical practices, as description in cartographic writing and, especially, in maps—in the form of symbols that represent a city, a river, or a chain of mountains—is understood as related to meaning rather than to a detailed or precise presentation of anything. The narrative use of topoi or motifs is but another way of referring to the same operation, shared by cartography and literature in this period.[36]

The knight, usually by himself, crosses the frontier of the known and traverses a space unknown. Every one of his battles is the result of an encounter, whether it be of love or war. The space in which he travels is articulated in contradictions taking the shape of opposing figures such as the forest and the court, the civilized place of origin and the savage lands traversed. The court is a sort of magnet that sends the knight forth into adventure but at the same time gives that space an order through finitude, for the knight is drawn inevitably back toward it.

Lefebvre specifically articulates this basic opposition between uncultivated land—the forest—and built space—the court—clearly at work in the structure of the romance; Le Goff confirms an essential difference in tone between Antiquity and the Middle Ages in similar terms, arguing that the traditional opposition between the city and the country (urbanity and rusticity) is not to be assimilated with how the medieval world expressed the opposition between nature and culture, for medieval culture expanded it into an opposition between built, inhabited, and cultivated spaces of community such as the city, the castle or the court, and the wild, uninhabited, primitive spaces of solitude, such as the sea, the forest, and the desert.[37]

This dualism is a source of themes and fantasies, which can be attested in both epic and romance and in the increasing fascination within these narratives with descriptions of towers, castles, palaces, courts, and cities. This fascination permeated the visual arts as well, which explains the explosion of images of the construction of the Tower of Babel, for example, from the twelfth century onward. Within religious life, the austere hermits would oppose monasticism by fleeing to the "deserts" and refusing the "built." Monastic orders responded by making the enclave in which fraternal communities could found their edifices a supernatural one, destined to such purposes by dreams or mystical visions, and by finding corresponding geographies in the rugged Alps, like Saint Gall, or on an island, like Reichenau.

The development of cities, parallel to the development of romance, conditioned the inclusion of the urban within the spatial ideology of romance, which saw the urban with both desire and contempt, for the archetype of the city evinces characteristics that mirror negatively the traits of the knight. In 1200 Jean Renart wrote in *L'Escoufle* that the city of Toul represented the vilest of temptations for the knight: a site of leisure, laziness, abundance, and riches. The city's features were obvious opposites for the conditions of adventure, and by the end of the fifteenth century, Fernando de Rojas would present an urban setting in his *Tragicomedia de Calisto y Melibea*, better known as *La Celestina*, where the figure of the knight is unimaginable, rendering visible an impossible coexistence of the two.[38] The marvelous, however, was intimately related to the urban as well, as part of the technological or scientific marvelous, thus presenting a dilemma for romance. It is easy to see this trait in the adjectives continually used to describe cities, such as grand, beautiful, the most wonderful, and so on. These modifiers most often concentrate on objects, buildings, and works of art. These terms were expressions of wonder in view of the urban and the cosmopolitan, but they were also a leitmotif, a rhetorical device. The city is there a *topos,* much like the forest, appropriated by the imaginary, losing its ties with a geographical reality.[39] The twelfth century, as the great epoch for urban development in the Christian world, saw from epic to romance, from the *Poem of the Cid* to the *Libro del cavallero Çifar,* how urban descriptions began to inhabit the literary landscape.[40] Outside the urban sphere, the other repository of "civilization" was the kingdom, which denoted the law, the right of the lord more than a territory by itself, and which from epic and historiography moved into the spatial ideology of romance.[41] Here, it was the castle that gave a shape to another built space, acting as a hinge for the desires of the knight, torn between love and battle.

The castle immediately refers us to its opposite, a space of wilderness and the uncivilized. This space is that of the forest.[42] The forest functions in the romance not only as a dark, negative setting or symbol but as the place for narrative resolution, the site where adventure takes place, thus bringing about the movement of the romance. In this sense, the forest is a technical, structural element of romance. But even within the romance, the forest is traversed by procedures that are not only literary. The forest is also a landscape of everyday life with a vast role in the medieval imaginary, not only because of its symbolic force but also because of its economic, juridical, and geographical reality.

In her study of the forest of medieval French and English romances, Corinne J. Saunders writes that already in the early romances the forest is a complex landscape in which many traditions converge. The first is that of the historical forest, which can be accurately documented in England by the Domesday Book of 1086, but which can only be approached indirectly on the continent through allusions, references and, most of the time, by inference.[43] Up to the twelfth century, the forests of medieval Europe impressed their dense, imposing reality on the medieval mind. This forest, however, was not a uniform landscape but a mixed series of woodlands, clearings, and pasture, and less solitary than one imagines. Hunters mainly, but also herdsmen, swineherds, charcoal-burners, woodcutters, and others inhabited the forest, along with marginals and wild animals. Parallel to the cultivated forest, a source of nourishment for domestic animals, as well as of wood, nuts, or berries, the forest held a juridical specificity in those parts of it that were set aside by kings for hunting, grouping a political set of conditions with paradisiacal descriptors that parallel it to a *locus amoenus*. In Iberia, the ties between sovereignty and hunting as territory and as policy were to become more complex as they sought to integrate different cultural perspectives. María Rosa Menocal has linked Alfonso X's notion of a kingly literary culture with the *Libro de las animalias que caçan*, a translation of the Baghdadi *Kitāb al-yawārih* from Arabic to Castilian, and Alfonso XI's *Libro de la montería* can be directly related to cartographic survey practices, as "it may be the first comprehensive toponymic survey produced in Castilian," in its modern editor's words.[44] This idea of the forest as a private, regulated territory linked to royal privilege was to merge with the general idea of the garden, finding expression in literature and developing the topos of the *hortus conclusus*, but above all, in architectural practice and visual programs that build on the links between monarchical power and hunting motifs.

To the historical characteristics of the medieval forest was added the material taken from the Bible. The forest, as the Western counterpart of the Oriental desert, took on the many traits of the scriptural desert, which was important not only to Christianity but also to Islam and Judaism. The biblical desert is a geographical reality, but one inextricably tied up with a symbolic space. The desert of Genesis is that of original chaos, the antonym of the Garden of Eden: it is a place of tests, of wandering, of exile, of solitude, but also of revelation. The image of the desert changes in the New Testament, making of the arid and rocky region where John the Baptist lives a place of temptation, rather than of trial; and it is also the place of refuge and solitude for Jesus. Throughout the Middle Ages, Christianity honed the great themes of hagiography in conjunction with the spirituality of deserted spaces. Saint Anthony haunted the literary and visual theme of temptation; while Saint Paul's desert was characterized by a mountain, a cavern, a palm tree, and a spring, paradoxically reminiscent of a *locus amoenus*. From the Greek *erēmía*, from *erēmos*, solitary, following the example of Paul and Anthony, the desert Fathers sought this space to find in it the power of exile and hardship, ideals the great medieval monastic orders would take up as their own.[45]

Through visions and temptations, the desert of Egyptian eremitism appeared particularly permeable to the ambiguity of the marvelous, at times marked by devilish temptation, at times the rewarding space of revelation.⁴⁶ Once again, we find that the working opposition is not that of the actual emptiness of the desert or of any other of its physical qualities as opposed to those of the city, but one that has to do with its wildness, with the absence of culture in this space: the Latin *desertum*, like the Greek *erēmoia*, from *erēmos*, means uninhabited. This cultural emptiness clearly marks the link between the desert and the forest. If the early Middle Ages chose the desert as its metaphorical space, the twelfth century took the desert's contents and relocated them to the forest. Characterizing the wild and nuancing it from the point of view of culture, itself determined socially, these complementary possibilities of the forest–desert were expressed in the figures of the savage and the hermit. The savage, or wild man, is a primitive man, but one who already dominates nature, while the hermit holds in interiority the most profound link to culture, which allows his inclusion in the community—in a variety of exile—as a sort of "saint." The savage, the wild then, is not what is absolutely outside but what lurks at the margins of humanity. In this way, culture is defined, limited, encircled by its margins, and it simultaneously draws those limits as well, it distances itself from its other in a necessary gesture pointing from the wild toward itself.⁴⁷

The forest also began to be discursively elaborated as a place for knowledge. Saint Bernard would write in 1172: "forests will teach you more than books. Trees and rocks will show you things that masters of science will not show you."⁴⁸ The force of the biblical transposition of meaning taken from the desert made the medieval forest, to some extent, a symbol of another world, one of spirituality and purity, opposed to the dubious image of the city. The medieval forest thus inherited from the desert, due to their shared characterizations as "wild," "savage," "uncultivated" spaces, the ideas of exile, penance, prophecy, vision, and temptation. But the forest also became a site where a higher level of spirituality *as knowledge* might be attained.

Saunders traces another thread that traverses the forest imaginary back to the philosophical tradition in the words *silva* and *hyle*. Plato, in the *Timaeus*, in reference to the chaos that gives way to order, uses the Greek word *hyle*, literally "forest." Aristotle, according to Saunders, used this concept in a more concrete fashion, making of it the "primary materials" from which everything is made: "Later neo-Platonic philosophers soon began to equate *hyle* with evil and *kosmos*, order, with good.... Chalchidius, in the late third century, combined the attitudes of Plato and Aristotle, adding a moralistic representation of the ordering of the *hyle* as the providing spirit of God working upon chaos."[49] Chalchidius would translate the Greek *hyle* into the Latin *silva*. The Latin term *silva* rendered a difficult concept, and to explain it, images of an angry sea or of malleable wax were often used in *conjunction* with it. Later on, classical commentators would use the forests of Virgil for the same purposes: Servius, Bernardus Silvestris, Guillaume de Conches, Jean de Meun, and others, all the way to the *Kitāb sirr al-asrār* or *Secretum Secretorum*, grappled with the concept of the *silva* as *hyle* in more or less specialized meanings.[50]

The deep symbolism of the forest is expressed not only in the poetry of the troubadours and epic, but particularly in romance. To the biblical tradition of the desert–forest, classic and Celtic, "barbaric" traditions were added to Germanic and Scandinavian ones, taken from the sagas and, most importantly, from the forest of the Tristan legend, imprinted with erotic connotations. Classical images were transmitted through pastoral, from Virgil's *Eclogues*, where the forest functions as a *locus amoenus*; and from the *Aeneid*. There, even if forest references are scant, the symbolic landscape of exile, where the uncivilized is linked to outlawry, was of great importance for medieval reworkings of the forest. Moreover, Virgil's forest—whether the forest of love where the gods set up Aeneas and Dido, or the forest of the Golden Bough, an access to the other world—is presented as a place where divinity might be encountered; not God, but pagan gods, what the medieval mind will interpret as instances of the marvelous, made possible by the lack of a boundary between the human and the supernatural.

The *roman d'Antiquité*, medieval reworkings of classical themes and characters, from the Alexander legend to the theme of Troy, in the parallel development of techniques it shared with Arthurian romance, elaborated on the forest as a motif that retained many of the classical traits, emphasizing some—such as the motif of the hunt for love or exile, but also the presence of the marvelous—that offered a more positive image of the forest for romance. The characteristics of romance description strip the classical forest of specificity and transform it into a codified, symbolic landscape.

As topos, mixed first with the idea of the forest in the circumscribed shape of the glade, was the *locus amoenus*, which also took the name of the "garden," *hortus conclusus*, the secret garden or paradise of Isidore's *Etymologies*, of Vincent de Beauvais's *Elucidarium*, of *Flores y Blancaflor*, of Pierre d'Ailly's *Jardin amoureux*, Hieronymus Bosch's disquieting painting *Garden of Earthly Delights*, of Fernando de Rojas's dystopic *Celestina*. In his classic study on the ideal landscape, E. R. Curtius traces the image of the *locus amoenus* back to Homer, in the shape of an island (*Odyssey*, book 9) or a simple garden (*Odyssey*, book 7). There, trees bear fruit year round, spring is eternal, and a fresh breeze from the West blows incessantly. In the *Odyssey* book 5, Curtius finds again these traits in the Calypso grotto, and in Ithaca, where there is another grotto inhabited by nymphs (*Odyssey*, book 13), thus linking island, cave, and *locus amoenus*.[51]

In the *Aeneid*, writes Curtius, *loci amoeni* are those that are useful only for pleasure, those that have not been destined for utilitarian purposes *(loca solois uoluptatis plena . . . , unde nullus fructus exoluitur)*. The term *locus amoenus*, however, was used as a technical term for the first time by Isidore as a concept of geological configuration, following Servius, in the company of forests, deserts, islands, and mountain ranges, rendering the link between the literary motif and the geographical obvious.[52]

This series of traits that characterize forest spaces in literature bear the mark of a rhetoric that takes them up, making these traits commutable, as is the case of the *locus amoenus*. The porosity of these rhetorical places makes them open to different contexts of production, to resignification, whether in literature or in cartography, where they must bear a minimal link of resemblance, an essential similarity or capacity of association with a number of places. It is this contiguity that allowed the content, that is, the sum of ideas, practices, and discourses associated with the forest, to be relocated to a similar space: that of the island. Romance, in particular, was the genre where this relocation became more functional, and the Spanish book of chivalry, the genre that made the archipelago structural to its composition.

Seascapes

The spatial tension that prevails in chivalric romance, as we have seen, is that between spaces of culture and spaces of wilderness, mediated by the knight through marvelous elements that often prove reversible, that are infernal and divine at the same time. In the structure of romance, the site for adventure is the binome *silva/desertum*, which we have seen are synonymous. The forest has a double value of desire and repulsion; it horrifies and gives peace. The forest is thus constituted as the space of isolation, for abandonment to solitude, as the ideal space, in religious terms, for penance, as some etymologies indicate.

The forest constitutes a matrix both literary and topographic that, at the end of the high Middle Ages, began a transformation due to various circumstances. From weather conditions specific to the Mediterranean, thus affecting the Iberian Peninsula in a much more dramatic way than the northern continental areas, to herding practices, the reality of the medieval forest radically changed while romance was being shaped in literature.[53] The dense forests Strabo had seen in Iberia in the second century had disappeared by the time Muslim armies crossed the Strait of Gibraltar, and Charles Higounet remarks that the forest reservoirs of which Islamic societies made use in the Iberian Peninsula consisted only of the Algarve—a great pine forest—and of the trees on the shores of the Betis, cork oak and chestnut forests. To the interior of the Iberian Peninsula, only the Campo de Montiel could still have been described in terms of "forest vegetation." Cuenca's range of mountains, the Tortosa forests, and, above all, the Balearic Islands were the other important forest repositories from 500 to 1200 supplying Iberia, when a heat wave favored the general expansion of forests in Western Europe, explaining the impact of the forest in the Western imagination. However, in all of Europe and particularly in the Alps and the Pyrenees, the return of a cold wave, aided by civilization, saw the great deforestation of the eleventh and twelfth centuries, spurred by the need to furnish crusades, cities, and transatlantic explorations.[54]

From 1100 on, the forest ceases to be a space beyond human control, and it will disappear as a "wild" space between the fifteenth and the eighteenth centuries. Zumthor equates this ecological reality to an erosion of the imaginary, debilitating previously established links between man and space. What is left, the "real," domesticated forest, no longer corresponds to the forest imaginary, replete with marvels and where adventure might be possible. Thus, the forest will be reimagined and set further into the fictional as the literary forest of Brocéliande.[55] The reality of deforestation can be traced already in chivalric fiction itself, as one of the spaces crucial to the narrative movement of Chrétien's *Yvain*, the "essart," or cleared forest, attests to the developing economy that would change the landscape radically as other spaces began to encroach on the forest in medieval romance.

Outside the symbolic, the sea began to infiltrate the romance as a new space. The biography of one of the Desert Fathers, Columban, written in the sixth century, illustrates the relation of similitude that made the relocation of the forest imaginary possible, as he tells us that the wandering monks hoped to find *desertum in pelago intransmeabili invenire obtantes,* "the desert in the unsurmountable sea." Such a space had been greatly anticipated by the same traditions informing the forest of the romance. The sea did appear as a transitory space in the Bible, in the *roman d'antiquité,* and in the *Libro de Apolonio,* but had remained unexplored as a backdrop, a setting, until the grim reality of the disappearing forest changed the potential of this landscape in the medieval imaginary.[56]

Romance thus began to represent the sea. The French *Estoire del Saint Graal,* written around 1225–30 and interpolated as the first or introductory part to the works that compose the Vulgate cycle (the prose *Merlin, Livre d'Artus, Lancelot, Queste del Saint Graal,* and *La mort le Roy Artu,* which were composed before), was translated into Portuguese and Spanish early on from a later recension, known as the Post-Vulgate, composed between 1230 and 1240. In Portuguese and Castilian it was referred to as the *Libro de Josep de Abarimatía.*[57] The *Estoire* makes use of a wide variety of genres, from fabliau to epic, Arthurian romance, hagiography, and *roman d'antiquité,* while it also retains ties to religious writing in a variety of ways. In terms of genre, the *Estoire* is the closest context for the elaboration of seascapes in the Iberian book of chivalry, if sea and islands appear in Iberian literatures in other genres, which I will discuss later.

After a prologue on the circumstances in which the writing of the book came about, the *Estoire* tells the story of Joseph of Arimathea, first proprietor of the Grail, and his journey to Great Britain. Michelle Szkilnik, writing a detailed study on nautical motifs in the *Estoire,*[58] characterizes the anecdote of the *Estoire* as a migration, as a series of voyages because the characters do not travel at the same time or live the same adventures, and classifies the characters into three traveling "groups." The medieval author does not narrate the travels of the first group: Joseph and his people leave Sarras, and we find them again just before their arrival in Great Britain.[59] A similar silence surrounds the character Chélidoine at certain points. Mordrain and Nascien will take longer to make the trip to Great Britain. These last three characters are of great interest to us: they all disembark upon an island, where they will be morally tested, and from which they will finally be rescued in order to continue to their destiny in the British Isles.[60] The premise reproduces the story of Moses, and through it the *Estoire* intimates a double allegorical meaning, one referred to Moses, the other to Galahad. Both of these point to anagogical or eschatological meanings, which Szkilnik assigns to the arrival in the promised land, to the possibility of death by shipwreck, to the idea of purgatory in travel, and so forth.[61] Overall, the text presents Great Britain as a promised land, making the West a repository for sainthood through the arrival of Joseph, his followers, and the Grail.

In the *Estoire*, the sea voyage takes up a third of the narrative, narrating the vicissitudes of the characters either on a ship or while they are imprisoned on an island.[62] While it is the ship that, in Szkilnik's analysis, constitutes the main image of the *Estoire*, based on the idea of the voyage, islands in a way already inhabit the narrative. Here, islands are all savage, deserted, and hostile places, inhabited by beasts, inspiring horror.

In the *Estoire* one can witness a first attempt at relocating the meanings of the forest to seascapes; however, islands in the *Estoire* do not yet have a multiplicity of possible meanings or interpretations. The island in the *Estoire* is never a place for paradise; even the pagan marvels of Corinth it describes or the magic of Hippocrates are cursed.[63] None of the islands is characterized in detail or even differentiated. The adjectives used to describe them are identical and their role remains the same: they are places for rites of passage, which is indeed the interpretation that Szkilnik gives them.[64]

Islands in the *Estoire* are only a point of view from which to see other ships; they are not a produced space. It seems as if the island, space of the marvelous but somehow fixed, functions only as a foothold for the spectator of ships and boats, floating spaces of the marvelous. Ships, such as that of Salomon, are different in presentation but not in function, for even if showered with adjectives, they are remarked upon solely for their symbolic value. In their symbology, ships are a motif much more developed in the *Estoire* than islands, or even castles. Ships are a meeting point, and islands pale beside their important role, sometimes even imitating their characteristics.

The islands of the *Estoire* are of particular importance, as they do point to an interesting change in the landscape of romance.[65] The island in the *Estoire* is a closed space, but one that is not really ever entered. It is just traced in its shorelines, a liminality precisely at the core of what the *Estoire* is meant to emphasize. This limit is drawn on the sea, and only momentarily, since the characters will embark as soon as possible. The narrative gaze, moreover, is not turned within: the island is not seen, nor does it function as a produced space, in the sense we have been analyzing. It constitutes, at most, a point from which to look back at sea or continent (or forward, in anticipation), a waiting area.[66] Islands in the *Estoire* are most frequently signs of conversion, of which the best example is Nascien's *Ile Tournoyante*. On this island, Nascien is tested as to the degree of his faith and his hope. From the island as a mere point of view, he sees Salomon's ship and doubts its divine origin. Christ himself explains the meaning and comforts him; thus, he is strengthened in his faith and confirmed in it by Christ himself. In addition, such a change of sign is not exclusive to islands in the *Estoire*: ships and castles function in identical manner.

Szkilnik parallels the experience of the island in the *Estoire* to that of the forest, common features stemming from overlaps between adventure and conversion. Adventure and conversion seem to coincide specifically in their "trial" quality, with the transformation that ensues. In all other senses, however, we cannot equate the forest as the space for adventure in chivalric romance with conversion and its location on insular spaces in the *Estoire*. Above all, one must remember that knights *seek* adventure, an adventure essentially defined by chance. But they are not compelled by divine or devilish forces to come upon adventure, as happens in the *Estoire* with these initiation rites that are commonplaces of islands, and which tend to result in conversion or confirmation of faith. This interpretation seems, in fact, to have been that of the Castilian translator, who seems interested in copying those episodes more laden with religious doctrine. "The *Libro de Josep de Abarimatía*," concludes Gómez Redondo, "thus constitutes a history of conversions . . . along whose thread multiple theological ideas and marvelous events are displayed, which are nothing but a demonstration of the power of the Church over human materiality."[67] Space—whether that of the sea or island, forest or ship—is thus subordinated to conversion, and the *Estoire* is interpreted in this way as a treatise of Christian doctrine in Spain.

Parallel to these translations, Iberia produced its own chivalric fiction. *Amadís* will take up the motif of the island before it becomes allegorized, before the geography becomes a sign of spirituality as an expression of the theology that the last Arthurian romances would propose, and work it into the core structure of the book of chivalry, whose main objective was the promulgation of an ethos and a politics. Within Spanish literary tradition, the island–archipelago will find its own development, its own metaphorization into a rhetorical device unsutured from strictly religious connotations.

In order to explain how the movement from mainland to sea took place, one must remember that this movement was not only produced by metaphor or poetics, by generic influences or literary tradition. From 1200 on, the structure of communities was reworked into *cercados*, closed fenced spaces, new establishments on the land beyond the village, closed-in spaces surrounding a house, reminding one of the etymology of *insula* as a block of buildings or to refer to a discrete place on firm ground, in the sense of an isolated patch of land.[68] At the same time, the development of cities rendered villages inoperative. In Castile alone, more than two hundred villages disappeared between the fourteenth and sixteenth centuries, in the reorganization of rural space that spanned all Europe.[69] The idea of isolation, linked to the concept of property, gained thus a new force. Technology and population increases occupy the real space of the forest, stripping it of the possibilities of housing a marvelous imaginary. The nearby forest, where the marvelous could be found, disappeared. The medieval imaginary lost its treetops, and, at the same time, a new rational urge began to scrape agency away from the marvelous. Humanity will, by the fifteenth century, be the agent of this marveling, resignifying it from ambiguity and difference to magic and spectacle, as Anna Bognolo has shown.[70] In between, Spanish literature would thus produce in the archipelago alternative possibilities for fiction.

Insular Wonder

Marvels were principally connected in the medieval mind, as we have seen, to a spatial perspective, that is, to the faraway. Thus, it would be in books of travel that marvels would be found, and for a great part, the reason they were read. The earliest books of travel to circulate in the Iberian Peninsula were related to pilgrimage, as guides to the Holy Land or itineraries. The *Fazienda de Ultramar*, a thirteenth-century document that has been defined as "a Bible fragmented by itineraries and descriptions of cities and holy places," merges two genres popular in Iberia: Holy Land itineraries and "romanced" translations of the Bible composed from the thirteenth through the sixteenth centuries.[71] The *Fazienda* is not a historical itinerary, yet it emphasizes its closer links to "fiction": the narrator travels the Holy Land in an imagined periplus that results in a personal description in which places are mentioned because of their role in an event or simply because of the narrator's proximity to them. The two criteria for the description of the Holy Land are thus event-relatedness and geography.[72] This is important, because it helps establish that links between space and events—which share etymons with adventure, and thus with the marvelous, understood as the fictional—were narrativized in different genres before the book of chivalry.

Other types of travel also found a written form, motivated by diplomatic efforts (Ruy González de Clavijo's *Embajada a Tamorlán*, 1420) or mercantile interests. Books of imaginary travels were composed (*Libro del conoscimiento de todos los reinos*, ca. 1450; *Libro del infante don Pedro de Portugal*, end of the fifteenth century) and translated (Mandeville's *Viajes*, fourteenth century; Marco Polo's *Libro de las maravillas*, translated first into Catalan in the fourteenth century), evincing the complex relation between the real and the imagined, the fictional and the historical.[73] Beyond this communication, the difference between medieval and Renaissance travel resided in the type of knowledge sought from the process of traveling, in what was perceived as truth and what had to be done to extract truth. Of course, the discourse on and of knowledge and travel had changed radically by the sixteenth century, and a series of technological developments—cartography and printing in particular—had affected it profoundly. By 1576 any traveler might put a hand in her pocket to find in it a *Repertorio de caminos*, composed by one Alonso de Meneses and printed as a *libro de faltriquera* in Alcalá for the comfort of its user.[74]

Sea travel had its own developments, which have been especially studied as leading toward the events of 1492 and following. However, as Fernand Braudel has shown, travel in the area of the Mediterranean during the late Middle Ages and the Renaissance had specific circumstances that should not be forgotten.[75] The especially dangerous conditions of the Mediterranean—

Prince Doria was still heard to say, in the beginning of the sixteenth century, that there were only three safe "ports": Cartagena, and the months of June and July, which thus limited judicious travel to the summer months—and commercial interests set the boundaries for seafaring at the Atlantic coasts between Morocco and Flanders, and many of these interests stopped at the exit of the Mediterranean, to which charts bear witness.[76]

But travel there was, at any risk, for curiosity or riches, historical and literary, imagined and experienced. By the time of Marco Polo, there was what one critic has called "an insular romanticism," naturalizing the bond between romance and islands, referring to a particular sensibility or traveler's imagination where mystery, visions, and literary and historical information coincided in navigators' sightings of islands in previously unexplored seas.[77] If, in the epic traditions of Orient, the Sumerian paradise of Dilmun already anticipated the isolation of Syria in the *Odyssey*, or if the island of Utnapishtim the Faraway prefigured Elysium,[78] the Middle Ages reproduced a marvelous insular tradition, which the Spanish book of chivalry structured into an "insular turn." From Isidorian maps and the mappamundi of Beatus of Liébana, to the invasion of monstrous and fantastic representations of the real discoveries of Henry the Navigator on the coasts of Africa in the fifteenth century, there are signs of the pendular trajectory of marvelous insularities spanning across history and literature.[79] Every one of these islands was a setting, a "theater," writes Leo Olschki, of combats, enchantments, adventures involving giants, monsters, a fabulous fauna that coexisted with a vision of the natural world also described for its marvelous resonances. Thus, the islands of the encircling limits of the world, loaded with the contents of many literary traditions, reinforced by erudition and religion, traditionally located in the Orient—a localization that provided still more added motifs and interpretations, such as that of Paradise and the general images of the rich East, as has been pointed out before[80]—began to move on charts and maps in two directions by the end of the Middle Ages. First, they moved further into the West, into the Atlantic, as new incursions into these waters gave territories to old myths in the shape of the Isles of Man (the false and the real one), the island of Brazil, the Canaries, the Azores, all the way to Antillia, now called the Antilles. And, simultaneously, they retreated to the center, into the Mediterranean, ascribing the contents of these marvelous insularities from the limits to very well known islands of the sea *between the lands*.[81] In the 1497 Castilian translation of Bernardus of Breidenbach's *Viaje a Tierra Santa*, for example, there is a description of Crete that follows book 14 of the *Etymologies*, as an island in which no evil beasts (such as wolves or serpents) can be found, and where these in fact die if taken there from other lands, illustrating the relocation of the marvelous from the margins to the center—and mirroring accounts of travels in the Greek islands.

To tie the production of insularity in the late medieval Iberian imaginary to the chivalric even tighter, it should be noted that books of travel from the fourteenth century onward respond, in the words of Miguel Ángel Pérez Priego, one of the genre's best scholars, "more than to a clerical, learned ideology or a mercantile activity, to the chivalric mentality and lifestyles of late medieval Spanish society." Pérez Priego goes on to quote the prologue to Pero Tafur's *Andanças e viajes por diversas partes del mundo avidos* (ca. 1454) as proof of this ideology, where faraway lands and people are linked to individual courage and deeds, requiring and enhancing the virtues of the knight: "Travel literature should be ascribed thus to the literature of chivalric ideology that still presides in the Castilian fifteenth century."[82]

As an effect of this close-knit web between space, the marvelous, and the chivalric, there was an "insular turn," that is, the production of an insular imaginary specific to this period that was elaborated in the book of chivalry, which brought all of these motifs, genres, and meanings together. Other genres experimented with this space, and the need for an exhaustive inventory of "insular models" in Spanish literature—and the absence of monographs on the subject—has been pointed out by Nicasio Salvador Miguel.[83] Salvador Miguel looks at four possible models, each a fragment with "insular descriptions," taken from the *Libro del cavallero Çifar*, the *Laberinto de Fortuna* by Juan de Mena, the *Andanças e viajes de Pero Tafur*, and the Castilian translation of the *Voyage to the Holy Land*, by Bernard of Breidenbach.[84] The critic stresses the combination of verisimilitude and marvelous elements in the description of these islands and what takes place in them: verisimilitude given either by the conventionally fantastic frame of the episode, as in the *Çifar*, or by the bookish nature of the information, as in Mena's *Laberinto*; or in the genre itself as narration of lived experience, that is, the travelogue or the itinerary. All of these texts provide island descriptions with marvelous elements taken from tradition and supported by classical *auctoritates*, in a manner that is reminiscent of the assemblage of *isolarii*, as we shall see in the next chapter, exhibiting a simultaneous tendency toward the encyclopedic and the humanistic, which thus characterizes what I have called a late medieval insular turn: "The accumulation of elements coming from ancient mythology stands out in the description of insular universes, because if such references increase for some readers the fantastic nature of the islands, for others they provoke images and allusions of an erudite nature ... contributing to create for the majority of readers a sheen of verisimilitude due to the frequent indistinctness between mythology and history."[85] Salvador Miguel rightly highlights the fluid condition of these insular models, between historicity and fictionalization, which is precisely what will put the space of the island and its contents at the center of a debate on poetics a few decades later.

Insular descriptions in medieval Spanish literature are not only permeable to various articulations between history and literature, but also between different signs. Paradisiacal islands, whose characteristics include the abundance of natural riches, the beauty of flora and quality of water, combined with benevolent weather, serving as a refuge and, most important to our study, inhabited by *mirabilia*, are common in Spanish literary insular descriptions even if, as Salvador Miguel points out, the existence of cold or unhealthy islands was not ignored, as Alfonso X, Juan Fernández de Heredia, or Pero Tafur remind us.[86] And Spanish literary islands are also open to both the miraculous and the marvelous, pointing to the popular and cultivated elements and the various genres that participate in their production.

At the very beginning of the fourteenth century, just a few decades after Alfonso's *Cantigas* and Berceo's *Milagros*, which elaborate marvelous insular episodes themselves, the best-known occurrence of marvelous events on an island is the *Ínsulas Dotadas* episode in the *Libro del caballero Çifar*, the first chivalric text of prose fiction in the peninsula, if a hybrid of other genres and motivations.[87] James Burke listed a series of sources and motifs that make up the episode, which deny it any originality but allow us to catalogue the many traditions that already come together in the image of an island.[88]

Cristina González has observed in this episode, along with the episode of the *Caballero Atrevido,* the idea of a ritual initiation in the travel to the Other World, the meeting with the fairy, interpreting it along the general lines of personal, individual merit.[89] This interpretation establishes the link between the idea of an individual (compared to a community), with the idea of merit (earned esteem, value, or power) in the setting of a particular geography, the island, that we will find again in chivalric texts and, particularly, in *Amadís*.[90] The spatiality of this episode of the *Çifar* has been studied by Reynaldo Ayerbe-Chaux, who discusses the fantastic episodes of the text—the voyage of Grima, the adventures of the *Caballero Atrevido* in the *Lago Solfáreo,* and the *Ínsulas Dotadas*.[91] His interpretation is supported by the analysis of the 11 illuminations illustrating this particular episode in the Paris manuscript (out of a total of 242 illuminations), where Ayerbe-Chaux notes the emphasis on the imprisonment of the lover.[92] The contrast in the images between a spatial openness (the eighth illumination, where even the dog smiles, as the critic points out, representing the knight's departure to hunt) and confinement are interpreted as a symbol of the constraining elements of love, whether carnal or ideal: "the main symbol the illuminator has left for the passage is the wall, the enclosed space with which he captures the essence of the episode: the exercise of courtly love limits and blocks chivalric action, a theme central and present already in two of Chrétien de Troyes's novels," whose *Yvain* is read to our knight as he travels to the island.[93] This analysis can be extended to the illuminator's insistence on closely following the text through the surrounding wall as way of emphasizing isolation, and the insular nature of both the kingdom of Nobleza and of the episode, otherwise left out of the general interpretation of the book as a whole. Such insularity, along with the geographical traits of the other marvelous episodes in the *Çifar,* has led critics to relate it to the Byzantine or Greek novel, traits all determined one way or the other by sea travel. Both Byzantine novel and the travelogue have been frequently mentioned as overlapping generically with chivalric romance.

As later versions of the *matière de Bretagne* make sea voyage more frequent, and as these texts make their way into the vernacular languages of the Iberian Peninsula, insular models begin to take shape and inform the production of the archipelagic imaginary of books of chivalry: the Kingdom of the Islands, the Island of Happiness, the Island of Gold, the Turning Island, and the Lost Island appear on the Arthurian landscape, many of them not specific to one text but present in many of them. The Kingdom of the Islands, for instance, is a different territory situated in the Orient, which marks its difference with the Hebrides, such as the marvelous kingdom of Brangemor in the *Perceval* continuation, apparently a free land not paying tribute, bringing in a politico-economic context that will recur in the Spanish book of chivalry. The Island of Happiness is the refuge to which Lancelot takes the daughter of King Peles and twenty damsels who happily dance around a green pine tree where Lancelot's shield is hung, thus the name. Upon their departure, the island changes its name to Dry Island of the Green Pine Tree. The Island of Gold is a fundamental space in Renaut de Beaujeau's *Li beaux inconnu*, curiously also called Turning Island. Very interesting in its relation to our *Amadís* is the enchanted palace in its center and the domination over the island through a particular adventure. The Turning Island has in some versions a reference to a fortress located upon it where Merlin is imprisoned by the magic of Abinor's daughter, in parallel to the *Ínsula Firme*, as the characters there will not be magically liberated until the time of Arthur, as is narrated in the *Esplandián*, *Amadís*'s continuation. Finally, the Lost Island, to which I will refer in relation to *Amadís*'s *Ínsula No Fallada* later on, is one of these recurring insular spaces in the chivalric romance.[94]

Beyond the peninsula, the enchanted island of Alcina in canto 7 of the *Orlando Furioso* is probably the best-known insular landscape in the period, along with the allegorical archipelago that Pantagruel travels, satirizing the insular exoticism that contemporary discoveries had triggered. The articulation between insular episodes in this vast panorama of texts and their constitution as an absolutely necessary topos in the Spanish book of chivalry is to be found in the *Amadís*.

2

ISLANDS AND MAPS
A Very Short History

> So Geographers, in Afric-maps,
> With Savage-pictures filled their gaps;
> And o'er unhabitable downs
> Place elephants for want of towns.
>
> —J. SWIFT, *On Poetry*

Spaces are constantly in the process of production. They are thus characterized by change, substitution, and replacement. However, as Lefebvre reminds us, spaces never disappear: they leave traces behind. A space like the forest is crisscrossed by traces, from the paths that are trod upon in order to traverse it, whether trails through pastures, footpaths, or merchant routes, which link up glades, springs, and inns; islands are loaded with mythology, colonization practices, marked as safe ports, or stepping stones in a commercial route. All of these spaces are imprinted with values of safety, riches, danger, and adventure, added on to the series of cultural build-up that they support. Space is dialectical. It is result and cause, product and producer, but, most importantly, it is a stake: "the locus of projects and actions deployed as part of specific strategies, and hence also the object of wagers on the future—wagers which are articulated, if never completed."[1] In the movement from continental space to the sea, the experience of the space of the Mediterranean must be thought of as the object of such speculation.

Before being traversed by sails and routes, the Mediterranean was for the longest time an obstacle. Navigation worthy of the name, writes Fernand Braudel, only occurred before the second half of the third millennium B.C. with Egyptian travels to Byblos or, more accurately, with the rising popularity of sailboats in the Cyclades in the second millennium, boats that, provided with a keel, were able to find a way to root themselves in the waters.[2] Fear of the sea was not only a reminder to use common sense, but a serious philosophical question.[3] One can even hypothesize that sea travel was possible among these islands because, at all times, at least one of them was in sight. In this sense, the sailor was never really engulfed, *empelagado*, or *engolfé*, as Spanish and French put it. In fact, throughout the sixteenth-century, ocean travel was still a feat, one that was only attempted when a profitable result was sure to come of it. Even though the compass was available from the twelfth century on, it was not generally used in the Mediterranean, where travel generally consisted of small mercantile trips, buying here, selling there.[4]

What the sailor could not afford to lose sight of was the shoreline, the limit of what constituted the access to stability, to safety, to the reliability of land. For it is the sea that sets limits to the land; or, as Strabo put it, it is the sea that "shapes and defines the land," emphasizing the inscriptionary gesture in the Greek word *geographei*.[5] This limit line, the reality of which anyone can witness in the trace of sea foam left on the beach by an ebbing wave, becomes in the process of being imagined or abstracted the primary cartographic gesture.

I suggested in the first chapter a series of relationships between spaces of the material world and spaces of fiction, their interaction and mutual influence. Any reflection on space, however, would not be complete without the perspective granted by cartography, which I have only gestured at until now. Cartography is relevant here not only in relation to discourses on or about space. It has a direct relationship with the development of the romance. In the pages that follow, I consider some lines in the development of cartography especially from the twelfth century on, in order to arrive at a particular cartographic genre that disembarks, as does the book of chivalry in Spain, on an island. As another manner of interpreting the imaginary, maps focus on insular geographies as the fifteenth century draws closer. Marvelous, palimpsestic, insular cartographies will allow for a theory of islands in which both cartography and narration serve as mirrors of the world.

The limit traced by the map was in ancient thought bound together in one single notion, that of *peirar*, which designated simultaneously the boundary of limit, the distant, and the shoreline or coast surrounding an island, especially in the context of the image of the island-earth surrounded by the Ocean.[6] A line drawn on the sand imitating that of the coastline is a gesture of imitation, but it is also one of appropriation. Cartography, it has been suggested, has one of its origins in this "domestication of remote regions, this association of unknown and reputedly dangerous lands with familiar territories, bringing them within a single homogeneous space," into the representation of a space where the unknown becomes merely "remote," fixated at a distance that is thereby made thinkable: "The map is thus an instrument for overcoming the fear of the unknown by slowly integrating the outer regions into the visual schema of the world,"[7] writes Christian Jacob. The map objectifies a space, and in the same process, it dissociates itself and the spaces it represents from the consciousness of the subject. As an object, then, the map recreates the world it visually replaces: "The map confers a new, analogous yet symbolic reality upon the world, in accord with a relationship that pertains either to the argument of authority, or the power of perception . . . or to a social convention validated by usage: at a given moment and in a given society, the country and the world where one lives are to be identified with a certain graphic configuration."[8] Some even argue that the map exists before the space, as the territory cannot be imagined until the map exists.

The power of the image—which the map shares with all visual arts—is one the map uses in order to turn an expression of subjectivity into an object of knowledge. The map's subjectivity derives both from the social convention on which the image of a certain space is founded, and from the cartographer himself, who serves as a vehicle for the expression of the convention. The map is thus always a sort of narcissistic gesture, as it returns to the onlooker that which she already expects—the map being a product of the onlooker's society. As such, it becomes an instrument of knowledge through confirmation, obtaining thus a sort of pleasure. The map is an instrument of knowledge, not only pertaining to geography but to the natural sciences, to history, to mythology.

A world terrified by the sea, particularly by those waters from which the shoreline would no longer be visible, produced a cartography of the world within that enclosed horizon. Thus Strabo, at the beginning of our era, thought the cartographer need be only concerned with the *oikoumenē*, the known world. Plutarch established a similar link with history, sketching the same kind of line between what is pertinent to history and cartography and what is not, between regions of established knowledge and regions of myth: "On the map, the latter are the zones at the world's borders; it is impossible to draw them, and the honest cartographer will content himself with writing on the margins of the earth as on the edges of the sheet: beyond, there exist only arid sands and dark swamps."[9]

Herodotus, in his *Histories*, mentions a map for the first time within a literary source: Aristagoras, a Milesian, brings a map to convince King Cleomenes to join him in a military expedition against the Persians, around 499 B.C.[10] Herodotus mocks this representation by calling it a *periodos gēs*, which could also mean a literary portrait of the earth, but he was essentially criticizing the clear boundary these descriptions presented (whether literary or cartographic) through the Ocean.[11] Herodotus proposes a varied new terminology that introduces the figure of the informant in the composition of a worldview—but paradoxically relies on the same mythic and legendary contents the boundaries/boundlessness of Ocean had offered before.[12] Almost a thousand years later, the commentary by Ambrosius Theodosius Macrobius on Cicero's *Somnium Scipionis* from the *De Republica* introduced the climatic zonal map. Macrobius's is a schematic map: it makes no claim at producing what we would now deem a realistic image of the earth. Many medieval maps share this characteristic. Perhaps this is one of the reasons why Macrobius's, which divides the world into climate zones deemed habitable or inhabitable, remained popular throughout the Middle Ages, in conjunction with other images of the world. Macrobius is of interest for the cartography of islands as he shapes his worldview by accepting Eratosthenes's (third century B.C.) argument for the sphericity and the measurement of the Earth, and taking the concepts of the ocean and land masses from Crates of Mallos: "separating us from the people of the southern hemisphere, Ocean flows along the whole extent of the equator; again, as its streams branch out at the extremities of both regions, it forms two islands on the upper face of the earth and two on the underside."[13] This "world-as-island" view is recurrent, for even after Herodotus had mocked it, Strabo would affirm in his *Geographies* that the Homeric island-earth vision had been proven right, so that Ptolemy will have to refute the boundedness of the Earth once again six centuries after Herodotus.[14] One of the Greek terms for a map, *periodos gēs*, mentioned a few lines above, could mean not only the visual but a verbal description of the earth, but in a literal sense it referred to a journey around the world, meaning both the entirety or encyclopedic representation of the world and the traveling around it to accomplish such a description. This genre of Greek and Roman literatures, due to its appearance within other genres of varying literary ambition, might also be labeled a *strategy* that authors could employ in a visual or verbal medium. In the second century A.D. a *Periēgēsis* attributed to Dionysius "enshrined the Greek view of the whole earth for late antique and (in Avienus's Latin translation) medieval readers and students."[15] The appropriate expression for a world map was then "circuit of the earth," emphasizing thus the contour, the circular shape of the earth as if following the Ocean's course and its traveling. Latin used the expression *orbis terrarum* to express this double meaning in close relation to the Greek words.

In geographic writing, islands, especially from the early Middle Ages onward, received separate treatment, as in Orosius, who treats island groups separately according to location after the continent they are adjacent to is described (northern islands after Gaul and Spain, Fortunate Islands following the description of Africa, etc.). In Isidore's *Etymologies*, islands are linked to land rather than sea and thus described in book 14 in a separate section devoted to islands, promontories, mountains, and inferior areas—caves, gorges, and so forth.[16] But cartography proper will not, until the fifteenth century, produce books of islands that prove that this detachment, this distancing had managed to break with the continent.

As a way of rationalizing the world through representation, perhaps the most symptomatic of the differences between the cartography of today and ancient cartography is the absence of a grid of latitude and longitude in medieval maps, which conceived the organization of space in different ways.[17] Hydrographic features were what articulated location in medieval maps of the world. The Red Sea of the Nile, the River Don, and the Mediterranean thus figured as the main boundaries within the tripartite world represented in medieval mappaemundi. Around the entire world, conceived as a great island or group of islands in classical tradition, as I have said, was the Ocean.[18] The reliance on water in the medieval period is not merely traditional, or convenient, it also responds to the Bible as master text: "On the third day you ordered the waters to collect in a seventh part of the earth; the other six parts you made in dry land" (Ezra 6:42),[19] hence the idea that all of the earth's waters were somehow connected. These schematic maps, dividing the world into a three-part image, are known as T/O maps. The name refers to the geometric abstraction that produces a graphic image, the "T" representing the three bodies of water mentioned above, crossing the land and dividing the three continents. These are placed as "islands" in this water system—Asia, the largest, depicted above the bar of the T, with Europe and Africa occupying the smaller spaces—while the "O" is the Ocean surrounding and containing the world. That such an abstraction corresponds to letters is interesting in terms of how these maps were reinterpreted for use within a particular mentality. The fifteenth-century idea that these letters correspond to the words *Terrarum Orbis*, follows and complements the earlier idea that the T should be read as a figure of the Crucifixion, making the map thus a symbol of sacrifice and salvation.[20] This kind of map, though inherited from the classical world, has its earliest version in Isidore of Seville's *Etymologies*, following Isidore's description of the division of the earth in book 14, 2.

From the link of early Greek words for maps intimately related to a description of a voyage, to the graphic quality of the T/O maps, an original intimacy between maps and language, both seen as narration, as something to be read, can be postulated. This play between cartography and narration is articulated in different ways according to the nature of the map in question: T/O and zonal maps share a certain elementary, minimalist quality that has even led some to question their status as maps. Their recurrent presence is explained by the fact that they can be easily memorized and thus reproduced in a form that will not suffer from deformation in the process of transmission.[21] They are figured in a circle, which offers a form of delimitation and containment: the shape of enclosure and totality. This shape reemerged in every encyclopedic project as a form of the "itinerary of knowledge" or of "knowledge in the form of a circular voyage," but also as the vision of a mastered territory, as a finite object of knowledge in which the medieval ideas of macrocosm and microcosm have a precise expression.[22]

The outside circle or border of the map is a circumference for which a center, an *omphalos,* or navel must be provided with special value. It was, in fact, the most valued place of the map: the Greeks placed Delphi there; most Christian mappaemundi revolved around Jerusalem (sometimes Constantinople), while al-Idrīsī's world map for Roger, king of Sicily (twelfth century), has Mecca as its center. From this center, the circle figures a series of oppositions: center and periphery, the concentrated and the dispersed, focalization and marginality, themselves originating corresponding oppositions. Even in the shape of perfection, the sphere or the circle, these oppositions suggest the fragmentation of geography, of knowledge, of a prelapsarian unity visually reinforced by the emplacement of Earthly Paradise upon an island at the top of the East-oriented map, or even walled up, inaccessible.[23]

Within the circle, following the Bible, the medieval world associated the three continents with the three sons of Noah: Shem, Ham, and Japheth. The division of the world among the sons entails a symbolic meaning that is reminiscent of George Dumézil's well-known trifunctional model of *oratores, bellatores,* and *laboratores.*[24] In his *Imago mundi* (twelfth century), Honorius of Autun explicitly associates the division of the earth among the sons as a division of labor, and Alfonso X's *General estoria* (second half of thirteenth century) does the same in the chapters devoted to Noah and the Ark. As representing both a physical and a symbolic reality, maps, in an intimate relation with history established by Sallust and the Iberian Orosius, reiterated throughout medieval historiography down to Juan Fernández de Heredia, figured a representation of a reality in geographic terms that revealed a spiritual meaning related to space, both in the past and in the present. Edson writes that, particularly in the context of historical works, maps of the high Middle Ages merge past and present time within a geographical framework.[25]

The Middle Ages developed an elaborate type of mappamundi in accordance with the didactic, intellectual, and spiritual desire of representation, as conveyed by the excruciatingly detailed Ebstorf, Hereford (both thirteenth century), and Fra Mauro 1459 mappamundi. The Ebstorf—destroyed in a World War II bombing—was a thirteenth-century drawing 3.5 meters in diameter representing the body of Christ. His head was drawn at the top, coinciding with the East and with the terrestrial paradise; his hands to the

North and South of the earth, while his feet were drawn below, on the West. Crucified, his body (and his sacrifice) became the surface of the earth—perhaps a reflection on the materiality of maps, here resymbolized by a divine skin—and Christ's gaze met the onlooker's, offering him his body—the world—for contemplation and spiritual reflection. Symbolically all-encompassing, the Ebstorf map offered complete knowledge to the spectator, both of the physical and spiritual worlds, spatial and historical, sacred and profane, geography and salvation, origin and end: the limit or ends of the earthly. It *was* the Encyclopedia. As such, it shared characteristics with other discursive genres, such as universal histories, which emerge in Spain roughly in the same period through royal patronage, with mirrors of the world, or geographical treatises such as the *Semejança del mundo*. As a figure of total knowledge, the encyclopedic map serves as a catalogue, as a form of inventory of the world. A catalogue of *mirabilia* as much as it is an inventory of known things, past and present, it offers samples of the world's diversity, it summarizes infinite difference in a microcosm. It contains the verified, the known, and the possible.

Yet another type of map was produced during the Middle Ages, perhaps the most influential of them all, contemporary with the mappamundi: the portolan chart. Although their totalizing effect can be very convincing, medieval mappaemundi correspond to only one kind of knowledge, they "are the cosmographies of thinking landsmen. By contrast, the portolan charts preserve the Mediterranean sailors' firsthand experience of their own sea, as well as their expanding knowledge of the Atlantic Ocean," opposing cartographers of the central, firm land to those of the marginal, moving seas. Portolan charts are sea maps, depicting coastlines carefully along with the names of harbors, bays, rocks, cities, and rivers. They are not concerned with the detail of landmasses, but with the accuracy of a shoreline on which the survival of sailors, the users of portolan charts, depended. If a difference must be noted here between mappaemundi and portolan charts, it would be one of emphasis: the first are mostly concerned with a theologico-historical message, the latter are with a practical knowledge, even when the qualification of "accurate" or of "realistic" does not fit portolan charts, for as Campbell observes, many legendary features can be found in charts, isolated in little known continental interiors or around the edges of the map.[26]

Medieval maps called for a reading that implied not only a spiritual result or a practical use. They also called for the imagination to travel the memory of stories taken from history, from classical authors, from contemporary—real or imaginary—travels, from Pliny to Marco Polo to Mandeville. While the contents of mappaemundi drew on biblical references and on miraculous stories triggered by toponomy or iconography, portolan charts represented in their margins the monsters and marvels that used to inhabit the islands of the encircling Ocean in the Beatus, Higden, and other generally encyclopedic maps. From the thirteenth-century Ebstorf and Hereford maps, where they populated Africa, to Juan de la Cosa's universal map of 1500, where they have moved to the northeastern tip of Asia, as the edges of the earth were extended—into the Atlantic, into America—marvels and monsters traveled along islands and disembarked on the new continent. Portolan charts were key in this process. Witnesses to the growing knowledge in the fourteenth and fifteenth centuries of the Atlantic and North Atlantic archipelagoes, they played an important part in the theories of the marvelous and the imaginary islands of Man, Antillia, and Brazil that would find a figured reality in the Americas.[27] Islands, especially from the fourteenth century onward, serve as laboratory for the emergence of "a new relation between the bookish and the real, between classical space and modern space," a relation that we have seen links geographic and historical genres, cartography and politics, and, in later chapters, various literary genres, and which, in Bouloux's words, "leads to interrogate the real in a different way, according to more complex processes than the simple opposition between authority and experience, imaginary and real."[28]

Whether schematic or encyclopedic, medieval mappaemundi inherited a cartography from antiquity that inscribed the known world as the central island surrounded by a peripheral Ocean. From antiquity as well, legendary islands are depicted on the margins, this "space open to imagination, where dreams and hauntings take place in their floating contours."[29] Almost all medieval mappaemundi represent these legendary, imaginary, mythical islands; and all of them represent them in their margins, whether in a Ptolemaic projection or in a mandorla-map, along with the Mediterranean archipelagoes. Such is the case, for example, of the mappamundi found in the mid-eleventh century *Commentary on the Apocalypse of Saint John* by Beatus of Liébana, where islands reproduce the form of the overall earth, while fish fill the encircling ocean. Another depiction of islands can be found in the Miller Atlas. While the first sheet displays the Azores archipelago in an Atlantic no-man's-land, the map devoted to the Indian Ocean is saturated with an exuberant insular geography. In Jacob's description, "the oceans are filled with luxuriant archipelagoes, with lively colors and aleatory forms, as if these islands were being represented *metaphorically* as precious stones, the dream of which continued to haunt both travelers and sailors."[30] This is the cartography of Le Goff's *"horizon onirique"* (oneiric horizon). The islands of the Miller Atlas do not strive for a geographic reality. They are there for at least two reasons: to entice the imagination into reveries of riches and exotic fantasies, and to obliterate the blank spaces of the map. They also mirror the allure that marvels had for a number of genres, from Hellenistic paradoxography to Indianographic writing, where the wonders of both Asia and Africa were often melded, a lust and pleasure in wonder writing that was simultaneously denounced and copied by Strabo, and especially by Pliny. This last one wavers in his *Natural History* between the writing of unquestioned wonder catalogues and arguments on diversity being the result of nature's games, between discussions on causality and attempts at subordinating the charisma of marvels to some form of scientific objectivity. Thus, like Strabo had done before, he presents Alexander's military expeditions into the East as simultaneous data-gathering explorations, which he buttresses through Aristotle: "By way of this imagined partnership of omnipotent commander and omniscient philosopher," writes Romm, "a cognitive dominion is established over the East, allowing the light of Greek rationalism to be shone under every rock and into every thicket." In his expansion of this partnership's achievements, Pliny anticipates the relation among cartography, marvels, an adventurous hero, and narration that medieval romance about Alexander will take up and elaborate in myriad forms: "I ask that my readers give them a warm reception, and with my guidance, wander at leisure amid the universal worlds of nature and the central passion of the most illustrious of all rulers."[31] Romance, that is, will elaborate precisely the wandering Pliny demands from his audience.

Other cartographers used the depiction of islands for different purposes. Ancient Greek or Islamic cartography had used them for mnemotechnical and denominative processes, a purpose the Renaissance atlas by Joan Martines (1587) takes up in an unusual fashion. Martines shapes his islands in the form of letters. The viewer identifies the forms on the map as floating signs, or isolated letters that do not constitute a language but that nevertheless stress the continued relationship of maps with language and with a reading.[32] Among those represented are the Fortunate Islands, later identified as the Canarian archipelago; the Island of Saint Brendan; Antillia or the Island of the Seven Cities; the island called Brazil which would later be identified as part of a continent;[33] and Green Island, today Greenland, in the middle of the North Atlantic.

Portolan charts also emphasized these islands in their Atlantic location—that is, when they found it fitting to depict them. For most commercial seafarers the Atlantic coasts were not interesting, thus, most charts would stop at the end of the Mediterranean, thereby excluding Scandinavia, distant Atlantic islands or western African coastlines. The Canary Islands were among the first to be consistently depicted; the Azores and Cape Verde archipelagoes would follow. Lanzarote and Fuerteventura, both part of the Canarian archipelago, appeared with these names on Dulcert's chart in 1339, three years after their discovery was documented.[34]

Each of these Atlantic and Oriental islands, in a group or by itself, has been surrounded by a considerable bibliography. The existence of most of these islands has been questioned at one point or another, which leads us once again to the ambiguous nature of insular space. Real or imaginary, islands are always lurking in the margins of the medieval map. As exuberant manifestations of a medieval imaginary, they crowd the waters in the Miller Atlas, signifying abundance through metonymy: spices, riches, wonders of all sorts are thus evoked. In the Atlantic, in the Ocean, islands play a multiple role. They figure there as a margin, as an "edge of the world" that borders the unknown; they confirm an ancient knowledge of lands beyond, be they Atlantis, Antillia, or Paradise; they cipher in their shape an unimaginable other, the ultimate wonder, a repository of that which cannot be verified anywhere else but which still haunts the imagination as possibility.

Both in the imaginary and in its projection onto the map, the island is a mix of the fabulous and the historical with a particular proclivity for politics. F. Lestringant finds that "the island appeared in all these cases as the privileged element of a malleable geography, in which form and design can be indefinitely rebuilt in terms of particular political projects. The uncertainty of the island, its essential aptitude to anchor itself for a time on a determined point of the mappaemundi will serve the divergent interests of rival colonial powers."[35] Lestringant thus highlights traits of mapped islands that expound possibilities that literature also saw in this geography, such as their malleability, the possibility of arranging them in different ways, ambiguity and openness to relocation, all related in one way or another to political operations. Islands are also one way to approach the map's intrinsic relation to fiction, which can be understood from at least two viewpoints: a historical one, which we have referred through Edson's reflections on the framing of the past within geographical structures, but which can also be analyzed as a projection onto a future in which the stumbling upon America confirmed the fabulous dimension of Western cartography and its imaginary in general; and, secondly, in the very nature of the map, closely related to literary texts in the very operations of fiction. In "What Is a Map?" the question that heralds Christian Jacob's best-read chapter in *The Sovereign Map*, he writes that the map is essentially a metaphor that describes human relations, power relationships, and hierarchies. The very process of composition of a map, its selection of traits to be represented and the process of symbolization that brings the map into existence, homologizes map and literature; it is the same process by which the map becomes a sort of model of "reality" that makes it into a work of fiction. The *hic est* refers both to the materiality of the map and the space painted on it and to the referred space, exterior to it, that must be imagined.[36] This trait of the map, not merely understood in its linguistically deictic possibility but in its narrative production of spaces within the text and outside of it, is shared by "fiction": "simultaneously, the narration figures an exterior 'real' and represents itself as discourse: sign at the same time of 'something' and 'for something,' the temporal representation explodes...a tension is established between the time proper to the narrative and that of a word it fictitiously assumes," writes Zumthor of medieval narrative—but he might have been writing of medieval maps.[37]

The reader of a map seems to be identical to the reader of romance, as she is forced to move from the legible to the visible, from the now to a then, from a here to a there that all exist simultaneously. Both texts, map and work of literature, demand of the reader a doubled consciousness of self-presence, one within the text—a fictional one, one in the historical space/time when the reading is occurring. Both discourses, moreover, share a bond of intention and legitimation with a hybrid genre that mediates between them: the travelogue, a genre intimately associated with the marvelous as fiction. As both historians of cartography and literary critics seem to suggest, map and travelogue use and legitimate each other; they are codependent, especially in relation to the marvelous elements they reciprocally incorporate. By 1400 the map was essentially a collection of *mirabilia,* lavishly glossed or visually represented on its surface. Besides the wealth of representation these marvels convey, they are markers for a paradox of cartographic representation, for they simultaneously occupy space and denote its emptiness. Figures of monsters are supplemented in these spaces with writing. Within cartography, as experience and technology converged, rhumblines first, then compasses substituted monsters in the absurd emptiness of space. The margins, in their chase of monsters around the map, one day forced their disappearance from it.

In a manner similar to Western vocabularies on cartography, Arabic did not have a specific word for map. Instead, "a number of words were used, sometimes simultaneously or in juxtaposition to each other, to refer to map artifacts . . . terms that derived from well-known Arabic roots" with meanings that range from form and figure, to drawing, graph, and painting, perhaps already allowing in this way for the permeability of genres that share a concern with geography.[38] The Islamic world, in a way that the rest of the medieval world tended to share, presented insular geography in a variety of texts and in a range of genres not easily discernible from one another. Descriptions, catalogues of wonders, travelogues, cosmographies, and geographies all dialogue with one another. As for islands, these genres share an odd consistency: they all seem to relate them directly with the marvelous, which further supports the links between insular geographies and fiction, but also with politics, for the term *djazīra,* comparable to the Latin *insula,* designates both islands and peninsulas, but also territories between rivers or maritime countries, oases, or districts.[39]

Angelo Arioli has studied a great variety of texts and assembled a catalogue of marvelous insular spaces mentioned by ten Arabic authors throughout the Middle Ages, from Sulaymān in 851 to Ibn al-Wardī in 1457. The entire commonplace spectrum of marvelous places is arranged in this vast archipelago, including nudity, riches, primitivism in nutrition, a prodigious nature, spices, gems, and sexuality. Among them, the most familiar to Western culture are the Island of Women, the Fish-Island, and the Mobile Island, which are common motifs of travel literature, cartography, and all sorts of collections of *mirabilia*.[40]

The Island of Women, versions of which are taken by Arioli from Captain Buzurg ibn Shahriyar, Shams al-Din al-Dimashqī, and al-Khwārizmī, is located in the Sea of China and evokes the long-standing tradition of the Amazons, also present in a great variety of texts in the Western tradition and bequeathed to the toponymy of the New World in the name of California through the Spanish book of chivalry.[41] The Fish Island is taken from Sulaymān, and with this text his (contestedly attributed) narration opens. The fragment chosen by Arioli speaks of a fish that, when it emerges, seems to the onlooker as if it were an island. At times this fish will put out one of its wings—a fin—which then seems like a sail. While this fish is not dangerous, sailors make huge noises, sometimes using bells like those of Christian churches, in order to scare it away and avoid the risk of shipwreck, the text tells us. Arioli footnotes that the fish referred to here is the finback or red whale. This Fish Island has a parallel in Captain Buzurg's Tortoise Island, with links to clas- sical images of the world, and to the *Navigatio Sancti Brendanis Abbati*, a Latin text of the tenth century that Benedeit would rework into the *Voyage de Saint Brandan*, mentioned in previous pages. Taken from Saint Brendan's legend, this island would be mapped as late as the seventeenth century, in a representation that mixes a tale with geography in the sixteenth-century map of Novae Francia.[42] By way of this Anglo-Norman text we find yet another common ground with the Arabic island imaginary in the shape of the Mobile Island. Arioli finds examples of this island in Ibn Wasif Sah and al-Ḥimyarī. It is a geography that upon sighting provoked in the sailors the desire to disembark upon it.[43] Arioli plays on the illusory character of the moving island by qualifying it as a "mirage." If in the desert the mirage is an oasis, its logical reversal—the mirage in the sea—is an island, a vision of earth in the desert of sea.

The overlaps between desert and sea—open, seemingly infinite spaces, lack of civilization, inhospitability, and so forth—are thus also present in the

Islamic insular imaginary, where they bear relations with mysticism. The marvelous, as intrinsic to the relationship between these spaces, presents another way of establishing links among them, as a way of exploring their transposition of meanings. We have also seen that the production of a space—in the form of distance, established by the adventurous knight galloping toward the beyond or by the traveler searching for the other, or by the eremite seeking a personal encounter with God—is essential to the encounter of the marvelous. It is interesting then here to note that *sarāb*, Arabic for *mirage*, is related to walking, to going on one's own way, particularly related to desert scenes and interpreted as deceit or instability.[44] Marvelous, in turn, refers mainly to a literary tradition in which travel literature, cosmography, natural sciences, and the supernatural met. The words came to refer to God's creation and power, encompassing the physical world, the human body, the heavens, and so on. Al-Kazwīnī, notes Hunsberger, distinguishes between *ăjīb* (marvel, wonder) and *gharīb* (strange), "in that the former impairs the human being in his ability to understand the cause of anything, especially the familiar (such as the sun [q.v.] rising), while gharīb consists of unusual things (such as earthquakes)," a distinction that bears resemblance to Alfonso X's definition of natural phenomena and miracles: "Thus, by contemplating even the everyday occurrences of life—the growing of plants, the digestion of food, the flowing of the tides—the believer marvels at the real, has a sense of wonder and amazement, and is thereby led to an awareness of the transcendence of God."[45] Writers, such as Ibn Baṭṭūṭa, undertook great journeys in an effort to catalogue these marvels, mirroring the example of the men of antiquity and of the Christian Middle Ages.

In Arabic geography, the Ocean is the limit of the Earth, and in the Sea of Darkness—also called Embracing or Encompassing, External Sea, Green or Black Sea, Tenebrous Sea—is the Throne of the Evil One, whose prison is an island. The Embracing Sea of Ocean surrounds a circular Earth, crossed by two gulfs: the Sea of Rum, or Mediterranean, and the Sea of Fars, or Indian Sea. The center of the Earth is Mecca. In one of these extremes lies the Island of Masfahan—identified as Tenerife, Pliny's Convallis, as al-Ḥimyarī writes. He takes the reference from al-Idrīsī, probably the most famous of Spanish Arabic travelers and geographers (1099–1165 or 1180).[46]

Within the Mediterranean, the signs for the end of the Earth are in Cádiz: the Columns of Hercules, a monument that al-Zuhrī, geographer from Almería, claims to have seen destroyed in 1145.[47] Sprinkled across these two seas, multiple islands present their wonders to the merchant, geographer, and traveler: the island of the Androgyne, the Island of Reason, where one can drink water from a spring that produces surprising effects on the mind;[48] the island of Malakan, a monster the size of a hill with many man-eating heads; and the Island of Little Ones, where people the size of a cubit—already referred to by Homer in the *Iliad*, Pliny, and Aristotle in his *Book of Animals*, picked up famously by Swift for the land of Lilliput—fight cranes in a legend with counterparts in Chinese and even North American Indian cultures.[49] There are islands reminiscent of Circe's island, and islands whose carnations will allow their possessors to never age or grow gray hair; islands of wonderful riches and well-being, and islands of cannibalism and incest. But perhaps the most original to the Islamic world is the Island of the Waq-Waq, found in many Iberian texts and mapped onto the Mediterranean, as in the Egerton map of the "Inhabited Quarter" from the *Shāhid-i ṣādiq*, an encyclopedic work in Persian by Āzādānī Iṣfahānī.[50]

The Waq-Waq have been variously identified with Japan, islands of southeast Asia and Africa, the Seychelles, and others. The Waq-Waq as an archipelago is mentioned by Buzurg, Ibn al-Wardī, al-Ḥimyarī, and consisted of sixteen hundred islands so called because on them grows a tree whose fruit resembles young women attached to the tree by the hair: when the fruit is ripe, a "waq-waq"–like noise can be heard, which the inhabitants take as a good omen. From al-Idrīsī's account, one might assume that the word renders click-speakers; from the more imaginative accounts, they are especially related to India and its catalogue of wonders; and from other accounts, one gathers that the Waq-Waq designate not only a land, but also the very edge of the knowable world.[51]

These are islands taken from works of various authors, books of travels to China and India, compendiums of marvels, travelogues, cosmographies, and geographies. The close relation between what is seen and what happens there is transmitted in two ways, one is by way of *images*, and the other is through *language*, in narration. Al-Idrīsī does both simultaneously in one of the most incredible works of geography of the Middle Ages, the *Kitāb nuzhat al-mushtāq fī ikhtirāq al-āfāq* (The Pleasure Excursion of One Who Is Eager to Traverse the Regions of the World), written in the service of King Roger II of Sicily.[52] Etymology seems to point us once more to suggestive territory for comparison. In Arabic the words that mean "to narrate," "novelty," and "event" all derive from the same root. The first two were later merged into the same word, as if to suggest that it is the event—that which is new—that is worthy of narration. Conversely, anything that is the object of narration is postulated implicitly as an event.[53] Furthermore, the relationship with space is already there: the primary meanings of the root *h-d-th* are "to be recent, new" and "to occur, to happen, to take place."[54] Islands seem to conjure in the Arabic geographical imagination this narratability linked to the notion of adventure as expressed in romance, adding one more element that buttresses the coupling of insularity and fiction.

Insularity thus moves in two directions, from extreme openness to extreme concentration. The island conjures a power of miniaturization for the real, the imagined, or the armchair traveler. Historic and imaginary travelers, like Mandeville or al-Idrīsī—when at sea—found themselves in solitude and desperation, in an *isolated* place. This experience of space marked by exile and displacement, by traversing and appropriation, takes the form of a discourse on space that is intimately tied to narration.

From *Isolario* to Atlas

In the late Middle Ages—when travels to the East were a matter of everyday conversation because of the wide popularity of the stories of Marco Polo and Mandeville; when marvels were known by all and had at least been confirmed by an acquaintance or by a close friend worthy of trust; when books of chivalry triumphed in Spain and new seafaring heroes were born; when the European gaze concentrated so much on the East that it would be a while before it managed to get a perspective on the West—the modern traveler began to make his way into the world. One of the first kinds of books this late medieval traveler wrote was a book consisting exclusively of descriptions of islands accompanied by maps: the *isolario*.

Isolarii are books that articulate diverse materials about islands, organized thematically in encyclopedic form, generally presenting a map for each island and a corresponding text. Regardless of the variety in style and content of the twenty different *isolarii* that we know—ranging from atlas prototypes to personal accounts of a sailor or traveler—all claim an insistent relationship between text and map. Indeed, the latter is often a visual interpretation of the narration. Some *isolarii* contain regional maps or even mappaemundi that show the location of the islands they focus on within a larger context, showing the relations either among the islands themselves or to a continent. Yet others present specific illustrations of details of each island, such as floor plans of fortresses, or representations of the inhabitants in traditional costume, anticipating an anthropological gaze.[55]

George Tolias mentions Homer's *Odyssey* as a first *isolario* of sorts, but the classical precursor to the genre is Dionysius Periegetes's section on islands in his *Oikoumenēs Periegesis* (A.D. 124). Even though the image of the world offered in this geographical poem was fairly conventional, perhaps even outdated for its time, it became a standard textbook for the Middle Ages, first translated into Latin in the fourth century, followed by two sixth-century translations, and another, with extensive commentary in the twelfth. Within the humanism that characterizes the cultural milieu that gave rise to *isolarii* proper, Tolias points to Domenico Silvestri's *De insulis* (1385–1406), an alphabetical "learned island dictionary following the methodology of Boccacio's 'De montibus, silvis, fontibus,' to which it was a sort of supplement," as the immediate antecedent of the *isolario*, from which there are no extant maps.[56]

Christophoro Buondelmonti's *Liber insularum archipelagi* is the only known island-book corresponding to the period before 1470.[57] Even though the data presented in it was available for a long time before Buondelmonti, he seems to have been the first to undertake this task of assemblage, as Elizabeth Clutton has called it.[58] A compilation of facts and fantasy filtered through personal experience, hearsay, and a series of more or less accurately cited poetic and historical sources, his voyage is motivated by several desires; a humanist curiosity, the search for Greek manuscripts, an archeological interest, a passion for Greek, all probably influencing the itinerary that leads from well-known monastic retreats in isolated rocks to the urban exuberance of Constantinople (Figures 1 and 2).[59] His text seeks to entertain and please the armchair traveler, the powerful Cardinal Orsini in particular, to whom the work is dedicated. Thus, Buondelmonti interpolates descriptions of historical and natural marvels, stories of pirates and of miracles, complaints about food, quotes from Ovid and Virgil. The *Liber* quickly became popular, as the more than sixty extant manuscripts in three different redactions evidence; and, more importantly, it constituted itself as the model for future *isolarii*, which until the seventeenth century derived from it not only the content but also the structure itself, and, quite often, the maps.

The date for the composition of the work is given by the acrostic formed by the eighty-two letters that begin each chapter. Some of the copies show 1422, some of them differ by as much as nine years, but the date for the first recension has been determined to be 1420.[60] Buondelmonti left Florence, where he was born into a powerful family around 1380, in order to study Greek in Rhodes, where he must have spent some eight years, according to Émile Legrand. His travels among the Greek islands took him about six years. During these voyages he acquired at least seven of the Greek manuscripts he had been sent to look for, kept today in the Biblioteca Laurenziana in Florence, some of which he annotated, including the fourth book of Aristotle's *Physics* and a life of Plutarch.[61]

The system of sources that Buondelmonti uses in order to compile his "descriptions" has baffled readers and critics for many, sometimes contradictory reasons. For most of the information that does not correspond to that of the reader or critic, Buondelmonti has been corrected and judged as ignorant. But research into personal history and context and the provenance of his information often turns out to be, if not accurate, instructive, as Legrand concluded.[62] Buondelmonti himself lists events and the entertainment or pleasure of an errant writing and reading as the purpose of his book, describing it as "an illustrated book of the Cyclades and the various other islands surrounding them, with a description of the *events* that took place there in antiquity up to our own times. . . . I am sending this to you [Orsini] so that you can have the *pleasure* of letting your thoughts *wander* when you are tired" (Figures 3 and 4).[63]

Buondelmonti's sources include Ovid and Virgil, whom he quotes directly, and references to Cicero, Livy, Pliny, Aristotle, Gorgias, Callimachus, Terence, Demosthenes, and Varro, among others (Figure 5). Buondelmonti points out in his preface that he will tell of the shape of the islands, their greatness and, most important to us, the events for which they have been a theater or

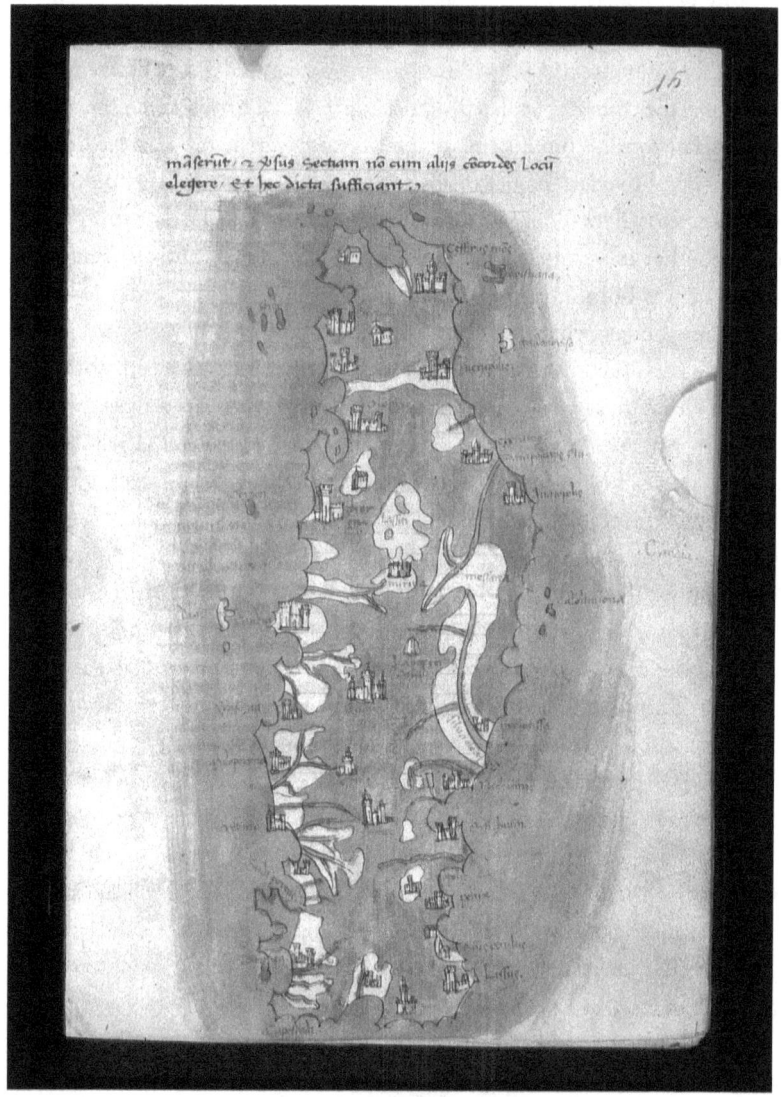

Figure 1. The island of Candia (Crete) depicts Daedalus's labyrinth at its center. Christophoro Buondelmonti, *Liber insularum archipelagi,* MS 18246, folio 15r. Copyright Biblioteca Nacional de España.

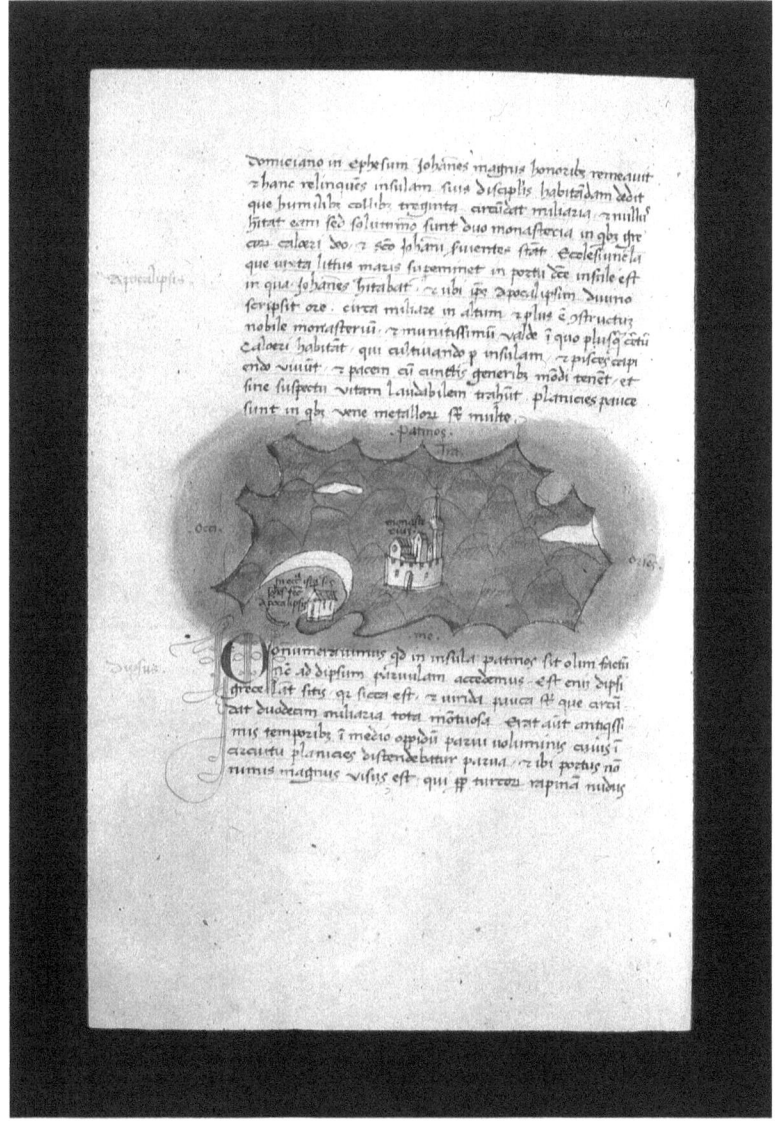

Figure 2. An inscription notes that Saint John wrote the Apocalypse while on this island. Christophoro Buondelmonti, *Liber insularum archipelagi*, MS 18246, folio 42v. Copyright Biblioteca Nacional de España.

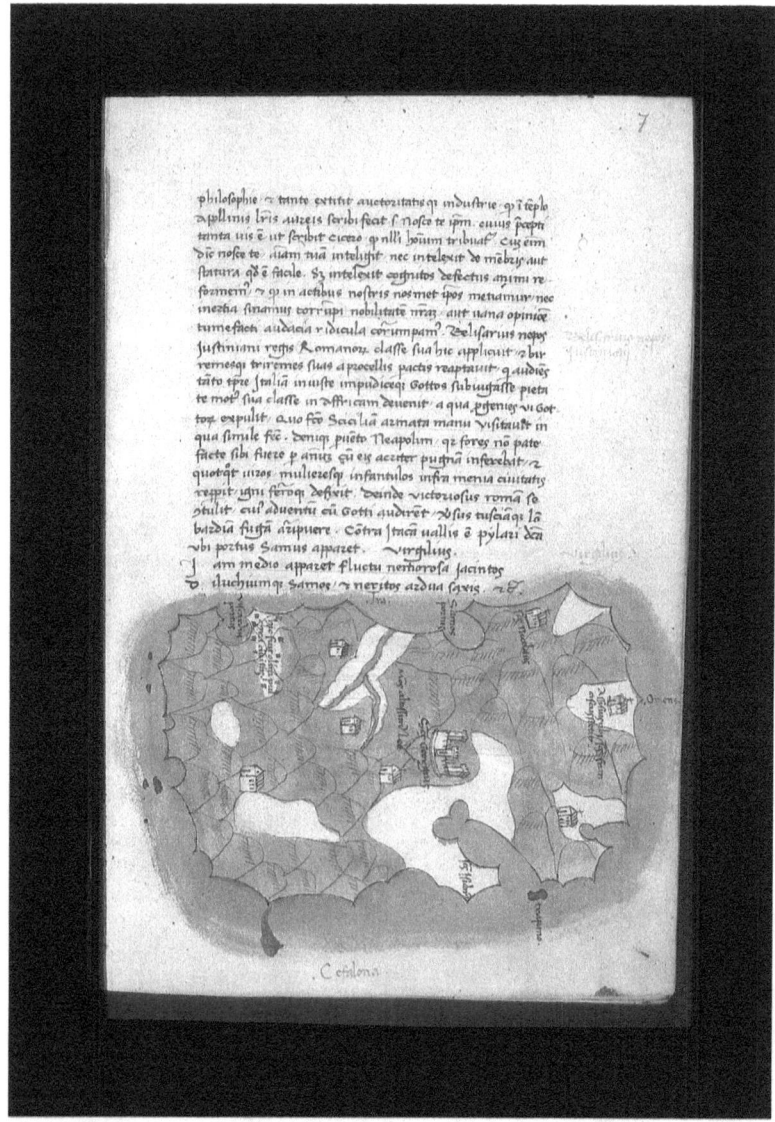

Figure 3. Mykonos, one of the Cyclades. In the text that accompanies the map, the author expresses doubt as to whether Saints George and Stephen were actually here. Christophoro Buondelmonti, *Liber insularum archipelagi*, MS 18246, folio 32r. Copyright Biblioteca Nacional de España.

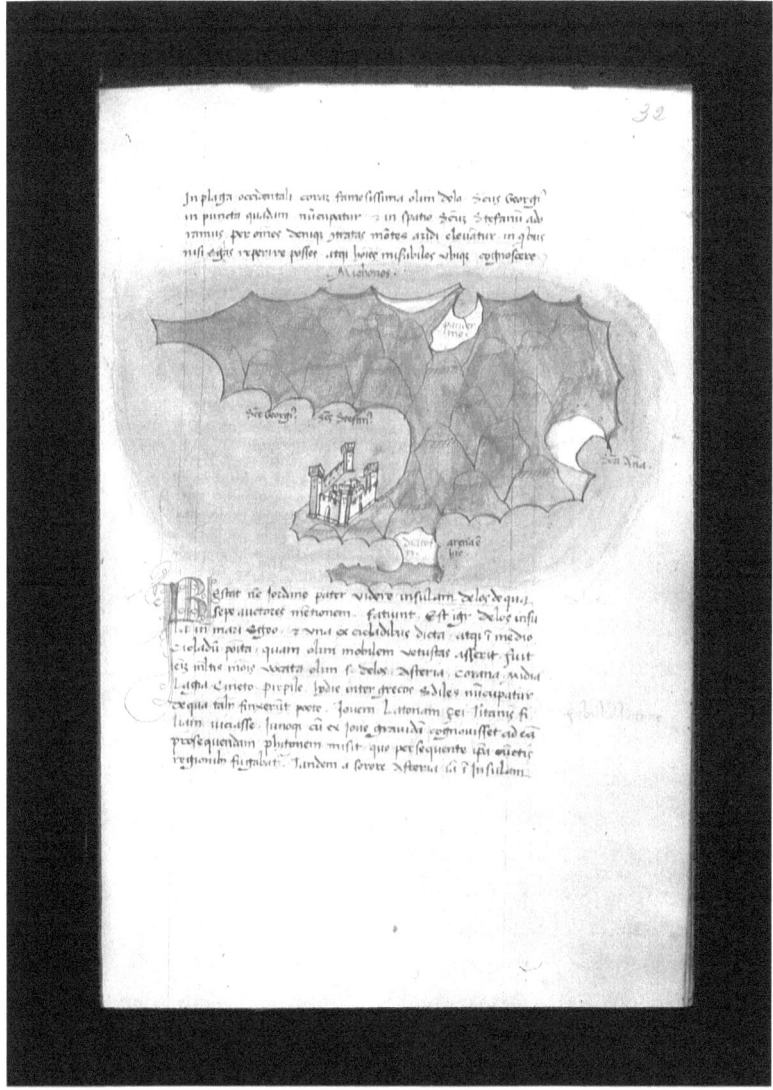

Figure 4. Cephalonia, represented laterally, proudly bears the inscription "Hic fuit olympica ciuitas." Christophoro Buondelmonti, *Liber insularum archipelagi*, MS 18246, folio 7r. Copyright Biblioteca Nacional de España.

a stage for a number of years, in his words. He remarks that his travels took place under the threat of tempests and enemies of the faith (Figure 6). The description of the Greek islands, divided into seventy-nine sections, begins with Corfu and ends with Aegina. Buondelmonti considers the Greek archipelago as the *arche pelagos,* stretching the etymology to mean the archipelago of first importance, as "master" or "leader of the sea."[64] The texts are interpolated among the maps of the islands, watercolors where green corresponds to the sea and the rivers, white to the plains and dark ink to the mountains, as is specified at the end of the preface itself, emphasizing the maps' integral role in the composition of the book.[65]

The island maps are intriguing reflections of the texts that accompany them. These are not maps suited for sailing, but neither are they precisely for the learning of a highly cultivated armchair traveler, as the illustrations are not rich enough nor do they convey any information that the curious mind of the time would not consider commonplace (Figures 7 and 8). It has been often remarked that the *isolario* as a genre and, specifically Buondelmonti's text, is to be inscribed in a tradition of encyclopedic knowledge, an attempt to encompass all information available for a specific space, in this case, a series of islands. Hilary L. Turner, in an article devoted specifically to the maps but which traces the manuscript tradition of the *Liber,* argues that Buondelmonti's work would be the result of two converging traditions. The first, the encyclopedic tradition, from which classical sources derived knowledge that was then passed on as geographical knowledge, was typical of the fourteenth century. Yet, this tradition never included maps, and it never attempted to present detailed or even generally accurate information. The other tradition, which would explain the inclusion of maps, would be that of portolan charts, confirming my observations above that the space of the island seems to be especially apt for conveying new forms of interrogating the real through the incorporation or assemblage of a variety of discourses.[66]

If encyclopedic indeed, the idea of totalization entailed in Buondelmonti's project is of a different nature than that of a *summa* or an *imago mundi.* His *isolario* is a kind of guide of *common sense* knowledge combined with clichés, an array of funny stories; obvious historical information; a series of archeological, anthropological, but, most of all, economical observations; unspecific tales of miracles; and a compilation of widely known classic legends and myths. He is a traveler: not a sailor, or hermit, or a saint determined to convert the infidels, or a man of commerce. I would say that he is one of the first learned tourists, with an eagerness to demonstrate his intellectual capacities, and particularly observant of his "creature comforts."[67] He even has pictures. His maps, which he drew with his own hand following Ptolemaic principles, are drawn according to the conventions of the period and are close to actual island shapes, though for no map is there an idea of scale or a uniform orientation. Maps are there to illustrate his text, to mirror the information, to visualize the stories: to provide a setting.[68] This collage includes stories of islands inhabited by monastic communities, or by oracles who used to reveal the future, or by harpies, flying griffins, and other monsters; stories of islands prolific in wine as a gift from Bacchus, and miracles that can be obtained after sleeping one night on the skin of a wild ass in the island of Sikinos; stories of cities entirely inhabited, in the past, by giants, like Sardopolis, in enumerations that inevitably remind one of Calvino. He tells of the labyrinth in Crete and of the miracle in Polycandros, where the death of a monk living in a cave is avenged by a voice in the sky.[69] On a more historical note, perhaps evidencing a personal sense of community, are his mentions of monks in Les Strophades, Mykonos, La Panagia, Polycandros, Nio, Le Caloyer, Athos, Patmos, and the islets around Constantinople (Figure 9). He sometimes questions his own information, as in the localization of Homer's tomb in Chios; other times he will credit anonymous people with his information, as he has not seen the island himself.[70] He describes Thira poetically as "spread like the hem of a garment" and Ikaria as a sinking ship.[71] And there are stories of monsters inhabiting Naxos and Kos, and of marvelous things happening in the times of the ancient Greeks, which he always introduces with "It is said . . . ," evading responsibility for their marvelous nature. In fact, the only times Buondelmonti uses the adjective "marvelous" to describe anything, the object is neither monster nor miracle, but curiously, architecture, specifically ruins, that anticipate the description of Constantinople toward the end of the book (Figure 10).[72] His archeological interest, coupled with his personal history, drive him to Christianized and allegorical explanations, as in the case of Pallas Athena, where he explains that she wears three colors that symbolize the three theological virtues, or the cases of Prometheus, Apollo, and Bacchus.[73]

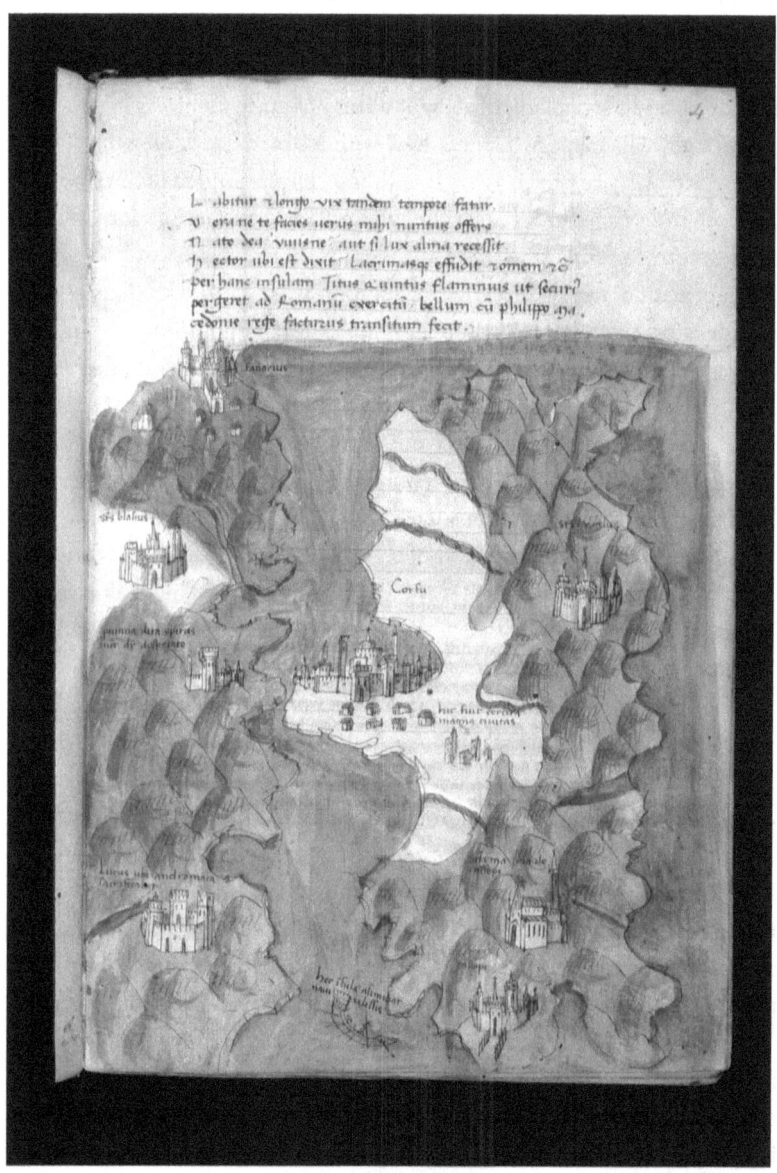

Figure 5. For Corfu, an Aegean island, Buondelmonti quotes verses from Virgil at the top of the folio. Christophoro Buondelmonti, *Liber insularum archipelagi*, MS 18246, folio 4r. Copyright Biblioteca Nacional de España.

Ostendimus insulam Leucatā dictā, siue ad Dilichi
am insulam transitū preparamus, que antiqs tpo
ribus hec itacha uel Dilichia dicta erat. hodie no ualde capi
te nominatur. ad trionem aūt Leucata supradca prope
ad duodecim miliaria elongatur. ad meridiem uo hec pro
pinqua insule Cephalonie altis distenditur ripis atqз per
totū montuosa et inutilis hētur nisi in medio exiguus
planus protenditur aliqbus arboribus fructificantibus.
circūcirca in portuosā satis appet. que de oriente ad oc
cidūi trequisita sunt miliaria. In latitudine uo ad quat
tuor tantū ampliatur. O uay qdem duo extremi in du
obus apiunt cornibus. corū qbus in nocte piculose nau
te transeūt ne in medio illoz brachioz in scopulis nauē
impingant. Asseriūt aūt auctores qз de hac insula fuit
ille eloquētissimus τ eximius grecoz vlixes qui p suā
sapientiam qi ad omia modum inueniebat. penelopen

Figure 6. On Lefkada, Buondelmonti represents a battle. Christophoro Buondelmonti, *Liber insularum archipelagi*, MS 18246, folio 5v. Copyright Biblioteca Nacional de España.

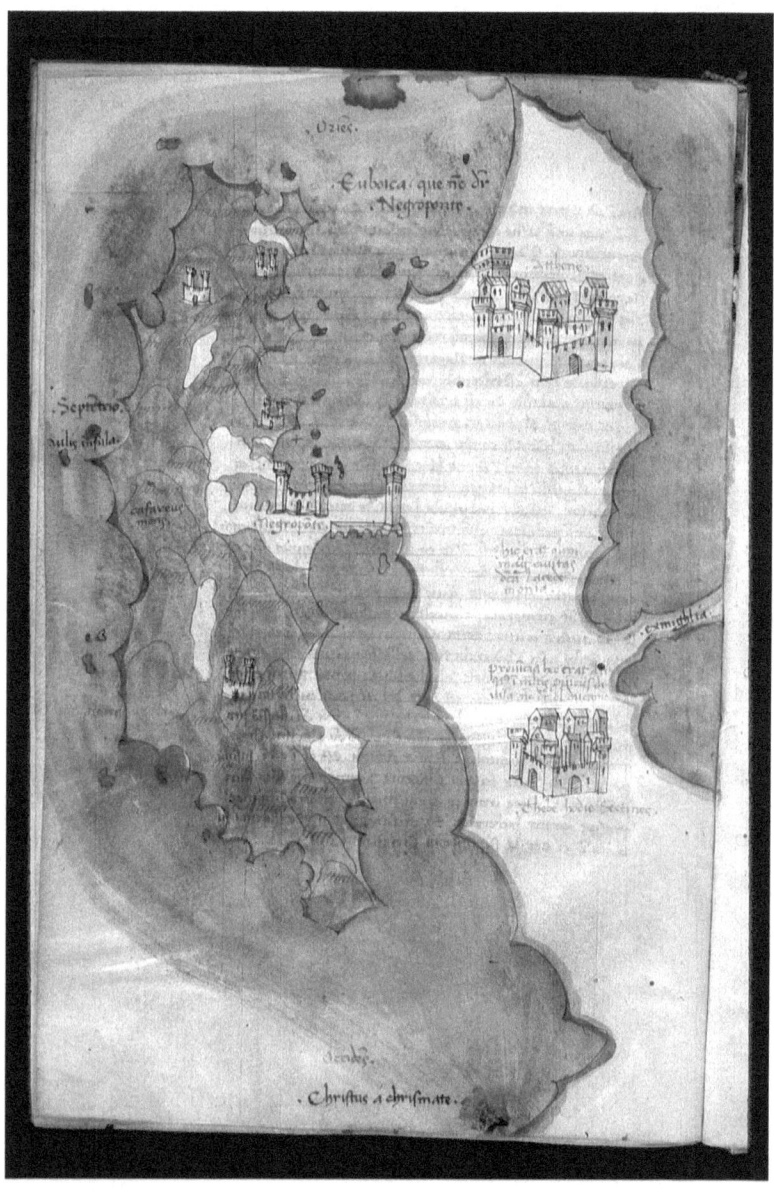

Figure 7. Athens and Negroponte face off on this map of the Saronic islands. Christophoro Buondelmonti, *Liber insularum archipelagi*, MS 18246, folio 61v. Copyright Biblioteca Nacional de España.

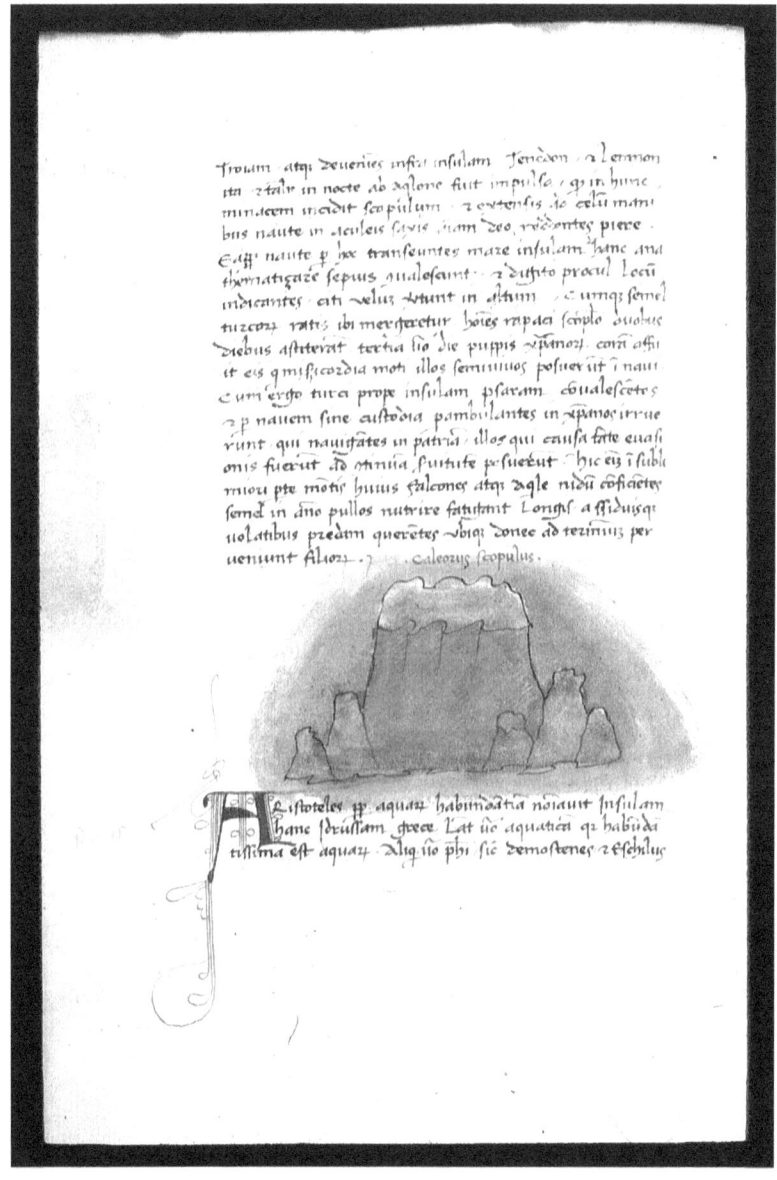

Figure 8. Islands and cliffs can be deserted and seem inaccessible. Christophoro Buondelmonti, *Liber insularum archipelagi*, MS 18246, folio 30v. Copyright Biblioteca Nacional de España.

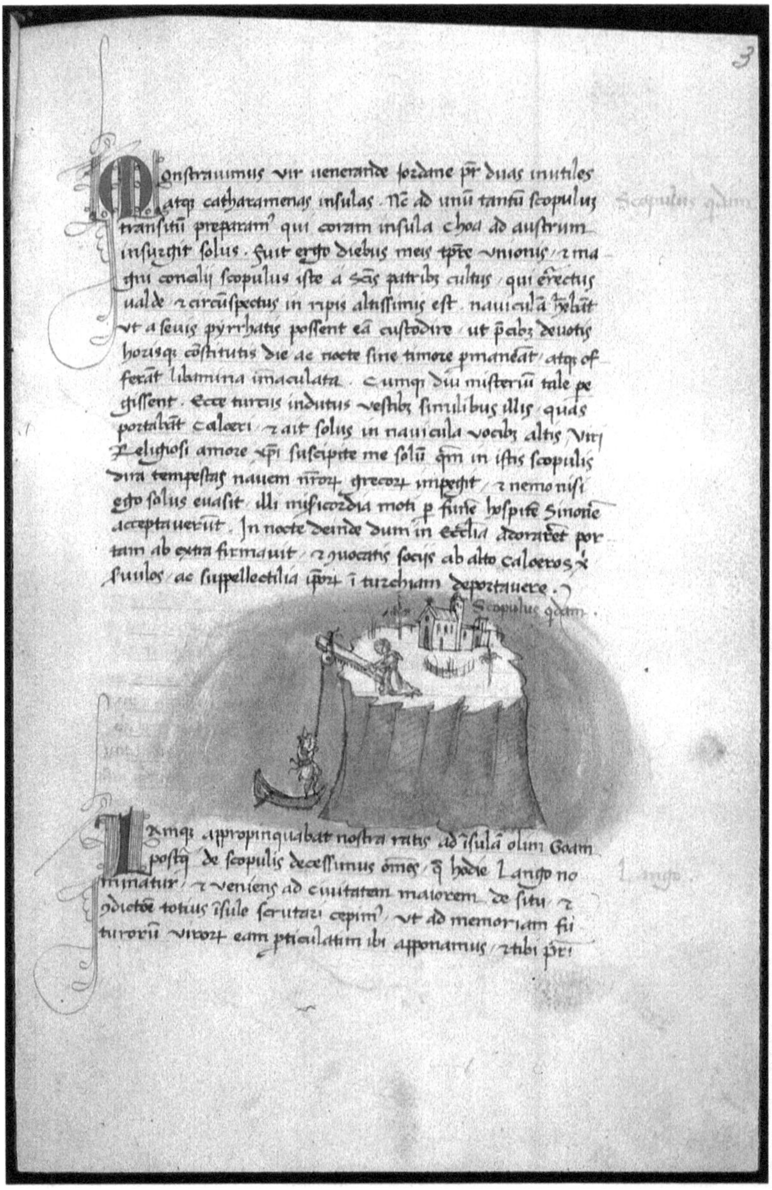

Onstrauimus vir uenerande iodane pr duas inutiles atq̃ catharamenas insulas. Nec ad unū tantū scopulus transitu preparam̃ qui coram insula choa ad austrum inspicit solus. fuit ergo diebus meis tp̄e vnionis, ĩ ma gn̄i cenalij scopulus iste a scīs patribꝫ cultus, qui erectus ualde ⁊ cireuspectus in ripis altissim̃ est. naui ul̄a tolut vt a seuis pyrrhatis possent eā custodire, ut p̄abꝫ deuotis horisqꝫ cōstitutis die ac nocte sine timore p̄maneat, atq̃ of ferat luamina imaculata. cumqꝫ dn̄i misteriū tale pe gissent. ecce turcus indutus vestibꝫ simulibus illis quas portabat calcerꝰ ⁊ ait solus in nauicula vocibꝫ altis, Viri ⁊ eligiosi amore xp̄i suscipite me solū qm in istis scopulis dira tempestas nauem nrōꝗ. grecoꝝ impegit, ⁊ nemo nisi ego solus euasit. illi misicordia moti p fūre hospite sinone acceptauerūt. In nocte deinde dum in ecclīa adorarent por tam ab extra firmauit, ⁊ inuocatis socijs ab alto calceros x fuslos ac suppellectilia ip̄oꝝ in turchiam deportauere.

Scopulus qdam.

Scopulus qdam.

Langho.

Cumqꝫ appropinquabat nostra ratis ad insulā olim Coam postq̃ de scopulis decessimus omes, q̃ hodie Langho no minatur ⁊ veniens ad ciuitatem maiorem de situ ⁊ obiectꝭ totius insule scrutari cepim̃ vt ad memoriam fi turoꝝ uiuoꝝ eam pticulatim ibi apponamus, tibi p̄r

Figure 9. Buondelmonti uses a different projection to depict Skopelos, showing the prominence of cliffs. Christophoro Buondelmonti, *Liber insularum archipelagi*, MS 18246, folio 39r. Copyright Biblioteca Nacional de España.

Figure 10. The text ends with the land, at the shoreline where the ancient city of Troy is marked through some ruins and the text that refers to it. Christophoro Buondelmonti, *Liber insularum archipelagi*, MS 18246, folio 50v. Copyright Biblioteca Nacional de España.

Via text or map, the *Liber* provides the reader with many traveling possibilities. One can read Buondelmonti and take his own itinerary as a guide among the Greek islands, or one may choose a different route. In any case, the alternation between text and map gives the whole a sense of continuity, of progress in the illusion of an itinerary created through traversing the pages. It is precisely the movement through the book that threads it together, "the book as a container or frame, comes to guarantee the integrity of the *isolario* as an encyclopedic book of the world, as the heroic travel of an individual humanistic (Buondelmonti) or courtly (Pigafetta) body in space ceases to define the parameters of the book of islands genre," where the initial movement of the author (Buondelmonti), paralleled by that of the reader, comes to disappear to leave the reader of the *isolario*, paradoxically outside the book, as its only guarantor of narration and travel.[74] Even if the alternation of text and map continued to be used in the genre, the role the insular model would play changed considerably from Buondelmonti's first assemblage to the last of *isolarii*. The combination of a literary enterprise with a scientific one, prefigured in Buondelmonti, took over the thread of the genre and, combined with new techniques, from print culture to woodcutting to rhumb lines, and with the revival of arts of memory, produced the printed *isolario*. Already in the first printed *isolario*, published in Venice in 1485, Bartolomeo dalli Sonetti's forty-nine maps were accompanied by a particular recasting of the information provided in Buondelmonti. The maps in Sonetti alternate, appropriately, with seventy-one sonnets, emphasizing in a poetic genre what is visible in the cartographic representation: brevity, enclosure, and miniaturization. Theodore J. Cachey argues that this transition to print is the "key moment in the history of the 'book of islands' genre, between the end of the fifteenth and the beginning of the sixteenth centuries."[75] Benedetto Bordone completed his manuscript in 1524 and published his *Libro di Benedetto Bordone nel qual si ragiona de tutte l'isole del mondo* in Venice in 1528. His is once again a tour of the Greek isles, which occupy a symbolic center, but he then displaces this center to Venice, making of that city the vantage point from which to gaze upon the world: "In Bordone, the 'fiction' of the book of 'all' the islands of the world and the fiction of some kind of objectivity and encyclopedic totality is belied by the disequilibrium in the proportions of the book which is heavily centered in the Mediterranean and within the Mediterranean is heavily anchored by the classical islands of the archipelago originally described and mapped by Buondelmonti."[76] From this privileged standpoint, Bordone then multiplies the "centers," in an insular production that seems to spin out from West to East, from Mexico to Venice as a series of archipelagoes. This proliferation and multiplication is a sign of the changing role of the island in *isolarii*, from geography to metaphor, of its increasing capacity for expansion.

Venetian mapmakers thus initiated a genre that would have a profound influence in Western culture still largely to be assessed outside the history of cartography. Through Bordone and Sonetti, Tom Conley analyzes the influence of the *isolario* as genre in Rabelais and Thévet,[77] and Lestringant traces the changes through the writings of Thévet himself, from the *Cosmographie universelle* to the unfinished *Grand Insulaire et pilotage*, where he finds it to be a strategy, a structure, "a laboratory enlarged to the dimensions of geography."[78] By emphasizing the island's microcosmic quality, these printed *isolarii* returned to the idea of an encyclopedia through the presentation of a "specimen," thus giving a new function to the genre's initial drive. Its contents seem to strive for an idea of totality that had, in its world-map version, been rendered impossible by Columbus's travels.[79]

The encyclopedic approach of the *isolario* after Buondelmonti, however, is not the same as that of medieval mappaemundi. The *isolario* is an atlas composed exclusively of islands. It is as *atlas*, then, that the drive for totalization of the *isolario* must be understood. The atlas is "a device that can reconcile the desire for an overview and for detail," writes Jacob: "The multiplicity of maps turns it into a site in which all the geographical knowledge of a period may be recorded. . . . It offers a symbolic mastery of space."[80] The *Liber* circulated widely, and served as a model for future *isolarii* but also influenced a variety of genres, one of them the atlas, in particular the production of nautical atlases out of Venice. Tolias, in his overview of the genre, writes that for the period between 1528 and 1571—precisely when the vogue of books of chivalry would take hold of readers' imaginations—there is only one manuscript *isolario* known, the nautical work by the Catalan cosmographer Alonso de Santa Cruz, "clearly intended as a practical guide to navigation. . . . In spite of its title . . . the Catalan cosmographer's guide to the islands covers much more territory than an ordinary *isolario:* for all intents and purposes it is an early world atlas. Although islands account for most of the material, there are also maps of most of the known parts of the old and new worlds."[81] That is, Santa Cruz extends the structuring principle of the *isolario* metaphorically to include all territories subject to that gaze that the island elicits, beyond a strict geographical definition.[82] The atlas, one could claim, is but the extended metaphor of the *isolario*, sharing with it three essential traits: its dependence on print culture for the development of the genre; the betrayal of a fear of omissions that might jeopardize the totalizing effect of the work; and the insufficiency of the image, which led to the interaction of the map with the description of the map: a text, a narration.

After Bordone, the *isolario* chose between worldviews and regional cartography, between a small group and a selected few, fragmenting the thread of the voyage, that is, the oneness of the single traveler, in a series of random organizing principles. Leandro Alberti's *Isole appartenenti alla Italia* (Venice, 1567), Tommaso Porcacchi's *L'Isole più famose del mondo* (1572), Boschini's *L'Arcipelago* (1658), Vicenzo Coronelli's *Isolario dell'Atlante Veneto* (1696)—the last of the *isolarii*—all respond to different, unrelated principles: to Italy, fame, and cultural prestige.[83] Cachey compares Antonio Pigafetta's *Isolario* of 1534, in the tradition of Buondelmonti—that is, articulated by an "order of travel"—to Bordone's, which has an "order of sequence," which sought "to make accessible to his readers, as they turned pages of his book, the illusion of the recovery of an edenic state of a direct knowledge of the archipelago of the world."[84] In Thévet, the *isolario* has detached the text from the context, the island from the map: "In the *Insulaire*, an atlas of islands, no continuous voyage can be envisaged. Or, more exactly, Thévet breaks up the continuity of real navigations; he retains only its 'punctuation,' these insular stages that he disseminates along the thread of the chapters of his world. Segmentation and ellipsis are clearly the ruling principles."[85] Such detachment and fragmentation of any continuity between islands, and between map and text, results in a revelatory different emphasis. Conley writes, "over and over again, Thévet underscores how much the discovery of strange object, flora, fauna or myths pertains to 'singularity.'" In the process, the *isolario* is questioned as a possible genre to represent the world. In Thévet's *La Cosmographie universelle*, the book is presented as "mythic continent and island-world of worlds," so that the image of the mappamundi, which seemed to haunt the *isolario,* returns in a typography that Conley analyzes in detail: "The printer ends *La Cosmographie universelle* in a conventional typographic flourish, in a *cul-de-lampe* design that leads the margins of the text toward a verbal vanishing point. A last island off the coast of China, Quinsay, is being described before the text comes to an arbitrary end."[86] This whimsical point of arrival is the ocean, *l'Océan.*

As happened with the book of chivalry and the emergence of the novel, "the appearance of the first world atlases toward the end of the sixteenth century did not spell the end of the *isolarii:* in fact they enjoyed a second heyday in the seventeenth century, in spite of the dominance of atlases." The reason for this was that *isolarii* had never competed with formal geography and cartography. The information that *isolarii* contained (except those that had specific practical intentions, as Santa Cruz's) was not directed at a particular audience or a specialized reader, but for the common person "eager for geographical facts and fascinated by tales of adventure and descriptions of marvels and wonders." Furthermore, early printed atlases incorporated features from *isolarii,* in a further parallel with the relation, which I shall detail in later chapters, between book of chivalry and the novel.[87]

The best known of early modern atlases, Ortelius's *Theatrum orbis terrarum* (1570), exemplifies the continued relation between text and map, a structure or strategy explored by all geographical writing from antiquity onward. Particularly attractive to the armchair traveler, the atlas combined the security of staying home with the excitement of travel and adventure, and, of no less importance, the knowledge obtained in the process. Reading the map is traveling, thus promising adventure. "It is a novel, somewhere between a travel narrative and a role-playing exercise," writes Jacob, while at the same time he underlines the link between the experience of the construction of the novel and the development of cartography: "The metaphor that Ortelius extended suggests a relationship between the atlas and the development of travel in the Renaissance, from literary accounts by travelers (Montaigne) to fantastic travel narratives (Rabelais). If Ortelius justifies his undertaking through the utility of maps for reading by historians, he does not neglect the pleasures of imaginary travel."[88] The changes from *isolario* to atlas indeed manifest the changing relations between image and language that informed the development of new genres. As Conley writes,

In their evolution toward a predominately pictorial form, atlases tend to jettison their textual baggage. Verbal decoration is reduced, set on verso pages, or suppressed. Like the repressed, the verbiage that flows from the cornucopia of cosmography does not simply evaporate. It returns in different forms. One of these, of course, is the encyclopedia, which will channel information according to artificial organizational schemes. . . . A second is the novel of travel, which uses the servility of the *isolario* to assemble discreet episodic units that are studied from multiple points of view.[89]

Encyclopedia and travelogue, knowledge and experience, bound in the *isolario*, take different paths in their separation, pointing to different possibilities in narration, such as historiography and fiction, and to a spectrum of pictorial presentations (Figure 11).

Theses on Isles

Traversing the Mediterranean would not be seen as a pleasure trip until well into the nineteenth century, when the steamship made the journey between Marseille and Piraeus a surprisingly brief nine-day adventure. Adventure—with all its promises of danger, heroism, and overcoming—characterized that immense sea, the sea of sails left to the mercy of winds, the sea of boats that took two months to go from Gibraltar to Istanbul and at least a week or two to go from Marseille to Algiers.[90] The measure of the world is, indeed, not only determined by technology, but is at once result and cause of a specific spatial imaginary. Thus, Braudel advises that, when looking at Arabic insularities, Western cartographic fantasies, or Greek island-hopping books,

> The historian must detach, whatever the cost, from this image that makes a lake of the actual Mediterranean. Dealing with surfaces, we must not forget that Augustus and Anthony's Mediterranean, or that of the Crusades or even that of Philip the Second's fleets is a hundred, a thousand times larger than those revealed by our trips across the air or maritime space of today. To speak of the Mediterranean of history is, thus—a first care and constant worry—to give it its true dimension, to imagine it in an oversized dress. By itself it used to be a universe, a planet.[91]

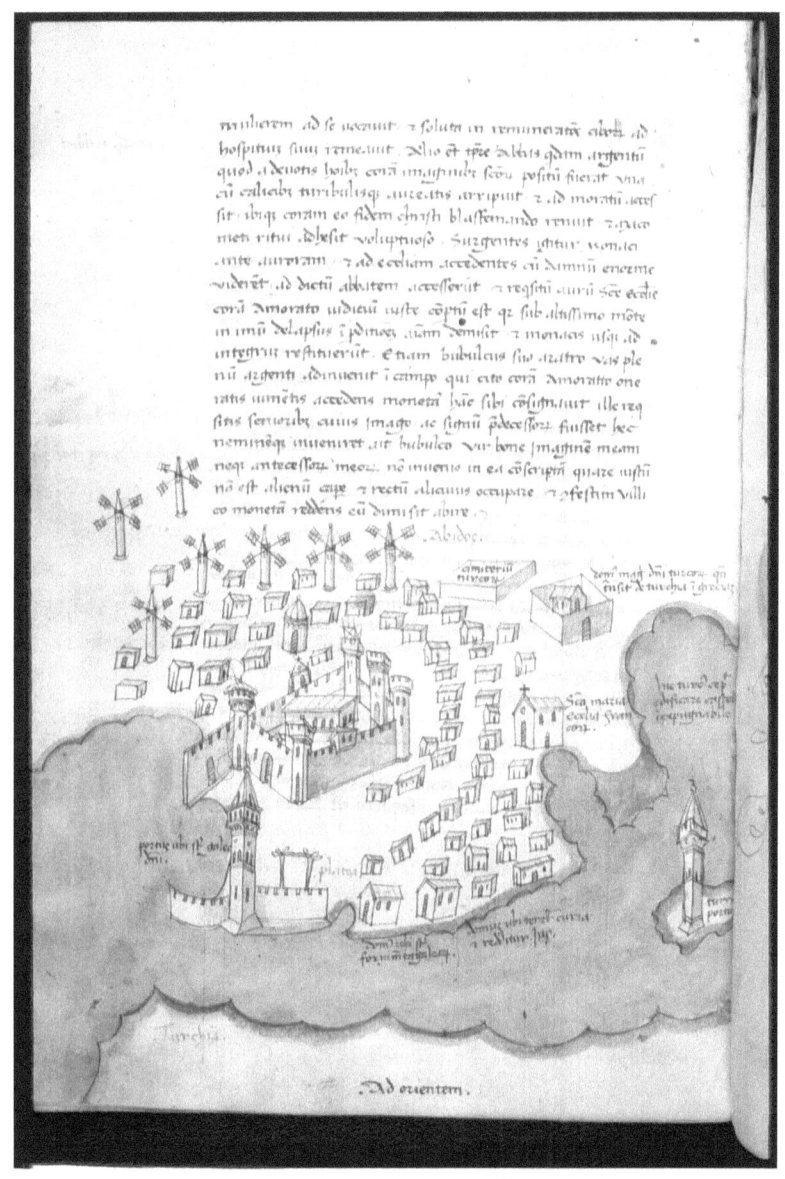

Figure 11. The ancient city of Abydos. Christophoro Buondelmonti, *Liber insularum archipelagi*, MS 18246, folio 51v. Copyright Biblioteca Nacional de España.

The Mediterranean was a world imagined and depicted in maps that conveyed a specifically produced space. The production of this space, as we have seen, corresponds to an amalgam of discourses on space that traverse that sea. Between the waves, the islands that dot these waters proved to be especially sensitive to the production of fictions.

Maps, and fictive maps in particular, or maps with fictive elements, are eloquent about the perception and use of insularity in the late Middle Ages and the early modern world. As Jacob writes, "in the typology of fictive maps, island maps occupy a privileged place. While landscape maps are given to a bird's-eye or a profile view, the island is a space suited par excellence to vertical, cartographical viewing."[92] Relying on the "closed" quality of the island, read as autonomy, the island map immediately calls on a verisimilitude that places it in the realm of the possible, even the likely. It is the minimal cartographic unity, providing the viewer or reader with all possibilities in a concentrated fashion. To look upon the map of an island is to conquer a point of view that is totalizing, comprehensive, and simple at the same time.

The impossibility of verifying in situ every detail of the map, let alone the islands themselves, is what left the debate of their *reality* very much up to the limits of a library that confirmed or denied their existence. The verification of a map was, until very recently, in the absence of images from space, the verification of geography *with* a fiction: the map. This verification depends on a social convention that precedes the production of the image—the map—articulated mainly in a series of texts, of narrations. We have already established the dependence between maps and texts and their claims—or absence of them—to a "reality." Fictive maps and the texts on which they depend share all these characteristics.

The *isolario* in particular bore an impact on writing that resulted in the "reshuffling of the taxonomies that order knowledge in the age of humanism." The cartographic move "from an inherited concept of a world mirror," to one of "subjective singularities," fathomed in part by every individual's experience of the world, as Tom Conley writes, is a change that can be traced in a parallel way in the development of romance into book of chivalry and into novel: "The way that cosmography *fails* to explain the world gives rise to a productive fragmentation that momentarily allows various shapes of difference to be registered without yet being appropriated or allegorized," as contemporary developments in sentimental fiction or the picaresque novel would do.[93] The structure of the *isolario* itself, in its new fragmented yet totalizing effect stands in close relation to the development of the structure of the modern novel.

Key to our study of the relation between insularity and fiction is Jacob's intuition that cartography can be defined more clearly as an effect of verisimilitude, backed by authoritative techniques and the power of representation as a form of mimesis.[94] The concept of verisimilitude emphasizes the crossroads where literature and cartography meet. On the one hand, the mapped or narrated island is the space of possibility, of likelihood; on the other hand, it is a historically produced space.

A series of abstractions govern the insular imaginary up to the moment when the Spanish book of chivalry comes into being. This set of paradigms, which can still be seen at work in today's island imaginary, can be enumerated as follows:

1. Otherness. The island, whether near or far, is the representation of a beyond that houses rupture, strangeness, and difference.[95]
2. Monstrosity. Related to otherness and to the sacred, to the other world and sometimes to femininity (through procreation), as a figure of the marvelous or of evil, increasingly as a figure for politics, monsters seem to favor islands as a habitat, from classical imaginations to fictions of our day.[96]
3. Lost islands. Beginning with Plato in the *Critias* and the *Timaeus* in the island of Atlantis, this idea was again taken up and emphasized in various degrees throughout the Middle Ages and beyond, sometimes coupled and even confused with other motifs, such as the receding or mobile island.
4. Supernatural. The dependence of the supernatural on a marginal space, or on a borderline space, is what determines its relationship to insularity. Giants and fairies are supernatural beings that usually inhabit islands, while islands are also particularly sensitive to enchantments.[97]
5. Otherworldliness. This refers to the afterlife, as exemplified in a way by the Arthurian Avalon, which through its subjection to the authority of fairies, points at an afterlife that, in Celtic culture, is characterized by femininity. This can be further emphasized through the Island of the Golden Apples *(Insula pomorum)* of the *Vita Merlini*, and the *Ínsulas Dotadas* episode of the *Çifar*, to cite examples from a general chivalric imaginary.[98]

6. Sacredness. Partaking of many characteristics, the medieval island inherits the concept of illustrious births on islands in Antiquity: Zeus is born on Crete, Hera on Samos, Hermes in Arcadia, in the center of the island of Pélops, Apollo on Delos.[99]
7. Femininity. Emphasized through the common image of the island of the Amazons, present in a great variety of texts, from Alexander texts to books of chivalry to catalogues of *mirabilia*, such as the *Liber de monstrosis hominibus Orientis*. Inherent to this feminization is the concept of desire, equating the desire to disembark upon an island with the desire to possess a woman. The coupling of eroticism and femininity give way, predictably, to a satanization of the island, making it a figure of evil, for which the best-known examples are Ogygia and Circe's island in the *Odyssey*.[100]
8. Refuge. Related to motherhood through the idea of femininity, the island as refuge is opposed to the ocean. It is a safeguard against drowning, but it is also a place of uncertainty. In the *Aeneid*, it ciphers the uncertainty of the future, as the island represents the moment where the hero does not yet know his destiny.
9. Exile. Set at a distance, the island is, in ancient Rome, above all the place of exile, for those banned from humanity. Pandataria in the Tyrrhenian where Julia, daughter of Augustus, and Agrippina, widow of Germanicus, were sent, where Octavia was murdered. Pianosa, Corsica, and Rhodes were also spaces that received all types of condemned men, from traitors to magicians to political exiles.[101] Also as an idea of exile, the island served as the "desert" for the monastic practices of early Christianity, relating the idea of exile to one of purification, sometimes through marvels and monstrosity, as in the case of Saint Anthony, and ultimately, to sacredness.
10. Origin. Related to the classic notion of "center" (Delos) and mixed with the Christian idea of Paradise, the island takes on the idea of "origin" or "beginning." Examples are to be found particularly in maps, where Paradise is represented as an island.

All of these traits are emphasized differently in texts and images, which configure series of relationships and reshuffle paradigms that characterize a period. A series of principles that articulate the motif of the island can be drawn from these characteristics, principles common to all uses of the island motif that illuminate, in their brevity, the instrumentality of the motif for a spatial narrative:

- Marvelous. Invoking inhabitants of islands can best convey this: gods (in Greek mythology), hermits, giants, the jinn of Islamic culture, monsters in general, women, prophets, and magicians. These are all marginal figures or related to marginality, thus making the marvelous their obvious way of expression.
- Miniaturization. As an object of knowledge, the island must be subjected to observation, best performed when miniaturization and separation from relations takes place: "The island gives in this sense the equivalent of an intimate or concentrated panoptism," writes Lestringant.[102] As the ideal legible space, the island provides a perfect site for images of the microcosm, often complemented or supplemented by caves or grottoes that were in any case contiguous in classical geographical writing. This principle is what Lestringant emphasizes when categorizing the world-island, a heterogeneous place where all variety is encompassed, harmoniously in the case of a utopia, contradictorily in historical cases.[103]
- Hyper-consciousness of a limit. This is the principle that sets off the island, both as a visual element in a map, signaled only by the tracing of its limit, or in a text, set aside by the narration of a journey (successful or ending in shipwreck) that leads to it. Either in complete isolation or in archipelago, where it emphasizes unity in diversity, the encompassing, achievable limit of the island distinguishes it from any other space.
- Reversibility.[104] Paradise-utopia/hell-dystopia.[105] Islands seem to be particularly sensitive to reversibility, often presenting both sides within the same text, the same presentation. But reversibility can also refer to a "function" of insularity that can be illustrated through synecdoche. In the same manner as this rhetorical figure, the island can be generalizing—gesturing toward totality—or particularizing—gesturing toward singularity—and often, it can do both at the same time, reversing its sign and transforming the meaning of what is set upon it.
- Totalization. This principle relates it to the idea of the absolute, figured on the island as a circle or a sphere: safe spaces, regular, perfect. It invokes the idea of the encyclopedia, of the world as island encircled by the ocean, of the possibility of encompassing everything by looking at the mappamundi and

encountering Christ's gaze on the way. It points not only to the microcosm of the singular island but also to the atlas structure of the *isolario*. It is also the cartographic legends that, framed as if they were islands and scattered on a map or a globe, occupy one space by explaining another, as pictorial metaphors.

- Inscription. "Islands, better than any other space, demonstrate most forcefully what is at stake with toponymy in cartography. Island names are toponyms associated with a form and a surface; they often constitute the only inscription within the island shape. The island is a toponym linked to a form. It is also the space par excellence that best lends itself to the pleasure of naming,"[106] a process best exemplified in the toponymy of the islands of the New World.[107] Inscription may come to the island not only as a designation, but also in the idea of authorship, where the cartographer draws his own name following a shoreline but, most frequently, upon a new island or rock just off the coast or well in the middle of the ocean.

- Singularity. This quality refers to the tendency to allocate one marvel, one monster, one species to the enclosed space of the island, to the possibility of cataloguing, of inventory, of taxonomy. Examples are catalogues of *mirabilia*, both in texts and in cartography, such as the islands of demons in sixteenth century portolans, the island of satyrs in the Indian Ocean or the Amazon islands in Thévet's *Grand Insulaire*, the island as a minimal unit for a repertoire, what Lestringant calls the monogram-island.[108] As "a minimal unit of cartographic space," the island in its very limitation "provides the guarantees of a maximal legibility."[109]

- Experience. Insularity is experimental in sets of oppositions, in binomes: experiences of the object in the singular island, of the exuberant microcosm contained in the world-island; experience of the catalogue in the multiplied island: the archipelago. But it is also an experience of the subject in the sense of a trial and in the sense of adventure.[110] The subject who actively, through traveling, seeks and is seized by the event that must then be narrated as experience.

These paradigms and principles are not present of course in every instance of insularity. But they are there as possibility. The presentation of insularity as archipelago invites both an author of *isolarii* and of books of chivalry to explore a variety of possibilities in relation. After Buondelmonti and Montalvo, who articulate a model for this exploration, the genres will evolve and dissolve, either because of an overextended metaphorization, or because of the ossification of a single-minded understanding of the marvelous island.

In the first assemblages of islands, many itineraries within and from the archipelago are offered. Christoforo Buondelmonti includes a long description and a beautiful map of Constantinople in his *isolario* (Figure 12): "We now arrive in the very unfortunate city of Constantinople. Even though it does not form an island, we will not fail, being here, to consecrate it a few lines so that the reader may get an idea of it."[111] Turner argues that one of the most important changes in the manuscript tradition of the *Liber* is the development of the drawing of Constantinople itself.[112] This anchoring of the *isolario* in the city of Constantinople is particularly curious, as it is also a city that holds together the archipelago in dalli Sonetti's (1485) and Porcacchi's (1572) *isolarii*. By then, however, a revealing substitution had occurred, which documented a critical change for the Mediterranean: the city that anchors dalli Sonetti's *isolario* is no longer Constantinople, but Venice. Bordone's Venice-centered perspective endured, as expression not only of a personal choice but as the obvious selection based on cultural, political, and economic reasons. It was at this moment, precisely when Venice had schemed and completed the sack of Constantinople, redistributing not only the material but also the imaginary contents of the most famous city of the Middle Ages, that the Italian city figured itself as the urban ideal.[113]

Bartolommeo dalli Sonetti inaugurated a type of *isolario*, the nautical *isolario*, which had multiple examples throughout the sixteenth century, including Valentim Fernandes's Portuguese *isolario* of 1506–10, connected to imperial expansion by way of its focus on Atlantic islands. Pīrī Re'īs's *Kitāb-i Baḥriyye* (1521) is the most spectacular example of this genre, exhibiting the deftness and seafaring knowledge in the Mediterranean of the Ottoman court, a work that belongs to the *isolario* genre but that has strong generic ties to navigation manuals, *artes de navegar*. After Sonetti and Re'īs, *isolarii* were ostensible commercial artifacts, as Bordone's. Porcacchi's *isolario* will develop yet another strand, forging the "topical *isolario*," which, set against the reformulation from book of chivalry into novel in Cervantes's *Don Quixote*, lends itself to further analysis. For while Cervantes will not be considered in direct relation to the developments of *isolarii*, but as a specular

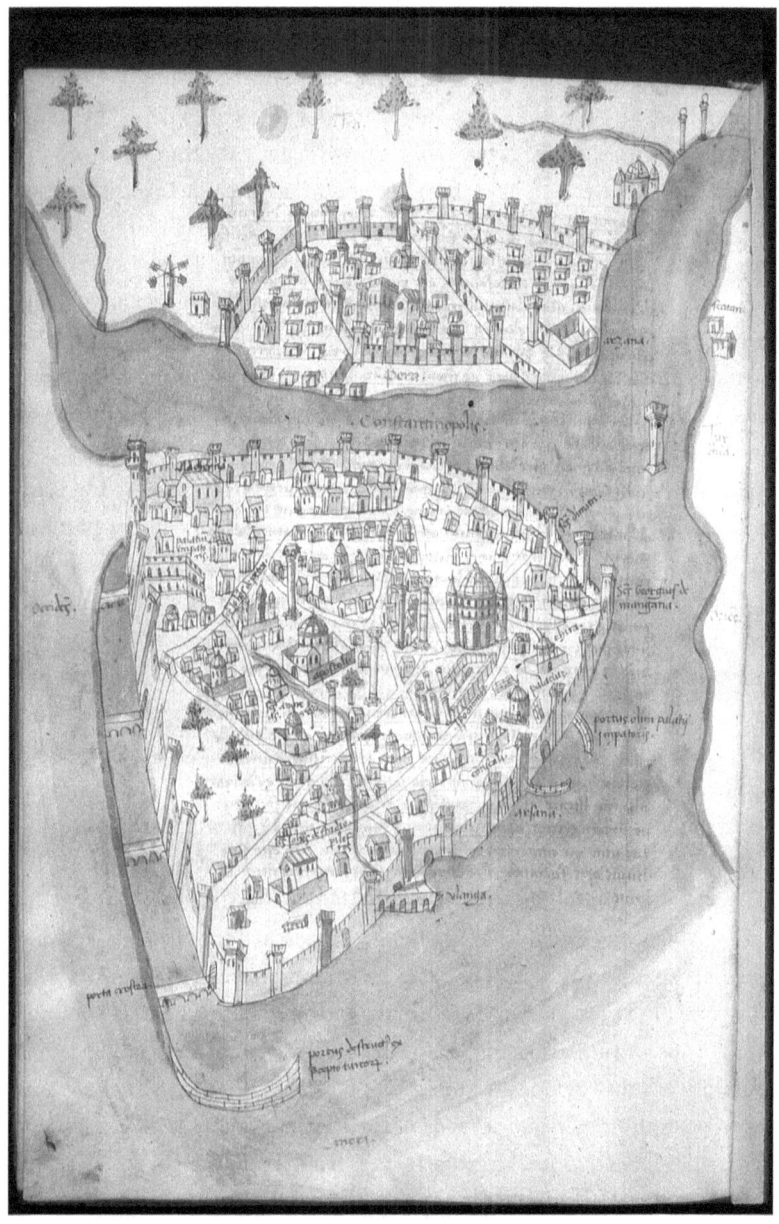

Figure 12. Constantinople is part of the archipelago, both an island and a city depicted in all its real, and fictional, wonder. Christophoro Buondelmonti, *Liber insularum archipelagi*, MS 18246, folio 55v. Copyright Biblioteca Nacional de España.

discourse, we should note here that his elaboration of the Amadisian insular model is in consonance with elements elaborated by Porcacchi. As Tolias writes, in Porcacchi the structural unity of space is ignored, fragmented in order for history and ethnography to come to the fore. The island becomes a pretext for the account of political situations, focused almost exclusively, as the times called for, on the eastern Mediterranean.[114] Other political enterprises, other expansionist interests took the *isolario* in the other direction, to the West, encompassing the entire world in a return to the universal *isolario*, which Coronelli produces three times within the thirteen-volume *Atlante Veneto*. Coronelli presents his work as a supplement to Blaeu's atlas, explaining its organization: "the whole work is divided into islands, starting with the four continents, which might be described as large islands, and ending with islands so small that they do not deserve the name and are called rocky islets" (Figure 13).[115]

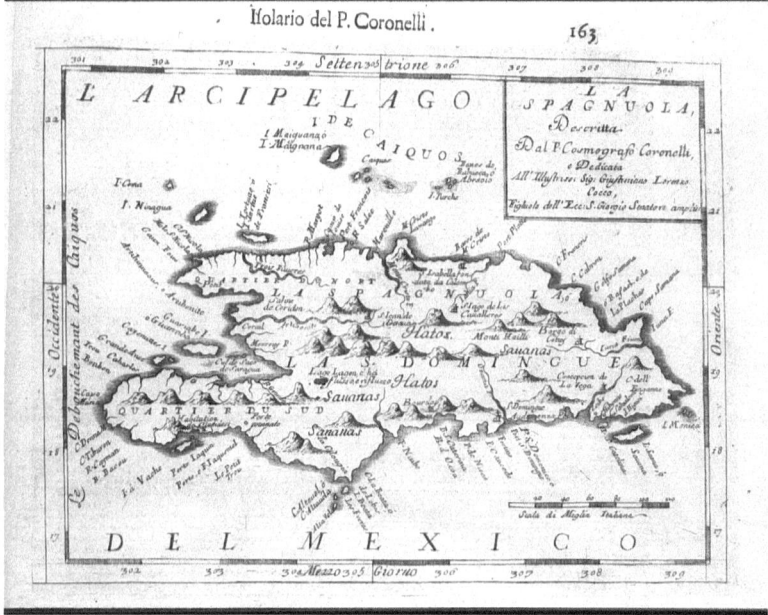

Figure 13. Coronelli's "L'Archipelago del Mexico" uses the metaphor of the island/archipelago to catalogue all diversity of the world. *Isolario dell' Atlante Veneto*. Ayer Collection, 135 C8 1696, p. 163, vol. 2. Courtesy of the Newberry Library.

Isolarii thus respond to and articulate a complex economic and political reality, even when parading their qualities of entertainment, adventure, and fiction. As a city that articulates the genre, both as center of the publishing industry and as content, Venice, real and unreal, as Braudel claims, is, of course, a concrete and known land. But it is a land only as those banks of mud and sand that in the lagoon barely emerge from the salt waters. To allow that land to sustain Venice, a consolidation of that land with rocks and, even more, with thousands and millions of tree trunks, of vertically assembled oaks was necessary: "Venice rises over an engulfed forest,"[116] writes Braudel, ciphering thus the palimpsest production of spaces, a forest, an island, a city. Such a coincidence of limits, of contents, of production, was not invisible to earlier geographical writing: Hugh of Saint Victor had listed Venice as an island off the Adriatic Sea in his *Descriptio mappe mundi*, and the Hereford mappamundi represented it as island as well, anticipating a new relocation of fiction.

3

ADVENTURE AND ARCHIPELAGO
Amadís de Gaula and the Insular Turn

> "Good friend, our enemies are here." And he said,
> "Let us arm ourselves and go see them."
> —*Amadís*, Book I

For the contemporary reader, *Amadís*'s positioning between Arthurian romance and Cervantes's *Don Quixote* is between a rock and a hard place. The unquestionable allure of the first and the celebrated status of the second have contributed to *Amadís*'s fading from the memory of readers, who for the most part will have never heard of it. To the late medieval and early modern audience, however, *Amadís* was very much a household name.

Amadís de Gaula is the first Castilian book of chivalry.[1] Emerging in the thirteenth century in the context of "molinismo," that is, in the precarious political situation that Queen María de Molina presided over, next to the *Libro del Caballero Çifar*, the first chivalric romance in the peninsula, the first medieval version of *Amadís de Gaula* adapted itself to a complex and generous group of traditions and interests. It had at least one other medieval version, of which there are some extant fragments, dated to 1420, kept at the Bancroft Library in Berkeley (ms. UCB 125), known as the Trastámara version.[2] At the end of the fifteenth century Garci Rodríguez de Montalvo, regent of the town of Medina del Campo, rewrote the story into four books (out of the original three) added a fifth, titled *Las sergas de Esplandián*, and gave them to the printing press. Adapted to the tastes and expectations of a Renaissance audience, in the political atmosphere of the reign of Ferdinand and Isabella, and tied to the development of print culture, *Amadís* inaugurated a literary and editorial genre with a success unparalleled by any other in the period.[3] Montalvo himself launched the genre's development through continuations that other authors took up, both in Spain and elsewhere, for the book of chivalry was not only astoundingly successful in Spain, but also in France—where François I sponsored the first translations by Nicolas D'Herberay des Essarts—and the success was echoed in translations into English, German, Dutch, and even a Hebrew version published in Constantinople in 1541, as well as in translation and inspiring original works in Portuguese and Italian. By this success, the book of chivalry came to substitute Arthurian romance in prestige and following, generating other new genres associated with it, such as the *Thrésors*, collections of quotations favored by courtiers throughout Europe. Among its famous readers *Amadís* counted Ignacio de Loyola and Santa Teresa de Jesús, and among the many who imitated him and his feats, whether privately or in ornate festivities, were kings and queens of many a European country. That literary taste indeed changed, favoring claims that already in the first French translations were present, trying to dispute nationality, but especially cultural prestige to the Spanish works in the context of imperial competition, cannot allow the literary historian to forget *Amadís*'s crucial role in the development of Western narrative fiction.

Developing well-known textual traditions, *Amadís* follows the paradigms established by French Arthurian romance, and of the Trojan legends, if in a lesser form, which had already entered the Iberian Peninsula by way of translations of the Vulgate and post-Vulgate cycles, a tradition that initially favored an attribution to a French original.[4] Already in the beginning of the twentieth century, Grace S. Williams, after a careful comparative study of toponymy, nomenclature, and structure, concluded that *Amadís* mainly followed the *Lancelot* and the *Tristan*, owing some of its traits to the Vulgate *Merlin* and other Spanish materials such as the *Gran conquista de Ultramar*, a source study that Lida de Malkiel supplemented with texts from the Trojan legend.[5] Spurred by these analyses, the geography of the *Amadís* has been looked at from many perspectives, ranging from critics who have tried to fix its places to a "reality,"[6] to those who have declared its existence to be absolutely imaginary. E. B. Place, in a passage that one might take to be a model for the rest of Amadisian geography, wrote that Gaula might be considered "one more Arthurian place name conventionalized through long use."[7]

Critics have called attention to the treatment of space in the *Amadís* as one of the ways in which the text drastically departs from the French romance tradition. Juan Bautista Avalle-Arce writes that, at the risk of being obvious, as chivalric literature required the horse, the romance was bound to land, and surprisingly the literature finds navigation merely supplementary.[8] However, the intensity of maritime orientation that governs the geography of *Amadís* from the third book on contradicts that assertion: this orientation does not rely on Arthurian materials—*Lancelot, Tristan,* and *Merlin* for the greater part—which have, for the first two books, marked most of the routes of the Spanish romance through fantastic geographies. In some way this maritime orientation can be traced to the *Estoire*, which as we have seen laid out the seascapes, as it were, for future elaborations in the genre, if Iberia in general preferred the elaboration of adventure in other branches of the cycles rather than the religious themes of the *Estoire*. Montalvo, as he rewrites and recasts *Amadís,* introduces glosses and moralizations to adapt the book to the new political and behavioral interests. Especially from the third book onward, where Montalvo's intervention is increasingly visible, seascapes enter the story and substitute interior continental spaces. Two of the most emblematic episodes of his version, the battle against the Endriago and the love penance on the Poor Rock, take place on an island.[9]

In *Amadís de Gaula* the hero's life opens with the motif of the abandonment of the newborn child to the waters, anticipating the maritime tendency that will become evident as in the middle of the third book, islands and littorals begin to clearly predominate over the mainland. While in books I and II routes of communication and places of adventure are roads and forests, *florestas* and springs (separately or in conjunction), Amadís's departure for the Orient inaugurates the charting of a new space. This space will be crossed by new routes, new means of transportation, new places of encounter and adventure.[10] *Ínsulas* are given this name in the romance because of the genre's archaizing tendency, but islands in the *Amadís* are not a metaphor, they are so in a literal sense: a geography, a portion of land surrounded by water. Individually, they serve different functions and perform different tasks within the whole of the narrative. Taken together as archipelago, they constitute the radical novelty of the Spanish book of chivalry—as an inventory of the marvelous, as an anchor with a chivalric reality in its political, economic, and juridical dimensions, as a structure for the construction of narrative fiction that prefigures the modern novel, and even as a spectrum for thought on fiction itself in its relation to philosophy.

The Amadisian archipelago, "the vastest and most eloquent example of this insular romanticism that appears in turn in legends and narrations of travelers,"[11] deploys a series of narrative strategies that, articulating a number of traditions, explore different uses of the sea and its islands in order to present variation in the notion of adventure that have important structural consequences. The presence of islands as sites of adventure has been noticed many times, and mostly interpreted as a group, at times dismissed as being scantly and monotonously described. The islands are in fact hazily individualized as geography except for the events that take place on them, mirroring the equally repetitive settings of forests and *florestas* of the first two books. This redundancy, while emphasizing the displacement of the function and contents of the forest to insular spaces, also highlights the ambiguity, the imprecision of a geography that may or may not be identified. As Cacho Blecua notes in his edition, "in no case can we analyze them as a wish to propose a verifiable geography."[12] Thus, if Olschki writes that although fantastic islands that from a variety of texts seem to predate the *Amadís*—*Ile Tournoyante, Isle Estranje, Iles Lointaines*—are located in the Ocean, in the West, that is, in the Atlantic, Amadís will travel to the East, thus forcing those cardinal points, those margins of the map, to coincide in his journey. The Amadisian archipelago brings the ambiguous marvels of Western and Eastern insularities together within the known sea, into the Mediterranean: it charts the unknown inside the everyday, making the unverifiable—fiction—part of the known or the real.

Parallel to the displacement toward the sea as a setting for adventure, *Amadís* continued a change in the meaning of chivalry, already present and paradoxically ciphered in its spiritualization in the realm of ideas and its secularization in the reality of chivalry's increasing absorption into state administration. Simultaneously, new structures and narrative techniques were needed to articulate the multiplicity of characters and spaces included in a general narrative thread, and as romance developed, these techniques became part and parcel of narrative advancement. This structural and technical problem is, crucially, a spatial one: the opposition between the space of community and the space of individuality, the space of courtly love and that of chivalric adventure. Critics have elaborated typologies of these spaces, which might be matched with categorizations of the narrative into "events."[13] Silvia Lastra Paz's structural analysis reveals the multilayered function of space in the novel, and the numerous overlaps, ambiguities, and contradictions that inform the use of space in *Amadís*.[14] Two ideas proposed by Lastra Paz are relevant to my analysis: First, that space constitutes a structure in the book of chivalry—a structure I relate to the technique called interweaving or interlacing; and second, that these spaces function through opposition, at times radical, but mostly through contradiction and ambiguities that contain both extremes.[15]

In spatial terms, the repetitive structure of separation, confrontation, recognition, and reconciliation, in Harry Sieber's concise formulation, articulates two basic spaces, one represented by the court, the other by adventure.[16] The hero, in his civilizing mission, travels farther each time, accreting the territories newly traversed to the romance's geography, and recreating an East/West opposition that culminates with the arrival of the hero in Constantinople in book III.[17] The motivation to move from court to the space of adventure may be personal, prompted by a letter, a lady's disdain, a rescue, kidnapping, and so forth. But what configures space as structure is the multiplicity of simultaneous spaces, which only becomes obvious when more than one character is involved. That is, if we take some distance from the hero's adventures and take into account the many other characters traversing the narrative, we can piece together what may be called a tapestry, following James D. Fogelquist's analysis of the relation between the secondary characters and the hero.[18]

For Juan Manuel Cacho Blecua, interweaving as a form of amplification implies a distance from the compositional models of Arthurian narrative and its folkloric roots. This critic argues for a "modernity" of the interwoven romance precisely because of its taste for multiple plots. Interweaving, then, would be a technique that allows new narrative models to come into being, to give way to this preference.[19]

Cacho Blecua cites two basic means of interweaving, one that formally indicates a change in plot and one that does not.[20] These marks aid the author in suggesting the simultaneity of events, even when a precise time sequence is not indicated or even remotely intended. The necessary rest follows the intensity of the moment of adventure for the knights wounded in battle, a pause that is the cue for interweaving. The formulation "dexa la historia," or "dexa aquí el cuento" (leaving the story aside), is common to both historiography and book of chivalry, suggesting a common solution for space–time problems in narrative contexts.[21] Space, coupled with adventure, functions thus as intrinsic to interweaving, standing at both ends of the process, motivating it, serving as setting for it, or providing a meeting place for the narrative threads at the end of a particular interweaving sequence. As Montalvo perfects his narrative techniques, new solutions come forth that include the narration of events remembered at the end of book IV, or the radical solution of making the protagonist a narrator of his own story in the *Sergas*.[22]

Once we have established that space is structural and key to the development of narrative techniques in the book of chivalry, we can look at geography proper. If the geographical domain of the *Amadís* is limited in the first book to vague but known places (Brittany, Gaul, Scotland, and Great Britain), in the second book the space of the romance is extended to new spaces that will take on greater importance as the text advances: *Ínsula Firme, Peña Pobre, Ínsula de Mongaça*, and so on.[23] By the third book, there is a great increase in the geographical reach of the romance, as it gradually displaces events to the East, reaching its climax in Constantinople, while the hero collects adventures in the kingdoms of Bohemia, the *Ínsulas de Romanía*—with extraordinary intensity in the *Ínsula del Diablo*—and Greece, to then, after Constantinople, make a hurried return to Great Britain. Book III's "amphibious destiny," in Avalle-Arce's words, marks a distance from *Amadís*'s Arthurian models and makes way for new motifs that will become models for the Spanish book of chivalry. The particularities of sea travel become decisive: navigation and its dangers, the most important among them being sea tempests, are key in the coming into being of adventures from this point on. In this particular setting, a newly conceived archipelago draws its silhouette.

The Amadisian archipelago is composed of rock formations and islands, reminiscent of Coronelli's definition of the islands that make up the world, from continents to rocky islets. These "cliffs" or "rocks" (*peñas*), which include the *Peña de Galtares* (I, 3),[24] the *Peña de la Doncella Encantadora* (IV), and the Rock of the Hermit or *Peña Pobre,* Poor Rock (II, 48), are distinguished from islands by their size. They are small, arid, and inhabited by serpents; denote austerity in one case (the Poor Rock); and stage a marvelous marked by tragedy in the three others. The case for some *peñas* as maritime spaces remains problematic, for in some cases it is not mentioned that a boat needs to be taken to get there, and at other times in the text, *peñas,* not singularized as a proper name, are just taken to be boulders, large and small. Most often, though, these spaces specifically articulate traits summarized in the previous chapter: the Poor Rock is described specifically as a hermitage located far into the sea, on a rock so steep that boats can only approach it in the summer, underlining navigational conditions; while the Rock of the Charming Damsel requires six days of sea travel to be reached.

Ínsulas are legion throughout the romance, so I will only mention here those that are individualized through a name: *Ínsula Gravisanda* (I, 41); *Ínsula No Fallada* (II, 59; III, 68); *Ínsula Dudada,* after *Ínsula Firme* (II, Prol and 63; 84 and 126 as the most important instances); Island of the Boiling Lake, or *Ínsula of Mongaça* (II, 54); *Ínsula Triste* (III, 65); *Ínsulas de las Landas* (III, 65); *Ínsula Leónida* (III, 68); *Ínsulas de Romanía* (III, 72); *Ínsula del Diablo,* later *Ínsula de Santa María* (III, 73–74); *Ínsula Gabasta* (III, 74); *Ínsula Profunda* (IV, 96 and 108); *Ínsula Sagitaria* (IV, 108); *Ínsula Fuerte* (IV, 109); *Ínsula del Infante* (IV, 127); *Ínsula de la Torre Bermeja* (IV, 127); *Ínsulas Luengas* (IV, 129); and *Ínsula Liconia* (IV, 132).[25] Of a total of seventeen named islands in the four books, thirteen appear in the last two books.

The *peñas* and *ínsulas* of *Amadís de Gaula* make up an archipelago where the whole spectrum of traditional, folkloric, scientific, and religious contents ascribed to islands is represented. From the space of penitence and sanctity inherited from historical monastic enclaves, to spaces of enchantment and magic, exoticism, riches, and spices; places inhabited by monsters and horrific beasts, home to giants, paradisiacal and thus utopian spaces, ciphers of the foreign and the strange: these rocks and islands of the Amadisian archipelago form an inventory of the marvelous. They are, in romance, what

Bordone and later *isolarii* would compile in cartography: as an *isolario* of all the islands in the world, the islands of *Amadís* constitute a catalogue of the universe of fiction. As the site for adventure to take place, as the situation of events through narrative, they thus present a theory of fiction.[26]

The marvelous takes on a series of meanings, often complementary and simultaneous in their occurrence in the text. The most immediate of these senses is the marvelous as the strange and ambiguous, as both weird and as foreign. Amadís as a child is described in this manner, his early feats are described in similar terms, and he identifies himself using the word in both senses: "soy un caballero estraño"; "I am a stranger knight" (I, 13, 358; 136), implying his own foreignness, his unknown identity.[27]

The term "marvelous" is used in many other less spectacular or intriguing ways, where the strange may or may not be implied. One of these is as a sign of quantity, of great numbers; often the concept is lexicalized in the untranslatable adverbial locution as "a maravilla," and related to this use, the word serves as an intensifier with the same formulation, sometimes changing the noun for a passive conjugation of the verb *maravillarse*. The meaning of "surprised" or "astonished" is represented by the verb *maravillarse*, its recurrence so systematic that it alternates with a noun form meaning "a thing to be admired." Paradoxically, the element of wonder remains uninterpretable for most occurrences because of the sheer number of times the word is used in this sense, rendering the supernatural natural.

Closer to what we might expect to be described in terms of the marvelous are all sorts of magical things, such as those events related to Urganda la Desconocida and Arcaláus el Encantador, often represented in the engravings, especially those of the French translation, where the events themselves are sometimes labeled enchantments. At other times even the wondrous effect of these events is subsumed under the marvelous presence of the enchantress herself, as when Urganda produces a sword for Galaor from a tree:

> "You shall not give him that one [sword], but the one yonder that is hanging in that tree, with which you will be happier."
>
> Then they all looked at the tree; they saw nothing. She began to laugh in earnest, and said,

"By heaven, it has been there for all of ten years, and no one ever saw it who passed by here and now everyone shall see it"

And again looking, they saw the sword hanging from a limb of the tree, and it appeared very beautiful, and as fresh as though it had been placed there just then, and the sheath very richly wrought of silk and gold. (I, 11, 339; 118)

The sword appears hanging as a fruit in the tree, highlighted by the author's description of the sword appearing "fresh," as a fruit would, contrasting the natural and the marvelous worlds.[28] By contrast, the magic of evil enchanter Arcaláus is tinged with treason and artifice. Even the architectonic marvel that is his palace is a *trick*, where the marvelous acquires negative undertones. While some other buildings in book I provoke wonder without suspicion, as the castle of the *Peña de Galtares*, Arcaláus's palace itself is an architectonic marvel that anticipates the development of the theme of marvelous architecture that will take on great importance from the second book on.[29]

The introduction to chapter 41 of the *Ínsula Gravisanda* and the marvelous events that take place in it—the battle and scene of recognition between Amadís's two brothers, Galaor and Florestán—is the result of a series of developments of insular space.[30] Even if islands and coastal spaces only begin to predominate in the third book, seascapes are present from the beginning of the romance, such as in this crucial scene. The most memorable of these irruptions is a structural, characterizing moment: Amadís's abandonment to the sea at birth, which gives him his name, from the moment of his rescue by Gandales to his recognition as the son of the king and queen of Gaula, with the name of *Donzel del Mar,* Child of the Sea. But the presence of the sea does not mark only the protagonist. All the main characters, notably Oriana and Amadís's two brothers, Galaor and Florestán, have a particular relation to the sea. Oriana is daughter of Brisena, "the most beautiful maiden to be found in all the islands of the sea" (I, 3, 268; 54), and is introduced in the text in chapter 4 of the first book when her parents, seeing that she is seasick, agree to leave their daughter with King Languines of Scotland, under whose queen the *Donzel del Mar* serves. Galaor, for his part, being two and a half years old, visits his father the king in a village by the sea called Banguil. There Gandalás, a kind giant lord of an island, kidnaps Galaor to fulfill the prophecy that told the giant the child would recover the *Peña de Galtares* for him. Galaor will live on the giant's island raised by a hermit until he reaches a knightly age and fulfills Urganda's prophecy. The third brother of Amadís is introduced as Florestán, the lover of Corisanda, lady of the *Ínsula de Gravisonda*, in the next-to-last chapter of the first book that has been discussed above. Amadís and his lineage are thus marked by the sea and insularity.

Islands and seascapes are referenced throughout *Amadís de Gaula*, through coastal itineraries and navigational remarks on sails, anchors, weather conditions, rivers, ports, ships, and harbors. The narrative stresses the changeable conditions of the sea, and the hero's self-definition links the sea to adventure: "que yo fue hallado en la mar por gran aventura"; "for by extraordinary chance I was found at sea" (I, 10, 327; 108). But most revealing is how this insular imaginary is lexicalized in expressions that make *todas las ínsulas del mar*, "all the islands of the sea"—an archipelago—into a figure for the world that recalls Alonso de Santa Cruz's *Islario de todas las islas del mundo*. In this vast and complex archipelago, I will emphasize three islands, as they seem to present models or paradigms for the narration of fiction: the *Ínsula Firme* (Firm Island), the *Ínsula del Diablo* (Island of the Devil), and the *Ínsula No Fallada* (Not Found Island), signaling various other places of the archipelago of the book of chivalry that reenact or reformulate these paradigms.

Ínsula Firme

The second book of *Amadís* begins with a justification for an *excursus* on the *Ínsula Firme*, or Firm Island, which argues that while this space is particularly important for events of the fourth book, it is pertinent to read about it at this particular moment of the narrative. This introduction is an obvious sign of Montalvo's intervention to expand and rewrite his own interests into the book. In fact, the immediate crucial events that take place on this island in the second, and not in the fourth book, undermine Montalvo's first assertions.[31]

There are several studies devoted to the *Ínsula Firme*, either on the general events that take place there or more specifically to the buildings, and general criticism on the *Amadís* must address it. A frequent approach to the *Ínsula Firme* has been to see it as a "center." Maier sees in London (by which he apparently means Lisuarte's traveling court) and the *Ínsula Firme* "symbols of the values which each character represents," that is, symbols of Lisuarte and Amadís, respectively. Following a folkloric approach, this interpretation has dominated as a method for reading *Amadís* and still conditions studies on the book of chivalry.[32] Centered on the main hero, studies tend to view space in the *Amadís* only as a sign of something else, as "symbol," or mirror of the character. Here, without overlooking the moral values that these episodes articulate in the configuration of chivalry, I want to emphasize a spatiality that can be further analyzed in terms of a political utopia and a reflection on law that has numerous parallels in contemporary debates on nobility and chivalry.

A few lines into the prologue we are told that once there was a king of Greece, married to a sister of the emperor of Constantinople. The first of their two sons, Apolidón, is described as having strength of both body and mind and of having dominated with his "subtle wit" the "sciences of all the arts," necromancy in particular. When the king of Greece must choose a successor, he divides his estate between the two brothers: the first-born will have the kingdom, the second shall have the treasure and books. After the younger brother complains, Apolidón generously gives up the kingdom and takes riches and library into a boat, having such favorable winds that he arrives by chance in the Roman Empire in no time (II, Prol, 658; 420). In Rome he falls in love with the emperor's sister, Grimanesa, and together they take to sea, arriving on the *Ínsula Firme,* ruled by a fierce giant (II, Prol, 659; 420). Apolidón fights and kills the giant, becoming lord of the island, where he and Grimanesa live for sixteen years, yielding to their mortal desires and building rich edifices with their treasure and knowledge.

The story merits close attention. We have moved westward from Constantinople to Greece to Rome and then, presumably still further west, to the *Ínsula Firme.* With the union of Grimanesa and Apolidón, the author has linked two empires, Constantinople and Rome, and the kingdom of Greece (later called an empire), with its political and cultural prestige, to the *Ínsula Firme,* and has given this union a realm of its own. This *ínsula,* previously ruled by a brave, cruel giant, is won over by Apolidón, marking a change in "sign" of the island that is eminently political, and which will be reenacted by our hero later on. The story goes on to tell us that after sixteen years, his grandfather dies without an heir, and Apolidón is summoned to occupy the throne. Before their departure, they arrange for a series of enchantments to guard the island and commemorate their love.

The entrance to the island is said to be by way of the castle. Castle and island are made synonymous, referring either to the castle as guarding the entrance-bridge to the island or to the castle located on the bay that looks to the continent.[33] But toponymy has other functions in the book of chivalry. Like Apolidón, Amadís is characterized by the steadfastness of his love. The trials in which he triumphs proclaim what knights around him who inhabit the island feel toward him as well, characterizing him as a leader who elicits loyalty from his companions and subjects: "And all were very firm in their affection for Amadís and determined to follow him in everything that he might will to do" (II, 63, 915; 658). Such harmony or "concordia," on the other hand, has been interpreted as an element revealing the idealized or paradisiacal characterization of the *Ínsula Firme*.

Maier uses Hesiod's *Works and Days* to look at these aspects of the *Ínsula Firme*. He traces the Golden Age concept, linked in Hesiod to the Isles of the Blessed, to *Amadís* through Juan del Encina's translation of Virgil in his 1496 *Cancionero*, to the *Ínsula Firme* episodes of the *Amadís de Gaula*. According to Maier, a contemporary reader of the *Ínsula Firme* episode would have been reminded of Paradise through "the wished-for return to an age of stability and justice," linking it to the reign of the Catholic kings, in a political reading not taken further by Maier.[34] Maier specifically considers the description of the garden in the *Ínsula Firme* as a paradise on earth, a *locus amoenus*, qualifying it as a mere rhetorical exercise that would have linked it to the paradisiacal tradition. This imagery is subsumed under a general "Golden Age concept" that permeates the entire work.[35] In this interpretation, the space of the island is made to signify a time, a period, and an age, and any meaning tied to its geography or more loosely spatial significance is subordinated or dismissed. Closely read, moreover, the idea of the Golden Age in the *Amadís* is in fact not articulated in the *Ínsula Firme* episodes themselves, but through a scattered authorial gloss vaguely linked by Maier to these episodes. Thus, even if the theme of the return of a Golden Age is a constant in Iberian literatures of the latter half of the fifteenth century, this "moral renaissance of the body politic" is figured in *Amadís* through the narrator/author but not specifically referred through the production of the space of the *Ínsula Firme*. As the place of reunion of these knights who defend the weak from the strong or proud, Maier claims that it emulates Hesiod's Island of the Heroes, in that the abundance and productivity of the place is a sort of reward for a chosen race.[36] However, Hesiod's semidivine beings hold exclusive rights to the space, while in *Amadís* it is only enchanted spaces, such as the garden beyond the Arch of Loyal Lovers and the buildings in it, that are reserved for the select few knights and ladies who are able to pass the tests. The rest of the island, as when it was ruled by the giant before Apolidón's arrival, was and is inhabited not by knights and ladies, but by common people. Amadís is to rule over them now, a people who, during the time they awaited the most perfect of knights, were governed by Isanjo, who in fact keeps this title under Amadís's supervision.

In pursuit of a political reading, Harney analyzes these episodes as willfully ahistorical, as the expression of a desire not to revolutionize the system that renders the institution of chivalry useless, but to become integrated into it. Thus, he reads the enchantments as "designed to fill the leisure characteristic of the noble habitus," while the abundance of fauna ensures hunting privileges associated with this class: "Firm Isle, like Eden, is a self-sufficient, enclosed environment, where economic necessity is supplied" in the form of jewels and treasure, which can satisfy everyone's needs.[37] This utopian place is not only a place where people are happy, but also where strict stratification is accepted and works to the taste and benefit of the knights, and where labor is ultimately taken for granted in the face of the knights' obvious superiority. Happiness, in the end, is not premised—or not solely—on the supply of food and water, on the isle's good weather, or even on endless riches, but on the possibility of locking out the threat to these struggling lesser nobles to stand their ground in a crumbling system. Their happiness, their utopia, lies in the locking out of history: "Forgotten are those things that impede household formation in real life: closed marriage market, money economy, bourgeois interests, fractious peasantry."[38]

This willful forgetfulness, this obliteration of historical political conditions that render the integration of the institution of chivalry into the establishment possible—an establishment that is crumbling down—makes the book of chivalry utopian *in general:* "It permits the trial—above all the exile or estrangement affording the pretext for a glorious second chance—that proves the worthiness of the protagonist. Looking at the chivalric narrative as an amusement park, each adventure, each geographical locale, is a ride or attraction that leads the reader (visitor) to the grand finale—the ride of all rides, the *pièce de résistance*—represented by marriage and living happily ever after."[39] In this analogy with Louis Marin's analysis of Disneyland, the role of the *Ínsula Firme*—as part of "the route of adventure"—becomes clear: it is the concentration of that utopian possibility that the romance offers its readers. In this sense, Harney reverses Marin's analysis in terms of chivalric romance: "we may ... describe readings by the audiences of chivalric romance as vicarious itinerations within the utopic space defined by the narratives."[40] We can extrapolate Harney's reading of the *Ínsula Firme* to the entire archipelago of *Amadís*, where reading the book would be just this kind of wishful journeying through a no longer existing political world.

Taking in the entire spectrum of island possibilities that the *Amadís* proposes, the Amadisian archipelago moves between the two opposing interpretations I have just summarized: one that sees chivalry as a call for a link with reality (Maier) and one that sees chivalry as utopian wish (Harney). These interpretations are possible and valid because they are supported by the historical contradictions between chivalric ideology and the institution of chivalry itself, contradictions that fueled the intense debates on chivalry throughout the fifteenth and sixteenth centuries. The period of expansion of chivalry, between 1390 and 1492, is preceded by a period of definition (1250–1350) and one of restriction (1330–1407), in Rodríguez Velasco's assessment.[41] The first is represented by Alfonso X's legal discussion in *Partidas* (XXI, II) and Don Juan Manuel's corrections to the Alfonsine idea of chivalry, in which the secularism that Alfonso had stressed in order to give chivalry a political dimension is revised and Christianized. Both figures represent a theoretical stage in the development of chivalry in Castile, as the institution of chivalry has no real systematic existence at this time. Rodríguez Velasco summarizes this "theory" in a series of propositions that are assumed or loosely laid out in the period itself: (1) chivalry is a company of noble men; (2) its highest virtue is prudence (which Alfonso calls *sanity*); (3) the lineage of these men is essential to their consideration in the institution, which identifies chivalry with nobility; (4) the origin of chivalry is essentially real and its character secular; (5) bearing the chivalric title is so important that not even the king himself may arm knights if he is not one himself; (6) the king is head of knights and he is tied to them in nobility through the shared chivalric title; (7) intellectual formation is indispensable for the knight, and it is provided through three kinds of text, hierarchically organized, from best to worst, as follows: historiography, oral narratives of chivalric deeds, and epic. The second period is represented by Alfonso X and his Orden de la banda (Order of the band or of the scarf), the introduction and dissemination of Egidius Romanus, and the work of Pero López de Ayala. During this period, knights begin to participate in state administration, and they dispute official posts to professional *letrados* or clerks (which calls into question, for Spain at least, Fuchs's remarks on the contradiction within chivalric romance triggered by the presentation of chivalric values by a clerkly author, for chivalric romance and chivalric institutions are, in fact, written and legislated by knights in Spain).[42] Knighthood gradually begins to be consciously seen as a political exercise ruled by *prudentia*, or discretion. Thus, the old chivalric virtue of *fortitudo*, strength, is driven out of chivalric ideology. From the invention of the institution of chivalry to its expansion in the fifteenth century, the existence of the knight as a specialist is regularly called into question, even during Alfonso XI's attempts to constitute his court in a center for knights and princes, which would serve as a symbol of political power. Chivalry, and the diverse interests that surround it, would work to adapt it. During the last period, two polemics, one concerning nobility and the other the model of knighthood, characterize the debate. While the fifteenth century is the period of maximum success for chivalric ideology, this same success casts a shadow that covers or overtly contradicts the decadence of institutional chivalry and a general disenchantment with chivalric values.[43]

Two factors—the gap between the desire for knighthood as an institutional reality and the historical conditions that split the idea of knighthood into the separate routes of nobility and state administration—account for the paradox of utopian and historically "symbolic" representations of chivalry in literature. Several traits of the book of chivalry itself support the ambivalent relationship with history found in the *Amadís*. Fogelquist argues that the greatest change introduced by Montalvo, distancing the romance from its Arthurian predecessor, is the fact that lovers do not fear the consequences of adultery, but live "under a sense of honor and justice of the woman's father."⁴⁴ Sieber suggests that a changing taste in the reading public accounts not only for the success of the book of chivalry, but also for its fall from grace: "In the very shadow of the romance, new literary tastes emerged and were satisfied by a new literature of immediacy.... The new fiction was set not in a remote land and the distant past but in contemporary urban centers—Seville, Toledo, Madrid—with recognizable geographical landmarks and street names,"⁴⁵ such as the picaresque novel, and the military prowess displayed in books of chivalry was also displaced by new technologies. This change, already reflected in *Amadís* in the change from individual to collective battles, also effects a change in chivalry's relation to and its effects on society. The old institution's perceived lack of legitimacy brings first a crisis and then a new social order. Ultimately, a general disenchantment would cancel both, the historically symbolic possibility and the utopian one.

If ideology is the "representation of the imaginary correlation between individuals and their real conditions of existence," as Louis Marin argues, then utopia is an "ideological locale," a place in ideology, a "theatrical setting" where ideology is put to the test. Marin's definition of Disneyland as "ideology in the form of a myth" helps Harney discuss utopia in chivalric texts: "The utopia of chivalric romances ... encompasses not one central locale, such as Çifar's Fortunate Isles or Amadís's Firm Isle nor the Near East and North Africa of the Catalan romances. It is, rather, the unbounded narrative space of notional topography, taken as a whole, which is utopic. The romances provide a mythogenetic playground for wish fulfillment—i.e., for an ideological resolution, on various levels, of the contradictions inherent in the *habitus* defended and justified by the fantasy."⁴⁶ In not so many words, Harney presents through this concept what I suggest is the archipelago's most interesting function: to "isolate" upon individual spaces types of adventure that address one or another aspect of these contradictions, while providing as a whole a set of possibilities to rearrange a wish or need.

Utopia is defined, however, not only by what it promises, but also by what *is not here in the present*, what lies outside it, beyond its limits. In this sense, it is not the pleasures offered by the space but the possibility of return, of a second chance that characterizes the chivalric utopia.⁴⁷ This is just what Utopus's literal ditching of the continent did for Thomas More: it established a distance and a difference. The active embodiment in a space, or in a persona of otherness, the setting of a limit that makes it an independent, isolated other is what constitutes utopia.

For Maier, the idealized realm of the *Ínsula Firme* is a temporal one, referred to in the past, and characterized by the respect, love, and loyalty of Amadís toward the king, Lisuarte, leaving other questions, such as economy, to the side.[48] For Harney, the utopian representation is motivated historically by the desire of lower nobility to gain prestige in a society characterized by the values of *epic*. The result is an economy that emulates that which is represented in epic itself: booty, the products of territories conquered. Harney terms this activity "economic predation": "wealth in the romances is gained through various modes of predatory appropriation, then used not to create additional wealth, but to reward, to motivate, to secure networks. The economy of the romances is, then, obstinately redistributive, in disregard of the contemporary monetary economy faintly reflected in the texts."[49]

Perhaps the fact that the economy implied by books of chivalry is not an exclusively monetary economy is what Sancho questions and Don Quixote finds puzzling, as Harney has suggested. Books of chivalry display a nostalgic tendency to represent a pre- or antimonetary economy in consonance with the long tradition that sees commerce and the amassing of wealth as not only sinful but also or otherwise vulgar. Privileged social status has never gone hand in hand with labor and engagement in trade, here emphasizing a transformation of the knightly into the courtly, aristocratic figure, a process ironically portrayed as well in *Lazarillo de Tormes*, the picaresque novel that inaugurates the most modern of genres.[50] This is precisely why Amadís's *Ínsula Firme* is characterized as a paradise of wealth and abundance without labor *for the knight's part*; knights are served by native inhabitants of the island, and their riches are those that Apolidón and Grimanesa left there. Amadís's contribution to the prestige of the island is his status as a knight and as a lover; and the wealth he brings with him comes from the epic system of pillaging, booty, and warfare. It is in this sense that the *Ínsula Firme* cannot be related to a *Cockaigne* or a *Jauja*.[51] It is not a place of magical abundance, but a place of absolute leisure, supported by a compliant, happy-to-be-there work force that serves the knightly ruling class. It is for the privileged alone that the *Ínsula Firme* houses a few more distinction-granting mechanisms, its things of mystery under the sign of luxury.

Constructions displaying mechanical artifices like the palace of Arcaláus el Encantador in book III, chapter 69, structures featuring robotic figures and other effects, are generally equated with pagan or evil characters. These mechanisms contrast with the wonderful buildings positively characterized elsewhere in the romance, which are related to knowledge—that is, to bookish knowledge—and magic. The buildings described in greatest detail in the romance are those found on the *Ínsula Firme*. Among them are the Arch of Loyal Lovers, the Defended or Forbidden Chamber, and four houses Apolidón built for himself: the building of the serpent and the lions, the one of the deer and the dogs, the Turning Castle, and the cave of the Bull. The culminating enchanted building is the round palace mounted on twelve marble columns that, when entered by the couple who can parallel Apolidón and Grimanesa in their love, will undo all enchantments of the island (II, Prol), a building that is forgotten in book IV, or more probably conflated with the Defended Chamber. Built with Apolidón's wealth and by his knowledge, these edifices are not only examples of the marvelous that characterize the *Ínsula Firme*, but also a political and social policy for chivalry. The buildings code a hierarchy among the most important characters, for example, between Agrajes and Amadís, or between Briolanja and Oriana. Each of the trials that serve to establish the differences between characters is minutely described, so much so that they might be read as manuals:

> Then he made an arch at the entrance to a garden in which there were trees of all kinds, and furthermore there were in it four vaulted chambers richly wrought; and the garden was fenced in such a way that no one could enter it except under the arch. On top of the latter he put a copper image of a man with a horn in his mouth as if he were about to blow it; and inside one of those rooms he placed two figures, one in his own semblance and the other in that of his mistress, so contrived that they seemed alive, with their faces and figures the same as his and hers, and beside them a very bright stone of striped marble; and he caused a column of iron five cubits in height to be set up, at half the distance of a crossbow shot from the arch, in a large field that was nearby. (II, Prol, 660–61; 422)

The human figure will produce surprising special effects (not only beautiful music, but sweet-smelling flowers flow from the trumpet) when the most loyal of lovers walks under it, and Oriana will also receive special treatment in book IV. The conditions for the test, not reserved exclusively for the heroic couple, are that

> From now on no man or woman will pass ahead if they have wronged those whom they first began to love; because the image that you see blowing that horn, with such an awful sound, amid smoke and flames of fire, will cause them to be paralyzed; and almost like dead they will be thrust forth from this place. But if there come here such knights, matrons, or maidens as be worthy of completing this adventure by reason of their great fidelity, as I have said already, they will enter forthwith and the image will make such a sweet sound that it will be delightful for those to hear who are present; and the latter will see our images and their own names inscribed on the marble, not knowing who inscribed them. (II, Prol, 661; 422)

The enchantments shall end, and all people are to pass under the arch when the island has a lord, and when a woman by virtue of her great beauty comes to occupy the chamber with the knight.[52]

The Arch of Loyal Lovers is the only entrance to an enclosed, wonderful garden.[53] The *hortus conclusus*, a variant of the *locus amoenus*, is a topos that follows strict rules: it is described as intensely desirable, located in remote places or behind barriers. Its original sources are in the garden paradise in the first chapter of Genesis, and in the enclosed garden that appears in the declarations between lovers in the Song of Songs or Songs of Solomon (IV, 12).[54] In terms of our analysis of an evolution of the opposition between savage and civilized spaces, the enclosed, idealized garden of the *Ínsula Firme* "embodies a harmony of city and wilderness, of reason and the nonrational faculties, and thus often constitutes the setting for the resolution of a problem involving the conflict of these elemental psychic forces."[55] The medieval gardens of earthly love, frequently rendering parodies of the Church's beliefs and institutions versus private morality, find in the Garden of Loyal Lovers a particular solution. By secluding Oriana in Apolidón's Tower, which distances her and all ladies from the knights in a kind of improvised monastery where their honor is guarded, Montalvo keeps parody at bay while still invoking all these references. The fragile balance between the savage and the civilized, between desire and reason, is maintained impeccably in the romance, displacing the erotic connotations of earlier Arthurian romances and focusing on the political construction of an elite within the elite.

The garden Cligés makes for his runaway mistress, Fenice, in Chrétien's *Cligés* (6259ff.) and the garden of the *Roman de la Rose* seem to be the most obvious direct antecedents for the garden guarded by the Arch of Loyal Lovers in *Amadís*, with changes derived from Spanish tradition. In *Cligés* the garden is a symbol of private morality, which nonetheless must account for a social morality. This elitist system of morals is betrayed by the pear that, falling from the tree, leads the lovers to discover Bertran's voyeuristic delight. The garden as a symbol of social elitism, manifested clearly in the *Roman de la Rose*, suggests the unavailability of courtly love to those who lack adequate leisure and the corresponding vulnerability of the idle to the assaults of sexual temptation. The symbol is more successfully developed in the Spanish romance. In *Amadís* the garden appears in terms of an *ethics*, rather than a morality. The enclosed garden is a symbol of a private ethics of an exclusive class, more anchored in an Augustinian idea of a spiritual paradise than in a biblical garden.[56] A wilder version of the garden is to be found in the *floresta*, where the encounter with enchantresses and the sensual ways of earthly love and deceit takes place.

Within this garden of perfect lovers, the marvelous serves to highlight individual merit, establishing a strict hierarchy, where achievement is minutely followed and inscribed. This "ordering of the world" only needs to take place until the best knight, Amadís, finishes the process of hierarchization, thus ending a phase of opportunity for the knights of his generation. The next generation will undergo similar tests, in order to settle in its own hierarchy established not through blood but through individual achievement.[57]

The hierarchy is notably visual and spectacular. When Amadís and his friends reach the *Ínsula Firme*, they go through the palace gates and they see in it many shields laid out in three layers according to the virtue, or *bondad*, of each knight: a hundred or so in the lower layer, ten set a little higher, and over these two more, one of them still a bit higher. Each of the shields bears a sign where the owner is commemorated. After they pass the columns, reaching the arch, a sign of the outcome is given through sound. What the inscriptions show is the name of the knight who has finished the adventure, and the name and title of his father, making the result of the *encantamento* and not the phenomenon itself what can be interpreted as a utopia. Amadís's inscription is equally extraordinary: "This is Amadis of Gaul, *the faithful man in love,* son of King Perion of Gaul" (II, 672; 431, my emphasis).

The *Ínsula Firme* is thus a space whose insularity makes it able to hold and contain at distance the most wonderful of pasts until the valorous lover Amadís can come and test the adventures and open the door for an order that is to come. It is a placeholder for a political future, it is the adventure that is to take place but that is already known will happen, the event of chivalric politics. As geography it also contains a number of marvelous adventures whose isolation give it a more special aura, where the extraordinary may be located. Specifically, the *Ínsula Firme* contains a number of marvelous and magical elements pertaining to the technical or scientific marvelous, the properly magical, the architectural, and even the miraculous, all enmeshed poetically through the collapsing of a number of topoi that include the paradisiacal, the *hortus conclusus,* the *locus amoenus,* and so forth. But most importantly, what the *Ínsula Firme* does is codify the production of a political space on an island within a very strict process of hierarchization that brings with it a visual program, a code of manners and behaviors, a project for the division of labor and the consideration of this fiction of politics as if it were already part of the world. As part of the world of *Amadís,* even if it is an island, it does not exist in isolation, but as part of an archipelago, with which it negotiates its meanings through the different possible itineraries.

Ínsula del Diablo

Opposite the paradisiacal island, the Middle Ages elaborated a counterbalancing space in the imaginary ocean: the island of Hell. The distancing and removal of the Other, whether as monster or angel, fairy or witch, are equally circumscribed. This distance produces a perspective, a distancing that refers not only to the horrific or the different, a motif more common to the travelogue, but also to the fantastic or the merely strange.

In the *Amadís* the encounter with an absolute Other takes place on an island ruled over by a monstrous beast, the Endriago, in book III, chapter 73.[58] The arrival at this island is equally clouded in mystery, haphazardness, and omens. We learn the island has been able to overturn the sailors' feelings of relief after being surprised by a fierce tempest they find themselves on shore. They have been moved from premonitions of death to feelings of life—literally, "como si de muerte a la vida tornados fueran" (as if from death to life they had been rendered), only to learn again of the dangers that await them on shore. The dangers of the island surpass the worst dangers of the sea, one of the most fearful experiences that could be expected, even at the time.[59] The island of the Endriago is identified, and fear of it supersedes anything the sailors have just gone through. Absolute danger—the absolute adventure—has been introduced.

The island is described as uninhabited. Some paragraphs later we are told that it once belonged to a giant called Bandaguido, who ruled over other giants who had territories around his realm. Bandaguido married a gentle giantess whose kindness balanced her husband's cruelty to Christians. Their daughter, Bandaguida, turns out to be a most beautiful creature, in fact more beautiful than any of her blood and size. Incest is introduced as a prelude to the story of the beast itself, linking beauty, vanity, and sin in the young giantess. Believing herself worthy of everyone's love but finding that no one attempts, because of her father, to court her, she decides to court her own father. Before the Endriago is born, another sin is added to that of incest, the sin of homicide, as the text suggests that one sin carries another with it. Father and daughter make up their minds to assassinate the kind giantess, wife and mother, and the giant takes his daughter as a wife. While characterized as proud giants, these are not the first to appear in the story.

Giants or their relatives are very popular in *Amadís*, and in the book of chivalry in general they are linked to a feudal lordship of islands that is against Christianity in some way.[60] From Gandalaz to Famongomadán (giant of the Boiling Lake and the *Ínsula de Mongaça*) and his wife, Gromadaça, Madanfabul (giant of the Island of the Red Tower), Cartadaque of the Defended Mountain, Albadançor, Gadancuriel, Ardán Canileo the Feared, Balán, Bravor, Basagante, Dandasido, Cuadragante, Lindoraque, Andaguel, Madásima, Barsinán (lord of Sansueña), Madarque (giant of the Sad Island),

and his sister Andandona are just some of them. It is at times difficult to discern just how much giant there is in some of the characters, since marriages between giants and shorter humans are common in the book of chivalry, which is a sign of how ambiguously the marvelous can function within the romance. Some of them are good, some bad, some gentle and kind, some horribly cruel, some beautiful and some particularly ugly. A good number of them rule over islands. Their character is revealed according to circumstances, not by their nature or their appearance. When the *jayán* who kidnaps Galaor is characterized as "dessemejado," unrecognizable, what provokes fear is not precisely his appearance, but the fact that the parents of the young prince cannot do anything to help their child. Afterward, we see how Gandalaz, the giant, is quite a nice fellow who raises Galaor appropriately and, leaving him with a hermit, sees to his knightly apprenticeship through books.

Eight chapters before arriving on the *Ínsula del Diablo,* and as a grand opening for book III, as Amadís sails from his *Ínsula Firme* toward Gaul, and after just five days of good and bad weather, they find themselves near an apparently beautiful island, covered with trees. Bruneo de Bonamar and Amadís decide to disembark in search of adventures, but a master warns them against it, telling them that it is the Sad Island, the kingdom of Madarque, most cruel of giants.[61] Not without fear, Bruneo and Amadís take up the challenge and go in search of the giant Madarque. Suddenly, they see Amadís's dwarf, Ardián, come running toward them, urging them to save Galaor and King Cildadán, who are fighting the giant's men. There is a brief digression on pride, built upon the biblical Babel episode and the mention of Nembrot, the proud giant, builder of the Tower.[62] All four knights then marvelously defeat men and giant, who is pardoned because first, he is the father of Gasquilán, King of Suesa, whom Cildadán loves dearly; and second, because Amadís makes him promise he will become Christian and build churches and monasteries. His pardon binds together two motifs: the topos of Arthurian romance to have the knight fight against *mauvaises coutumes,* or evil customs, and the motif of conversion that will become prevalent in later books of chivalry. The prisoners are liberated; they thank Amadís and are sent on their way to Brisena. As the knights prepare to leave, they stop by to check on the giant's recovery. He is being looked after by Andandona, his older sister by fifteen years, who presents a peculiar physiognomy: she is covered with rough white hair that cannot be brushed; her face is extremely ugly, so much so she seems nothing but a demon. She wears a bow and arrows for weapons, is dressed with the skin of animals she kills, and is a fierce enemy of Christians. She presents paradoxical qualities, such as being extremely large but also extremely light, while she also has the ability to tame all animals and to mount all horses, no matter how savage they are.[63] She is on many occasions confused with a devil, but she remains a woman, which will prompt Amadís, three chapters later, to charge his squire Gandalín with the task of beheading her, for she has tried to kill the hero, in an episode that is both courtly—knights do not fight women—and humorous, a paradox that Cervantes will take up in comments by Sancho when he compares his own wife to Andandona in chapter 25 of the second part.

The motifs of pride, cruelty, and ugliness are shared between Madarque and Andandona, though their end is very different. But we do not really encounter ugliness until we have read the description of the Endriago.[64] It is covered with hair and scales as armor, arms strong as lion's paws with hands strong as an eagle's talons, enormous wings, teeth protruding one cubit from his jaw, and eyes like red coals that can be seen at night from afar. Like Andandona, it is very light and can run fast, only needs to drink but rarely, and takes pleasure in killing. It screams in anger, smells like poison, and causes its scales and wings to creak so that it seems to make the earth tremble (III, 73, 1132–33; 164–65).

The Endriago itself is no giant. It is a monster, its wings covered in a "gleaming, hairy, leather-like hide black as pitch" and not in feathers, as angel wings would be. It has parts of lion and eagle, and blows smoke out of its nose. Not only is its appearance horrifying, but also the noises it produces make all things alive fear it like death. All these characteristics add up to a description of the Endriago as a machine of war, as Cacho Blecua has suggested. Its lightness, its meanness, its physical power and, most of all, its indifference to food or water or rest all make it apparently invincible. That is, until he faces our hero.

Amadís's adventure in the battle with the Endriago entails not only a victory over ugliness, following Ulrich of Strassburg's dictum in his *Summo Bono* that ugliness is the triumph of chaos over order, but a victory that would be the restoration of order in the world, perfectly coherent with the notion of events in this book.⁶⁵ It is also a triumph over sin. For, as the text carefully informs the reader, while the Endriago is the result of incest and homicide, its traits are also the result of a cult of idols. One of those, in human shape, bequeaths reason to the monster; another has the shape of a lion, which gives the beast courage and strength; while the third, in the shape of a griffin, gives it wings and talons and lightness. The participation of devils in the conception of the Endriago is explicit: "having been informed by his false idols, whom he worshipped, that if he married his daughter, there would be engendered in her the fiercest and strongest thing to be found in the whole world" (III 73, 1132; 164). The Endriago kills all the women who raise the monster from birth, except for the fourth, who does not offer the beast her breast but feeds it cow's milk for a year. When the Endriago's parents come to see it for the first time, the beast kills its mother and Bandaguido accidentally kills himself, while the Endriago flees. In a short time the island is deserted, bringing the geography to an appropriate staging for adventure.

Ultimately, the association of ugliness and depravity or sin is a commonplace, as Goldberg remarks, that takes its authority from the Bible (Leviticus 21:17–23), where the deformed are forbidden to approach the altar or to profane the holy sanctuary, and from a campaign that related historical events to the birth of monstrous children from incestuous relationships.⁶⁶ By the end of the twelfth century, writes Georges Duby, it was necessary to provoke the anxiety present in the population through the threat of teratological effects of sexual relations with blood relatives, necessary because simple prohibition was not doing much to stop these relationships.⁶⁷ This campaign took shape in the peninsula in, among other elements, the printing in the fifteenth century of the *Libro del Anticristo*, which associates the incest motif with the conception of the Beast itself, the Antichrist, through the sexual encounters of a father with a daughter and the participation of devils in the conception of the Beast, which clearly finds an echo in the conception of the Endriago, as Paloma Gracia notes.⁶⁸

Its appearance is that of absolute ugliness, according to Goldberg's classification; and this is what distances the Endriago from all other beasts, "animalias," or evil beings in the romance. The most common form of ugliness in medieval texts is exaggeration—such as being a giant or a dwarf. It is a question of size, but it is also distortion or deformity. The link with the beastly also brought with it the characteristics commonly assigned to animals in bestiaries, most of the time linking a moral dimension to the physical one. In *Amadís*, the example of Ardián Canileo, a giant who presents the ideally ugly portrait (thick neck, flat wide nose, snout like a dog's—which gives him his name—reddish freckled skin, thick lips, heavy, bony, and with hair and beard so curly he was unable to comb them), is an excellent example of this overlap, which can also be seen in Andandona.

Goldberg argues that along with the expected sensation of fright these descriptions produced in the reader, she or he also experienced a "*frisson* of delight," provoked by a relief and feeling of pride from surviving, vicariously, a perilous encounter, or, as Goldberg compares with De Bruyne's terms, felt the "expressive force" that with the intensity of ugliness produces beauty. The popular motif of the comparison between beauty and beast—in the episode of the Endriago alluded to only by Amadís's invoking of Oriana—a common situation in which one finds the ugly, suggests another interesting scenario: "The nature of the sexual fantasy inherent in the encounter of innocent, vulnerable beauty with an ugly, lascivious, unrestrained creature is evident."[69] The coupling of monster and hero or beauty and the beast does not put sexuality on the side of evil; it simply places a sign onto such sexuality, offering usually two solutions, one through moralizing and another through humor as in the case of Andandona.

The episode on Devil's Island enacts the defeat of evil and the conversion of a space: from its savageness, its "sinfulness" revealed by its deserted, uninhabited quality, to a change in toponym that reinscribes this space into that of Christianity. Amadís, as Knight of the Green Sword in these episodes, writes to the emperor of Constantinople—anticipating his own arrival in the city—informing him that the island has been liberated and is under his lordship, and that it can now be repopulated and renamed. The defeat of the Endriago is duly labeled not only marvelous, but miraculous, and as is common in the *Amadís*, the event is inscribed into the landscape in the form of architecture, in this case, statues and a monastery: "and on a large copper plaque I shall cause a description of the battle to be inscribed, together with the name of the knight. And I shall order a monastery established there in which friars may live in order to restore that island to the service of God" (III, 74, 1154; 182).

This episode is central to the structure of the romance. It is the most spiritual of Amadís's adventures, and the most difficult for him to achieve. The setting of the event on an island that the characters reach by chance and the reinscription of the island into Christianity not only because of the conversion—still not fully accomplished: that will be the task of the monastery—but because it is returned to its original ruler, the emperor of Constantinople, provide eloquent testimony to the role of insularity in our romance. As a space, Devil's Island is fundamental for the construction of the character's heroic, spiritual, and hierarchic—social—evolution. In spatial terms, the *Ínsula del Diablo* is important because of the many changes in relation to a community it offers. As we first encounter it, undifferentiated from any other sighting of land, it is a place of salvation; once identified it is charged with evil omens. The space's story has this duplicity embedded in it, for there is a change in sign from a temperate lordship of the island to the dismissal of morality that leads first to the opposition to the community and then the obliteration and banishment of all population. Amadís's conversion of the space through the adventurous defeat of the monster marks only a beginning, for the restoration of order after chaos entails two processes that he claims no responsibility for: a political repopulation obligation that is ceded to the emperor and a moral one with which the monastery is charged. In terms of the recuperation of a territory for the community—the empire, Christianity—it is especially interesting that what the archipelago offers here enlists the loyalty of others to sustain the process of reincorporation of that space, previously lost.[70]

Ínsula No Fallada

The images of loss and recuperation have manifest political, territorial, and religious overtones that can be related to contemporary interests in the East, or closer commercial interests in Mediterranean island territories, as well as in more symbolic interpretations. The idea of something being lost also brings in the idea of a quest, of a search for a lost object. But if what has been lost is a space, and especially a space that no one has seen, then the quest is in a way an interrogation of something's existence, that is, it is an ontological question. In a space lived as near and concrete, evil, according to Augustine, takes shape as "a lack in ontological space, an islet of nonbeing, an obsession that can only contemplate the image of a nonexistent island."[71] Such a definition would seem to anchor the realm of Urganda the Unknown, enchantress and protector of Amadís in a marvelous directly connected to evil, for her kingdom is labeled *Ínsula No Fallada*, the Not Found Island. Linked to the magical but marked positively, as it is closely connected to the hero's success, the Not Found Island is ambiguous, and it is also paradoxical. If an island has a name and someone rules over it, we can conclude it exists. But if it has not been found, how can it exist?

The territory of the enchantress is in fact the stage for only one episode in the entire first five books of *Amadís*: in chapter 59 of book I, Galaor and King Cildadán are mysteriously taken to a place where they are cured of their battle wounds. On opposite sides of a battle that confronts all lineages of giants against the knights of King Lisuarte, which include all three brothers Galaor, Florestán, and Amadís himself, Galaor and Cildadán have been victims of mortal wounds, found among the bodies after the cruel battle. Near death, unidentified damsels claim their bodies to heal them and forbid anyone to come with them, and Amadís watches them from the shore as they set sail. Galaor and Cildadán wake up to find themselves captive and healed in mirror places: a fenced-in house on marble pillars set in a walled garden with a single door as entrance and a high tower surrounded by the sea on three sides. Strange contradictory events follow, which do not assure the reader that they are there to be healed or killed, but after the events that have taken them there are revealed to Galaor, Urganda identifies herself and tells them she has brought them to her realm to be cured. The characters then leave the island, and nothing else is ever said of it.

The discourse on insularity, remarks Dubost, takes the concept of the phantasmagoric characterized by Saint Augustine as the faculty of speaking of that which has never been seen.[72] This confirms the enchanting and more properly marvelous nature of the Not Found Island, but the name is also a philosophical reminder, for the island that has not been found, the Lost Island, in fact became the center of an eleventh-century debate around the existence of God, promoted by Saint Anselm, who argued that the existence of a perfect island in the middle of the ocean, which no one had seen, was not to be denied ontological status. Gaunilon de Marmoutiers would famously rebuke his argument, a debate that highlights the vitality of the image of the Lost

Island in medieval imagination.[73] That which has not been seen is known, however, even if mediated by theology or the fantasy of literature or legend.

The geographical coincidence of islands with a Western margin plagued by marvels would frequently locate the islands of Saint Brendan, San Borondón, or San Brandano, in all cartographic forms, near the Canarian archipelago, as I anticipated in chapter 1.[74] The *Voyage de Saint Brandan*, a twelfth-century Anglo-Norman text, rewrites a tenth-century Latin text, the *Navigatio Sanctii Brendanni Abbatis*, which narrates the pilgrimage of Brendan, a sixth-century monk, in a sort of "Christianized Aeneid," as Marie-José Lemarchand calls it.[75] Read as adventure story, but also as a *libro de a bordo* or logbook, the monk's travels motivated the search for that island which Brendan and his mates found in the eighth year of their periplus: the Island of Paradise, Eden, the Garden of Delights. Brendan became the discoverer of the island, thus giving it his name. The popularity of this story was enormous, and it was translated into many languages. A testimony to its vitality in the Hispanic world is the 1479 Treaty of Alcáçovas, in which the kings of Spain and Portugal dispute the rights to the Canaries, conceded by his majesty to Spain, including the mythical eighth island "si la hallare," if it were to be found.

From classical times, the Canary Islands were given the diverse titles of Elysian Isles, the Blessed Isles, and the Hesperides. Pomponius Mela and Pliny in the first century called them Fortunate Islands. In medieval mappaemundi the Canaries, along with the rest of mythic and real Atlantic islands, kept their marginal, peripheral position up to the fourteenth century, when the knowledge of what was west and south of previous representations of the world started to permeate portolan charts.[76] Among the problems inherent to the identification of real islands designated by diverse toponyms, many of which had no geographical equivalent, Campbell points out that the Canaries, due to their position and shape, do not present any doubts as to their authenticity; Lanzarote and Fuerteventura already appear under these names in Dulcert's 1339 chart, only three years after their discovery, and are a staple of portolan charts from then onward.[77] However, portolan charts were themselves well inhabited by the marvelous: "It cannot be claimed, of course, that the portolan charts were totally free from what today we call superstition, but neither were medieval sailors. Yet Prester John, the four rivers of Paradise, the mythical Atlantic islands, and other legendary features found on some charts are all placed in the little-known interior or around the periphery."[78]

Brendan's lost paradise left a long cartographic trace. The *De imagine mundi* (ca. 1100), a text widely circulated in the Middle Ages, reads that "in the ocean there is an island called Lost, superior to all other lands for the amenity and fertility of all its coasts, unknown to men, which, found once by chance, has not been found again since its discovery, which is why it is called Lost."[79] Ebstorf's twelfth-century mappamundi reads: "Lost island. Saint Brendan discovered it, but nobody has found it since," and the *Libro del conoscimiento* also labels them as lost. In the famous Catalan atlas of 1375, the work of Cresques Abraham, two legendary islands are represented, Brazil and the false Isle of Man, both near Ireland. The Canaries are characterized there in such a way that they could be mixed with the description of Brendan's Lost Island, reminiscent of course of paradise, and thus repeatedly labeled as "found," or "again found."[80] The myth of earthly paradise figured during the Middle Ages through two main traditions.[81] One of them locates it in the East, in Asia, a location that allows the development of the theme of the four rivers of Paradise; while the other places it on an island, a motif that is fused with the Celtic Other World in the *Voyage de Saint Brandan*, making the name of Lost both a theme of discovery and one of theology. The description of the Island of Paradise or of the Saints bears a strong resemblance to the description of the Fortunate Islands:

> With beautiful forests and rivers they see that land blessed. . . . No thistles or brambles, nor nettle can prosper: among the trees and plants there is nothing that does not spread sweetness. . . . Rivers of milk flow and everything overflows in abundance. With the dew fallen from the sky, honey springs from the rushes. . . . The sun shines there with eternal splendor, because there is no cloud in the air to rob the sun of its clarity nor winds or breezes rustling the hair. He who lives there will not suffer any woe, nor know any hostile thing: neither stormy wind, nor heat, nor cold, nor sorrow, nor hunger, nor thirst, nor shortage. He will have such abundance of riches that they will overcome his desire, he will not be able to lose them because they are sure there, and he will be able to use them every day.[82]

Such is Brendan's island, while the Fortunate Islands are described in Cresques as abundant with fruit, and quoting Pliny, called "master of mappamundi," the chart reads that in that archipelago there is an island where all goodness of the earth exists, where no labor is required, where trees do not lose their foliage and fruit spreads about a wonderful smell.[83]

In the fifteenth and sixteenth centuries, Saint Brendan's Island was frequently depicted in cartography, from the *Novae Franciae* map, where it is placed south of Terranova, all the way to the *Map of America,* included in Ortelius's *Theatrum orbis terrarum.* In Pierre Du Val's *Mappe de Les Isles Canaries* of 1653, the long reputation of the island is confirmed. Here we read that: "To the West of the Canary Islands, some place those of Saint Brendan, one of which is the Inaccessible, which others call the Fortunate one, the Enchanted one, the Not Found one."[84] This cartographic itinerary identifies the "island of the saints" of Brendan with the name of Lost and, more interestingly yet, with the name *Non Trouvada,* not found. This tradition spans five centuries, fusing two of the seven islands that Brendan finds in his voyage: that of the whale or mobile island where the monk and his friends celebrate a Mass and that of the saints, related to paradise.

Those are some of the *derroteros,* or routes, over which Montalvo might have traced his emplacement of a space for Urganda.[85] While one can see the parallels between the *Ínsula No Fallada* and the *Ínsula Firme* in terms of a general utopia, the signs of the marvelous stake out differing interpretations for each that Montalvo carefully lays out. While the *Ínsula Firme* is a political utopia, marked by hierarchies determined by merit, the *Ínsula No Fallada* points to a marvelous abundance related to a different ontological status. Without claiming an influence, the itinerary traced above, from Isidore to Anselm and from Pliny to Cresques, does spell out a tradition, a diverse series of routes that converge in the paradigm for the Lost Island to which other layers might be added, such as the imaginary spaces of the *Critias* and the *Timaeus* in the shape of Atlantis, an island that Pierre d'Ailly would take for his *Imago mundi.* In this manner, the *Ínsula No Fallada* of *Amadís de Gaula* might be seen as a sort of wind rose, ciphering and signaling directions, discourses, different interpretations.

As a point of convergence of multiple meanings, the *Ínsula No Fallada* relays a particular function within the archipelago of the hero's adventures and in the chivalric program proposed by Rodríguez de Montalvo.[86] If for Saint Augustine the phantasmagoric is a way of talking about that which has not been seen, we can say that the *Ínsula No Fallada* is the location of an event that cannot be described because it has not been seen, but which may nevertheless be circumscribed. The only passages in which anything within the *Ínsula No Fallada* is described note this encirclement by isolating the spaces where the characters are kept not once, but thrice: within the island, on a tower encircled and walled, or inside a fenced building within a walled garden. Its existence is not left unquestioned, but in fact confirmed in its being named as "lost," in the insistence on mapping a space of which there is no certainty. And its ambiguity—the fact that it acts as both a place of liberation from death but where the characters are held captive, even by their own interpretation—mirrors the status of the space itself.

The phantasmatic existence of the *Ínsula No Fallada* seems to suggest the configuration of a different type of insularity than those previously analyzed: a nonplace.[87] To take this function of the *Ínsula No Fallada* as an indicator of the archipelago, in the same way that a system of nonplaces can be articulated through the relocations of a traveling circus or an itinerant market, islands in *Amadís,* in their probable but uncertain existence, might be postulated as a non-archipelago. The *Ínsula No Fallada* is perhaps the most transparent or self-conscious example of this function of the archipelago, as its anchorings in cartographic discourse rendered it "real" for at least five centuries, making the links between fictional, historical, and even philosophical discourses patent. Even the political interpretation might be read onto it, for in a sense, the distribution of maritime realms, remarks Olschki—the extreme case being, of course, *Don Quixote's Ínsula Barataria*—mirrors historical figures such as Portugal's João II, who "with a certain ironic generosity distributed the islands his subjects saw, but never managed to find."[88]

The Amadisian archipelago as a whole can be read as articulating a system of nonplaces in a phantasmatic geography that may *and* may not be identified with a "real" geography, supplementary spaces of fiction that make possible the affirmations of something within the real as if it were already part of it. In the different itineraries they follow, these fictions that the insular adventures offer articulate possibilities for hypotheses on truths on aesthetics, politics, ethics. Such a system, the geography of Not Found Island would suggest, constitutes the deep structure of the book of chivalry, taking the island as the geographic shape of the episode, and thus a theory of fiction. This theory of fiction, where the intent is not in showing real spaces or addressing historical geographies, uses insularity as a way of building within chivalric fiction's political and ethical program a series of hypotheses on the real. Insularity, especially because it is presented in archipelago form, where the itineraries between islands are enacted by the hero, thus comprises a laboratory of experiences for the subject—the knight—that, in their completion as adventures manage to change the situation by forcing a new reality onto it: whether by claiming a reserved political realm by merit *(Ínsula Firme)*, or by recuperating a lost territory *(Ínsula del Diablo)*, or even by forging the space for interiority, as *Peña Pobre*. The insular episodes that I have studied in these pages are but paradigms that the myriad islands and rocks in the book of chivalry provide nuance for in a variety of ways: for love, for government, for self. The *Ínsula No Fallada* is the nonplace that self-consciously points to the possibility of reading the Amadisian archipelago in this way by naming the possibility of the event without giving it a site, enunciating the possibility of event for all the other islands in the archipelago.

By way of such a system, the different archipelagoes in Hispanic literatures beginning with *Amadís* might be compared, analyzed, and studied. Just as nonplaces can present themselves as openings to immortality, they can be faces of the abyss, routes to hell. The *Ínsula No Fallada*, the space of a fugitive fiction, a fiction that wishes to remain unfound, is also eloquent of the ways in which space subordinates time to itself in the book of chivalry: at the end of the *Sergas*, the fifth book of *Amadís*, Montalvo has Urganda come out of the *Ínsula No Fallada* to rejuvenate (or turn back time for) the protagonists, and to enchant them (to freeze in time, to stop it) on the *Ínsula Firme*, which she then sends to the depths of the earth, only to reemerge when the appropriate time for them has come in time of Arthur. Space in the *Amadís* subjects time to its shape, it circumscribes it and contains it within the fiction for the fiction to produce more, later, in other books, other cycles.[89]

4

SHORES OF FICTION
The Insular Image in *Amadís* and Cervantes

> A self does not amount to much, but no self is an island;
> each exists in a fabric of relations that is now more
> complex and mobile than ever before.
>
> —JEAN-FRANÇOIS LYOTARD, *The Postmodern Condition*

Buondelmonti's account of his travels in the Aegean can be seen as the first of a genre, since explored in many different ways and cultivated well into the twentieth century. It confirms a model of modern travel writing inaugurated by Petrarch that is related to "the emergence of a subject that writes and records and memorializes the self," in Cachey's words, summarizing in a way the West's response to the Aegean, constituting one of the first cultural inscriptions of subjectivity articulated through writing and geography.[1] That coincidence between internal and external geographies is made possible by the inscription of the traveling and writing subject. In the *Liber insularum archipelagi*, this inscribed subjectivity gives the genre its shape, in the sense that it is the body of the traveler-compiler-cartographer that guarantees the text's continuity, between island descriptions, and between texts and illustrations, maps and legends.

The connection between geography and the writing of fiction through the mediation of a traveling subject in the *isolario* and the book of chivalry was manifest in many genres before, but in the fifteenth century a particular relation between chivalric fiction and cartography became evident. Historians of cartography and literature have noted as an oddity that the first mentions of the rediscovery of Ptolemy in the late medieval world would appear within chivalric romance. The cultural atmosphere from the beginning of the fifteenth century and continuing throughout the seventeenth century favored a relationship between chivalric fiction and its emphasis on geography and the discourse of cartography. "At the end of the fourteenth and in the first few decades of the fifteenth century," writes Gautier Dalché, "the people of Florence could hear the works of poets writing in local idiom recited and declaimed on the banks of the Arno."[2] An established singer of *chansons de geste* and compiler of chivalric prose romances, Andrea da Barberino has recently been labeled the "missing link between the early Italian reworking of the chanson de geste and the Renaissance epic masterpieces."[3] Especially interesting to us is Barberino's *Il Guerrin Meschino*, a chivalric prose romance composed at the end of the 1410s and the beginning of the 1420s, for scholars have pointed out Barberino's wide use of Ptolemaic toponymy in it (though whether it has been taken from the text or from the maps remains undecidable). The *Guerrin* tells the story of a knight whose adventures take him to Constantinople; unfit to become a serious suitor to the emperor's daughter because of his unknown identity, following a pattern closely related to both Byzantine and chivalric romance, he decides to travel the world. Chivalry, travel, and the interest in the East, represented by Constantinople, are, again, elements that bind the book of chivalry and cartography together. More interestingly, the connection reveals in Barberino, and in consequence, in *Amadís* and Buondelmonti, the popularity and permeability of cartographic discourse via chivalric fiction. The *Guerrin* links Italy and Spain early on, as it was translated and published in Seville in 1527 as *Guarino Mezquino* and thus entered the canon of books of chivalry, if linked to the Carolingian and not the Arthurian tradition, as is *Amadís*.[4] As Karla Amozurrutia Nava notes, the identifiable itinerary of Guarino—which distances the book from the ambiguous, isolated spaces of other books of chivalry—is traced, however, according not just to mere geography, but to an interest in going through places notable for their religious or literary relevance, such as Santiago de Compostela and the Purgatory of Saint Patrick; places related to the Carolingian tradition in Italy, such as the cave of the Sybil; and places related to other cultures and the marvelous, such as the Mosque and Arch of Mohammed or Alexander's Tree of the Sun and the Moon, directed always to the East.[5] The coexistence of these symbolic and fictional places alongside a verifiable itinerary make the text more akin to the structure of the portolan in its perplexing mix of medieval and Renaissance elements, of symbolic and real geographies. Gautier Dalché notes that in any case in Barberino, and in general in these first texts, the interest in Ptolemy, whether one regards it as encyclopedic or humanist, seems to be mainly connected to place-names. The preference is curious, since it benefits from the verisimilitude granted by the source (Ptolemy) but without any special regard to geographic precision.[6] In the *Guarino,* moreover, in contrast with other books of chivalry where interlacing guarantees the unity of narration while integrating other spaces and other characters' adventures, narration almost exclusively follows the protagonist and his travels, where adventure is more of a moral nature (rather than political) in the encounter with the marvelous—much more linked to a type of chivalry represented by Amadís's son, Esplandián, than by Amadís himself—from which the knight must learn and gradually rebuild his identity, the core preoccupation of the book.

Chivalry and cartography would continue to be connected and would constitute in Italian literature, in Cachey's words, the "fullest literary integrations during the Renaissance" of Ptolemy and modern cartography, culminating in Ariosto's *Orlando Furioso,* published a century later. Ariosto's precise use of maps contrasts with the marvelous voyages he invents, tying cartography and literary imagination together in chivalric epic: "Ariosto's cartographic conquests," as Cachey labels them, "thus represent an illuminating parallel or counterpoint to other more historical journeys of conquest and political uses of the map." *Amadís* is concerned with the East, and it will be later in the genre that the Americas will be gradually brought in; in contrast, the marginalization of Italian courts from the enterprises of empire and discovery effected a closing of the margins of the map in subsequent Italian epic, as in Torquato Tasso's exclusion of America in his *Gerusalemme liberata.* Not surprisingly, this displacement is predicated on a mobile island, as Tasso relocates the island of the enchantress Armida from the shores of Patagonia in the first version, to the Fortunate Islands or Canarian archipelago in the final version.[7]

These later elaborations confirm a continued relation between cartography and chivalric literature in the early modern world, and simultaneously reveal the political differences between Italian and Spanish literary traditions that would be imperially tied through Charles V's coronation in 1530, and especially differences within Italian literature between epic and romance.[8]

Published some twenty years after Montalvo's recension of *Amadís, Orlando* treads very different waters, even if the body of the hero still guarantees the narrative unity of the geographies traveled.

In *Amadís*, narration advances with the protagonist, its "subject," who transforms the space he travels through his adventures. Space also effects a change in the protagonist, a correlation between internal and external spaces that is most obviously expressed in nomenclature or toponymy. A mirroring between external and internal space is evidenced in the name of the *Ínsula Firme*, as I detailed in the previous chapter, or in the change in name from *Ínsula del Diablo* to *Ínsula de Santa María*. In this production of space, as Rosario Santana Paixão has pointed out, the goal of the genre is to "create its own space, where the fantastic side is presented as an end in itself," where the emphasis is not on the particular reality of a feat, but on the universal truth of heroism.[9] What Santana Paixão calls *essential truth* consists of a subjectivity expressed both in the body of the adventurous traveling hero and in his internal characterization—as firm, loyal lover and friend. In other words, his subjective truth resides in emotion, in the order of feeling and being that are taken as a universal knowledge, "which transcends the dimensions of the immediate and focuses on ethical or existential preoccupations, with the goal of nurturing human perfection, encouraging the pursuit of Virtue," expressed in a series of behaviors and gestures that will give *Amadís* currency in the courts, beyond its literary success, as a book of manners, and more collectively, as a manual for spectacles.[10]

While in cartography there is a gradual effacing of the author–traveler as the organizing thread of the *isolario*, no doubt in response to the transition from manuscript to print and the commercial success of the genre, in the book of chivalry there is no such effacing, but a shift from the hero's subjectivity to the author's. If in the *Amadís* it is the hero himself whose body, whose subjective experience and fidelity links the separate adventures—especially those at sea, for those on land convey at least visually an illusion of stability—in the process of development of the genre, this subjective experience will increasingly be that of the author. This displacement is expressed structurally in the topos of the finding of a manuscript that will then become the book.[11] This author's experience, let us note, is that of an explorer and a discoverer; but it is also an experience of a bookish nature:

it is the experience of the reader.¹² In some way, one might compare the displacement of the experience from protagonist to author to reader in the book of chivalry and the novel, to the displacement from traveler to explorer to cartographer as the atlas comes into being. A Renaissance idea, that of reading as traveling—linked through the ancient *topos* of travel as means for knowledge—makes its way into the chivalric genres as cartography disseminates its power through the printing press.

Buondelmonti threads his book with his own name in the shape of an acrostic, assembled from the red block letters that head the *isolario* and read: "Cristoforus Bondelmont. De Florencia Presbiter nunc misit Cardinali Jordano de Ursinis MCCCCXX" (Cristoforus Bondelmont, Presbiter of Florence sent by Cardinal Jordano de Ursinis 1420).¹³ In the book of chivalry, the acrostic can be paralleled to the genealogy of protagonists that characterizes the genre. Genealogies articulate not only Montalvo's refurbishing of the story but also anticipate the many books and the organization in cycles that will follow his remastering of *Amadís de Gaula*. The *isolario* has other manifestations of subjectivity, such as when the author of the *Liber* mixes personal data in the pseudo-historical narration that accompanies the description of islands, and above all, the extraordinary episode in which, having been shipwrecked on an island and about to starve, Buondelmonti engraves his own epitaph on a rock in the Furni islands.¹⁴ This engraving recalls the many inscriptions of Amadís's name and feats in many contexts, from toponymy in the *Ínsula del Diablo* to the marvelous engravings on statues and buildings both there and in the *Ínsula Firme*. Other authors of *isolarii* and books of chivalry followed this singular method of self-inscription, highlighting travel itself as heroic feat.

Buondelmonti makes use of all possible resources, from fiction to history, from legend to myth, even to his own testimony as traveler in order to write his periplus. That is, subjectivity in the *isolario* is not dissociated from the encyclopedic thrust that makes it possible, and is essentially medieval. The encyclopedic side of the *Liber* finds a perfect niche in the print culture that would follow its conception:

> Printed books increasingly come to be conceived as a collection of places that are arranged or organized in space. Increased spatialization of the textual

epistemology (vis-à-vis the manuscript book) coincided with a revival of the classical and medieval arts of memory whose practice involved a spatialized organization of knowledge. The repercussions throughout the literary system of this particular conjunction of technological and cultural factors (related to but distinguishable from the coeval conjunction between print and rhetorical canons of imitation) have just begun to be appreciated.[15]

A printed book of chivalry such as *Amadís* can be seen as a collection of places organized in space, but the idea of the book as a memory gallery can also be extrapolated to the chivalric in general, for example, to understand the reception of *Orlando furioso*, "which was reorganized into a kind of 'World Book Encyclopedia' by polygraph, editorial entrepreneurs like Orazio Toscanella."[16] Buondelmonti and Montalvo anticipated with their assemblages the development of their respective genres in this direction. Frequently, the notion of the book as collection of places was expressed visually in the composition of text and images. In its very makeup, the book of chivalry retained this characteristic, among many others, in its passage from manuscript to print.[17] The context of representation of insularity, however, from verbal descriptions to different forms of visual representation effected changes in the ethical and political project of chivalric fiction presented through the archipelagic structure in *Amadís*.

Images of Place

Common among illustrations in the book of chivalry were the richly dressed knight (whose illustration is not exclusive to books of chivalry, appearing also in heraldries, historical chronicles, heroic personal chronicles, ballad chapbooks, etc.), usually accompanied by his horse either in an open landscape or with the background of a castle, scenes of pledges of allegiance, heraldic motifs, knights and ladies, ladies with a lance, battle scenes, and tournaments (Figure 14). Particularly frequent were maritime scenes, repeated constantly within the same work and between books, reflecting the importance granted this motif. José María Diez Borque finds the scene of ships near a coast in the *Amadís* (Venice, 1533) and *Tristán* (Seville, 1538) repeated several times in each; the same happens with the scene of king and courtiers watching a boat and others (Figures 15 and 16).[18]

Figure 14. Gandalín, the loyal squire, follows Amadís on horseback on the title page of the 1533 edition. *Amadís de Gaula: Los quatro libros de Amadís d'Gaula nueuamente impressos et hystoriados* [Venice, 1533]. Houghton Library, Typ 525.33.138 F.

Figure 15. Three large ships send out dinghies to disembark on an island. Folio 9r, from *Amadís de Gaula* [Seville: Juan Cromberger, 1535]. Houghton Library, Typ 560.35.138 F.

Figure 16. A king and courtiers welcome or bid farewell to a man on a ship. The image highlights the opposition between the built space of the court and the unstable sea. Folio 169r, from *Amadís de Gaula* [Seville: Juan Cromberger, 1535]. Houghton Library, Typ 560.35.138 F.

Images used in books of the period may be classified in three general categories: illustrations proper, thematic images, and disjunctive images. Logically, images could be used as proper illustrations only once, because only once could they be illustrating the episode or chapter in which they were inserted. This *only once* is extremely important. From the moment of their first use on, these images will entail a change in the operations made by the reader/spectator of these images and texts. The juxtaposition between text and image cannot continue being a two-way mirror; after the first time illustrations appear, text and image stop being a repetition of each other, a summary, a duplication, or a commentary (depending on the value ascribed to certain visual characteristics in terms of what is valued or not of the episode illustrated). The relationship between text and image changes radically when this mirroring effect is absent. The reuse of images within one book, in a chapter or episode presenting a similar theme—a battle or a tournament, for example—or just to occupy the space for the illustration, results in a disjunctive relationship with the text. In a sense, the images in these last two situations become texts themselves, as they remind the reader of another text for which the image is a substitute. Transformation of the image into a text that must be remembered is what Marian Rothstein calls a "commemorative" use of the image. The commemorative use of woodcuts depends for its power on the reader's familiarity with an earlier, illustrative use of the image (Figures 17 and 18).[19]

Images juxtaposed to text are not only commemorative in the chivalric genre. They serve as guarantors of continuity, as another version of genealogy, established this time not by the protagonist or the author but by the printer himself, the chooser of the images. It has been pointed out that books of chivalry establish relationships among themselves, resulting from direct blood relations between protagonists or in an indirect manner through the reworking of names or the revisiting of spaces, as in the reelaborations by Juan Díaz or Francisco de Morais of the *Ínsula No Fallada* detailed in the previous chapter (Figure 19). The juxtaposition of images would in this sense have two functions. On the one hand, it would provide another kind of continuity to the cycles, reminding the reader each time of the link between the present text and others, forcing her or him to establish contrasts, to compare adventures and heroes, and to put them on the same

LE QVATRIESME LIVRE
Comme Amadis se partit seul

pour aller venger le Cheualier qu'vne Dame auoit em-
mené mort en vn basteau, & de ce qu'il luy
en aduint.

Chapitre   XXXII.

Madis & Grasandor hors (se leur sembloit) de tou-
te fascherie, ayant en leurs compagnies celles qu'ilz
aymoient de tout leur cueur, ne tascheret qu'a pas-
ser le temps auec tout le plaisir dont ilz se pouoient
auiser, quand fortune ennemye de trop grand ayse,
leur apresta nouuelle ocasion d'ennuy & melenco-
lie, telle que vous entendrez. Vn iour entre autres, comme ces deux
Cheualiers estoient allez courre vn cerf, ainsi qu'Amadis tenoit son
limier en relaiz, aperceut du plus hault de la coste vne barque en mer
aprocher du riuage, & estimant auoir quelque chose estrange dedans
comença à deualer la roche pour voir que ce pouuoit estre : Mais de-
uant qu'il y peut arriuer, la barque auoit prins terre, & estoient sortis
vne dame & vn marinier, lesquelz à bien grand peine tirioêt hors vn
Cheualier mort, encores armé de toutes pieces. Lors Amadis s'arresta
court, pour voir qu'ilz feroiét, se cacha derriere vn fort halier, ou il ne
se tint longuemét qu'il aperceut la Damoyselle & le marinier estédre
ce Cheualier

Figure 17. A walled city contrasts with the open space of the sea in this engraving from the French *Amadís. Amadis de Gaule,* book IV, chapter title 32. Special collections, case Y7675 .A 458. Courtesy of the Newberry Library.

Figure 18. Ships in the foreground seem to have traversed the seascape behind them in this framed engraving for the French edition of *Amadís*. *Amadis de Gaule,* book IV, folio 1r. Special collections, case Y7675 .A 458. Courtesy of the Newberry Library.

level. In this manner it also creates a sense of genre, in a very material fashion. On the other hand, this juxtaposition would support the interpretation of the "grotesque" nature of the romances, in the overlay not only of image over image but also of text over text through the image, in a series of translations between systems, as well as between languages.

The French *Amadís* (1540–44), for example, had the privilege of having most of its blocks cut specifically for it. They were used for the next ten years or so, and they were later found illustrating *Palmerín*, a different cycle. Rothstein writes that because of this special treatment, the *Amadís* is a good case for arguing that commemorative images referred constantly to it, following not only its extraordinary success but its normative, modeling role in the genre: "With some important exceptions, the woodcuts decorating the large folio pages of *Amadís* are small, roughly eight by ten centimeters. Woodblocks of this size were more durable, less prone to cracking, cheaper to have cut, and more commercially flexible since they could be, and were, used in octavo volumes as well as the luxury folios printed to meet initial demand. The first book of *Amadis* has fourteen woodcuts," complex, detailed visual narratives (Figures 20 and 21). These are invariably set between the explanatory chapter title and the text of the chapter itself. In this way, even if too vague to be sufficiently descriptive, the explanatory chapter title serves the image as caption.[20] If that is the first relation between text and image that the reader establishes, a second, in which the reader follows the events represented visually, contradicts the simultaneous presentation of the order of events that illustration offers by forcing the reader to find the proper sequence. This, of course, is only possible when the illustration functions precisely as a mirror of the narrative, for in the thematic or disjunctive use the images serve only as flashbacks or digressions (Figure 22).[21]

The most famous episodes of *Amadís de Gaula* were profusely and painstakingly illustrated in the luxury edition presenting Nicolas d'Herberay des Essart's translation into French, commissioned by François I (Figure 23).[22] The magnificent woodcuts, each set apart on its own page in an enormous folio edition, are decoratively framed and made to head a chapter. Among these lavish engravings, whose blocks were overseen by the translator himself, island episodes seem to be of particular interest. What is interesting about these island illustrations is not only their detailed presentation of the

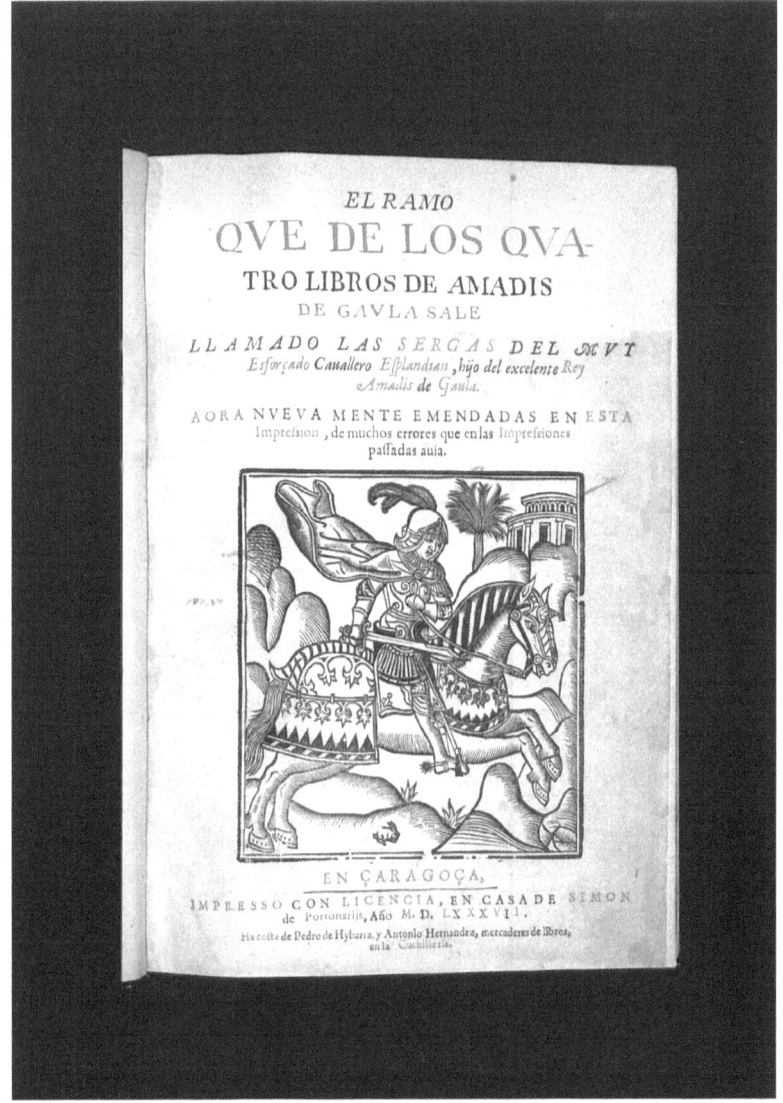

Figure 19. The title page of the fifth book of *Amadís*, narrating the story of Esplandián, his son. *Sergas de Esplandián.* Ayer Collection *438 M76 1587. Courtesy of the Newberry Library.

LE SECOND LIVRE
Apolidô gouuerner son Empire, pour vous declairer ce, qui aduint à icel
luy Amadis, & à ceulx qui le suyuirent au partir de la ville de Sobradise.

Comme Amadis Galaor, Flore-

stan, & Agraies, ayants prins congé de la belle Briolanie pour
retourner vers le Roy Lisuart, furent conduictz en l'isle
Ferme, pour esprouuer l'arc des loyaulx amants,
& les aultres aduentures d'icelle.

Chapitre II.

Figure 20. The Arch of Loyal Lovers rejects lesser knights, letting through only the most loyal of lovers. Folio 3v, from book II, *Amadis de Gaule,* Paris, 1550. Houghton Library, Typ. 515.46.138 F.

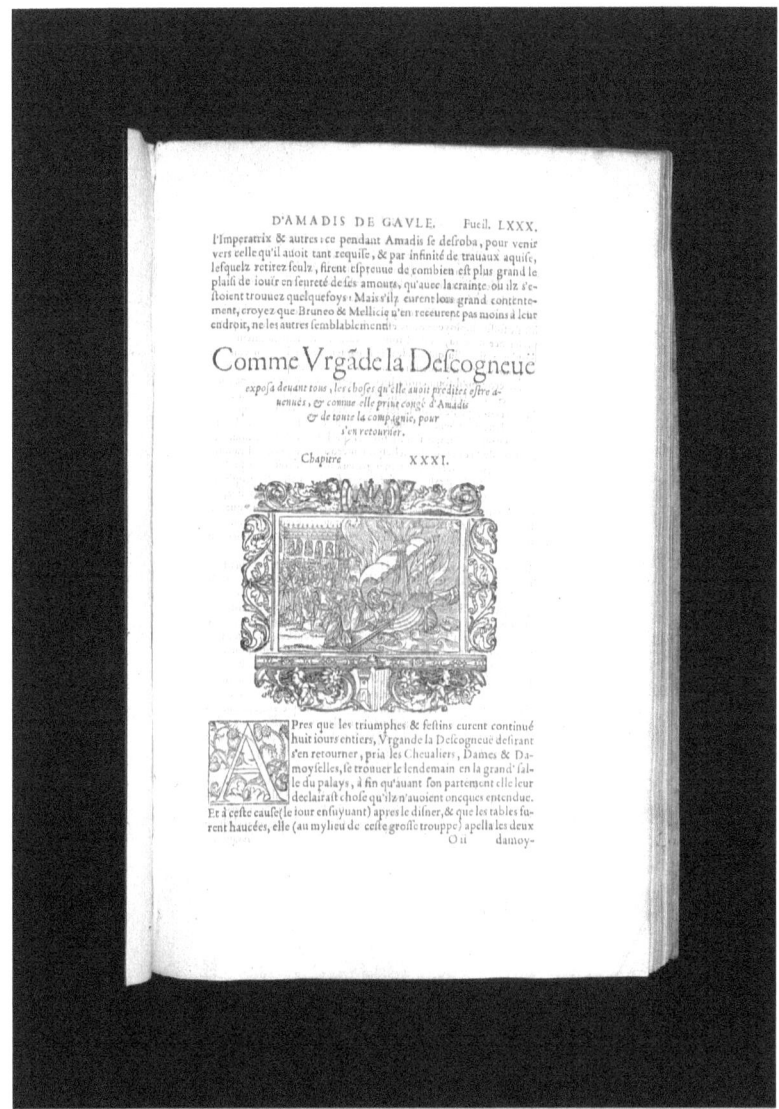

Figure 21. Urganda's ship is recurrently represented, in substitution for her realm. *Amadis de Gaule,* book IV, f 80r. Special collections, case Y7675 .A 458. Courtesy of the Newberry Library.

Figure 22. The engraving tells the entire episode of the battle with the Endriago, up to its death, and of the hero's delicate condition. Folio 49v, from book III, *Amadis de Gaule*, Paris, 1550. Houghton Library, Typ. 515.46.138 F.

sequence of events in the narrative, but also of the presentation of islands in relation to on another: on the horizon boats and islands appear to suggest this relationality of the Amadisian archipelago. For the beginning of the second book, the French luxury edition presents a two-page illustration of the *Ínsula Firme* laid out on the left as map, an architectural plan of the island's enchanted buildings that closely follows the description provided in the text (Figure 24). On the right, the edition offers a plan of a raised building of the *Ínsula Firme*.[23] In the plan of the *Ínsula Firme*, however, there is an interesting development, for the shape of the island seems to have given in to the shape of the page that sustains the image: the island is represented not as geography but as a floor plan, suggesting that the interpretation of *ínsula* is here much closer to its etymological definition as a block of buildings than that of a land surrounded by the sea. There is, in fact, no visual reference to the sea, and the lines detailing the topography of the island are controlled, rational limits signaling labyrinths, columns, corridors, and perimeters. The extremely influential French edition, whose popularity included the copying of its illustrations, coupled with *Amadís de Gaula*'s ever-increasing success within and beyond Spain's borders, would find its way into yet another expression of the romance's visual qualities: the tapestry.

Tapestries are specifically referred to in the *Amadís* itself: in book III, chapter 68, after the defeat of the Seven Kings has been narrated, King Lisuarte and his men enter the tents of his enemies: "That night Galaor and Agrajes and many others of their friends lodged in the tent of Arcaláus, which was very luxurious and beautiful. On it they found depicted in silk and embroidery the battle that he had had with Amadís and how he had enchanted him, and other things that he had done" (III, 68, 1052; 98). Cacho Blecua remarks that this scene might be included among the group of tents painted with the feats of heroes, such as the tent of Alexander in the *Libro de Alexandre* that has been related to the tent of Don Amor, in the *Libro de Buen Amor*. The romance does not specifically refer to the tent—the walls of the tent, as in the *Libro de Alexandre*—as being painted, but tells of a silk cloth upon which these feats are represented, which I take to be a tapestry.[24] The link with Alexander is productive, because it elevates the hero to the level of other heroes whose feats also have been represented in tapestries. Art historians have identified nine tapestries of an *Amadís* series, designed by Karel

Figure 23. A knight kills a giant, while in the foreground knights fight monstrous beings in this French *Amadís*. Folio 22e (F2r), from book V, *Amadis de Gaule*, Paris, 1550. Houghton Library, Typ 515.46.138 F.

van Mander the Elder and manufactured in the François Spiering workshop in the 1590s.[25] Two of them were shown as part of the 2001 "Vermeer and the Delft School" exhibit at the Metropolitan Museum of Art in New York, on loan from their London owner, one of which was later bought by the museum and is now part of its collection. Two others are in the Poldi Pezzoli in Milan, two more in private collections in Rome and London, and yet another is part of the collection of the Princeton University Art Museum; the remaining two are only known from photographs in sale catalogues (Figures 25, 26, and 27). Princeton's is particularly interesting, as a direct inspiration on the illustrations made for Herberay des Essarts's edition may be argued.[26]

Figure 24. This extraordinary double-folio illustration in the French *Amadís* is composed of a number of perspectives that underscore the motifs at work: Paradise, the labyrinth, *locus amoenus, hortus conclusus,* forest, and island. On the right hand, architecture between the historical and the fabulous. Folios 3v–4r, from book IV, *Amadis de Gaule*, Paris, 1550. Houghton Library, Typ 515.46.138 F.

The Princeton tapestry depicts the buildings of the *Ínsula Firme* from a slightly elevated perspective, providing thus the possibility of making it a narrative, following the text, or of reading it as a map. The Princeton tapestry works then not only as a commemorative image, but as a subjectivizing force, making the reader/spectator make her way into the image/text itself:

> The map is a microcosm that takes the form of a landscape, a geographical garden in which promenades can be taken. Only the traces of human occupation require recourse to symbols; the natural landscape can be reproduced by the mimesis of forms, matter, and colors in which the very material identity of the natural elements is preserved. . . . The promenade through the geographical garden is a voyage because the traveler goes from country to country, contemplating the mountains from above, following the course of rivers or the seashores. But a map of this kind also provides symbolic power over the space that it represents.[27]

Figure 25. Tapestry of the *Story of Amadís de Gaula*. The protagonists are depicted several times in the tapestry, representing different moments in the narrative. After Karel van Mander the Elder, Dutch, 1548–1606. Frans Spiering, 1551–1630. Scene from Amadis de Gaule. Tapestry 249 × 432 cm. (98 1/16 × 170 1/16 in.). Princeton University Art Museum. Gift of Hugh Trumbull Adams, Class of 1935. Photo: Bruce M. White. y1954-76. Courtesy of the Princeton Art Museum.

Figure 26. This detail of the Princeton tapestry depicts the protagonists, Amadís and Oriana, attempting the adventure of the Arch of Loyal Lovers. After Karel van Mander the Elder, Dutch, 1548–1606. Frans Spiering, 1551–1630. Scene from Amadis de Gaule. Tapestry 249 × 432 cm. (98 1/16 × 170 1/16 in.). Princeton University Art Museum. Gift of Hugh Trumbull Adams, Class of 1935. Photo: Bruce M. White. y1954–76. Courtesy of the Princeton Art Museum.

Figure 27. The magic of the chamber of Apolidón is represented by smoke in this detail of the Princeton tapestry. After Karel van Mander the Elder, Dutch, 1548–1606. Frans Spiering, 1551–1630. Scene from Amadis de Gaule. Tapestry 249 × 432 cm. (98 1/16 × 170 1/16 in.). Princeton University Art Museum. Gift of Hugh Trumbull Adams, Class of 1935. Photo: Bruce M. White. y1954-76. Courtesy of the Princeton Art Museum.

That is, the tapestry of the *Ínsula Firme* is a landscape where both nature and human action are represented, where the garden and its buildings sum up the contradictions between the civilized and the savage. Reading the tapestry is parallel to walking its world. The reader is thus taken within the image; she is made part of the tapestry. For, in the same manner that Jacob says is done with maps, the first question asked of this tapestry is for the reader: "Where am I? It is essential to define this fundamental landmark, this anchor and origin, this guarantee of the individual's identity, a central reference in respect to which all surrounding space is organized."[28] The reader, identifying her/himself as knight or lady, places herself within the *Ínsula Firme* as a traveler within the space; for the map is a construction from a subjective point of view, and not an impartial, impersonal mirror. The possibility of mobility within the tapestry is motivated by perspective—in this case eloquently called a "horseman's perspective," reinforcing the chivalric association—and the idea of promenading is bolstered because what is represented there is precisely a garden: "Bodily mobility was an aspect entirely integral to the pedagogical scenario," which we have seen the ethical utopia of the *Ínsula Firme* striving for, the education of a class. If in the nineteenth century, as Jacob writes, "Map-gardens still figured among the great pedagogical utopias aiming at popular education and the dissemination of geography," we can find one of their earliest examples in this garden of loyal lovers, this garden of delights reserved for a hierarchized class of ethical defenders of a merit-based order.[29]

Many island episodes were represented, both in the more rudimentary Spanish woodcuts and in the French illustrations. The absence of the *Ínsula No Fallada* in the many woodcuts and engravings that accompanied the text signals a particular difficulty in representing that which has not been found, that is, woodcuts and engravings mirror the marvelous status that the island retains for itself in the text. If in the first five books of the *Amadís* cycle— that is, those written by Montalvo—the *Ínsula No Fallada* is not described within the narration, maintaining the suspense of its marvelous existence, Juan Díaz will describe it in chapter 7 of his *Lisuarte de Grecia*, and later Francisco de Morais will revisit the space and give it a new name, that of the *Isla Peligrosa* or Dangerous Island as his protagonist spatially links his own adventures to the prestige of Amadís in the Portuguese *Palmeirim d'Inglaterra*.

This is not only testament to *Amadís*'s hold over the imagination, or of the prestige the spaces he had created for the genre kept and generated, but also of the change the marvelous in general had experienced, linked more to surface, to spectacle. This description, of course, made the island available for representation.

The tapestries depicting the *Amadís de Gaula* seem to refuse to represent all insular spaces. In the tapestries, islands are stripped of their relation to the sea, adventures reduced to their territorial, promenading possibility, pushing the very limiting qualities of the insular outside the frame of representation, voiding, in a way, the essence of insularity, as in the Princeton tapestry, which depicts the magic garden of the *Ínsula Firme*. In contrast with the book illustrations, there is no reference here to the seascape that contextualizes the island in the narrative, there are no boats, no horizon with other islands. The tapestry selects the smallest, the innermost *locus* of the palimpsestic insular dominion of the hero, taking only the garden, the *locus amoenus* and placing at its center the French invention of a labyrinth, while shedding the political utopia, the possibility of relation to the other islands, the other spaces of the *Amadís* fiction.

One of the reasons for this treatment of the representation of spaces is that the vastness that surrounds the islands, the ocean, runs counter to the rich elaborations and complex overlapping of episodes and detail the weaving of tapestries seeks. The very nature of tapestry weaving made it much more likely to represent the French translation, obsessed with textural detail and description, than the more action-driven Spanish original. But there are other reasons, as there are also other types of movement being opposed in these representations. While the tapestries and the spaces depicted there encourage courtly promenading, it is the closed, static space of the court and its monumental, overpopulated, spectacular imitations of chivalric life that frame the scenes. The most open of spaces represented in the tapestries, in which the action of the knight liberating Oriana presents the forest of their adventures, has as its image front and center one of staticity, of submission, of controlled, structured gestures.

Going back to the woodcuts and engravings, I want to underscore the possibility of mobility between illustrations, or of wandering within a single one of them, for many depict insular spaces with entire episodes represented in sequence, a double movement that suggests the possibility of travel of gaze and imagination located on a single island or between these islands of illustration through the sea of words, inciting the mind to wander off—what Buondelmonti stated in his dedication as possibility for his *isolario*. The Spanish woodcuts, in their lack of specificity, in their coarse inability to illustrate, as Rothstein might characterize them, further highlight such fictional possibilities for the reading, traveling subject. One might of course linger on one particular island, but one might also err among them, even imagine the possibility of inserting one's own island fiction in the archipelago.

In maps that depict islands, even fictional islands, such extremes are not so readily available for comparison, for, as Jacob suggests, in cartography the lines that delimit an island "suggest the essence of insularity more than any clear geographical identity."[30] This immediate trigger of imagination limits the possibility of lingering upon one, singular island, for the relation to the continent is always there. Perspective is crucial to these distinctions. While representation in tapestry and the French engravings, and to a certain point in the Spanish woodcuts, places the viewer as a potential protagonist, the maps depicting islands offer a vertical view. In these maps, moreover, the invention of a probable island by the casual spectator is impossible in the way it is possible for the reader of books of chivalry. In these maps, the possibility of charting a new course that includes one's own island is limited to the cartographer, and even then, the recognition of these invented insular spaces will not be available to the casual reader of the map.

Within cartography, however, *isolarii* offer the perfect format for the exploration of the entire spectrum of representation of insular fictions. The curious symmetry of material space and represented space in the *isolario*, that is, where the codex is the archipelago, and a folio is an island, a symmetry developed later in the genre equating even the form of the text itself to the island, making the text a sonnet, explains in part the enduring charm of the genre, and even its demise, as the metaphorical expansion of the concept of insularity into an ever-expanding space to be represented could no longer be buttressed by the material support of its representation. The ambiguous status of insular spaces between isolation and relation, between individual representation and consideration as archipelago, is resolved in the *isolario* through the very format, where the alternation of text and map allows for the transition between one space and the other. The text there serves as the sea, in a way, as the time of travel between islands, or as the space that takes one from the interior of the continent to arrive at the end of a paragraph and disembark on a new beach traced in brown ink. A user of these manuscripts would have, no doubt, held the volume and considered some form of totalization, of absolute power over a completeness, the satisfaction of a catalogue, of an ordered logic contained comparable to the encyclopedia—or the atlas. The experience of *isolarii*, however, also includes an opening to infinite repetition, of multiple travels reproduced and restarted upon increasingly abstract locations. That the space that provides this possibility of both totalizing experience and infinite repetition is an island is no coincidence, and the particular exhilaration one feels when perusing these manuscripts is one common to the genre in general, that of both extremes of experience simultaneously presented: the deserted singular island of self and the archipelagic, cosmopolitan relation of the unity of many islands, pure fiction and pure politics, with the reading, traveling subject enacting possible itineraries between them.

In literature, *Amadís de Gaula* provided the same paradoxical set of possibilities, detailing singular island experiences that determine the construction of the hero, and providing the possibility of infinite repetition. The emphasis on singularity offers the characterization of self through the emotional construction of the protagonist, as in the *Peña Pobre* episode, and through the archipelago, linking the episodes on the *Ínsula Firme*, the *Ínsula de Mongaça*, the *Ínsula de la Torre Bermeja*, and so forth, Montalvo articulates a particular political and ethical project that involves chivalric fiction within a specific historical context. Books of chivalry took pleasure in exploring the *variatio* that *Amadís* inaugurated and thus expanded the archipelago into the New World, into the fantastic or the dystopian.

Between the encyclopedic thrust and a humanism related to a more realistic, protoscientific, objective attitude, and the emphasis on subjective experience as a guiding thread of narrative in all these variations of Amadisian perspective, from the verbal to the visual, is the space of fiction. Fiction understood as intrinsic to the experience of travel that separates Buondelmonti's *Liber* from the purely cartographic and links it to the travelogue. *Amadís* is the literary version of the same operation: a marvelous periplus that transforms elements from history, literature, and geography to build not a scientific or rational archipelago but one linked through the experience and fidelity of the knightly hero, an experience that the visual interpretations of the book, whether in woodcuts or tapestries, transform into one readily available for the viewer/reader. Each in its own way, focusing on the experience of space, book of chivalry, *isolario,* or tapestry, illustrate that specter referred to by Bede, Diomedes the grammarian, Saint Isidore, or Jean de Garlande as *res ficta quae tamen fieri potuit* (fictional deeds that nevertheless could have been true), with different effects at the level of the political and ethical projects underlying each specific project. This is the third course of narration, astride between *res gesta* and *res ficta,* between the "done" and the "imagined," a frontier genre.[31]

The genres coincide in their spatial nature, bordering on cartographic discourse and in their Homeric hybridity between the historical and the poetic, both articulated through an impulse that finds expression in what I have called an "insular turn." This elaboration can be read from the point of view of philosophy in terms of what I anticipated in the discussion of Badiou in the introduction in terms of event. As complementary developments in intimately related disciplines, *isolario* and book of chivalry supplement each other's thrust toward adventure, both bookish and military, humanistic and colonizing, mercantile and imperial.

Amadís's travels to the East—in the Aegean, in the *Ínsulas de Romanía*— end in that paradoxical palimpsest of spaces: Constantinople. Frequently represented as a *peninsula,* that is, as *almost* an island, Constantinople lies at the extreme of the marvelous: as the urban, technological, wondrous other. Amadís's trip to Constantinople reworks a literary topos present already in Chrétien's *Cligès,* and follows a narrative tradition of the description of cities inaugurated in twelfth-century romances with the description of Carthage in the *Enéas,* followed by that of Babylon represented in the *Libro de Alexandre,* or the Babylon of *Flores y Blancaflor.* With the added imaginary value of wealth and magic linked to its Orientalism, Constantinople became a logical site for the marvelous, and a staple of books of chivalry.

Historically, the 1453 fall of Constantinople to the Turks rekindled for the city both the mystery and the will to penetrate that mystery. Half a century later, peregrinations to Constantinople, the Holy Land, and the East in general became very popular again, making the visit to Constantinople by

Amadís one that can be traced back, once again, to historical travel accounts.[32] Constantinople in *Amadís* is not only a place visited by the hero. In *Amadís de Gaula*, the city's marvelous thrust is distributed equally between protagonist and author. In the prologue we are told that the fourth book was found in "a stone tomb, which was buried under a hermitage, near Constantinople." This not only complies with a motif, but also mirrors the historical search for manuscripts that learned men undertook, either out of their own interest or following someone's request, as in the case of Buondelmonti. In a sort of balancing of the marvelous, Amadís's entrance into the city is triumphant, and the human and the urban complement each other's wondrous nature. In Amadís's battle against Lisuarte and the Roman Empire, the equation of Amadís's kingdom, of *Ínsula Firme* and the City of Constantinople will be complete, as the hero is acknowledged as an equal and those other emperors send their support. Constantinople, at the extreme of the spatial coordinates of the *Amadís*, is part of its archipelago (Figures 28, 29, and 30).

Figure 28. A queen on her knees bids farewell to a ship. Folio 15v, from *Amadís de Gaula: Los quatro libros de Amadís d'Gaula nueuamente impressos et hystoriados* [Venice, 1533]. Houghton Library, Typ 525.33.138 F.

At the end of the *Sergas de Esplandián*, fifth book of the *Amadís* cycle, which recounts the adventures of Amadís's son (the word *sergas* means "feats," but also alludes to a tapestry with the story of a character),[33] Urganda la Desconocida, sensing the death of the heroes is near, gathers the characters on the *Ínsula Firme*, rejuvenates them through magic herbs, and commands the island to disappear magically into the depths of the earth, whence they will return in the time of Arthur. With this sunken Atlantis as a legacy, books of chivalry will multiply archipelagoes, their characters hoping for the reappearance of the *Ínsula Firme*, reenacting forms of fiction (and politics) in their itineraries. In its wake, authors of many interests and skills produce books and cycles in the genre, texts that constitute a collection of places, an *isolario* of the sort on which the itinerary of the modern novel might be traced.

Figure 29. Islands are places to seek solitude and salvation, as hermit or as lover in penance. Folio 109r, from *Amadís de Gaula: Los quatro libros de Amadís d'Gaula nueuamente impressos et hystoriados* [Venice, 1533]. Houghton Library, Typ 525.33.138 F.

The numerous recurrences of marvelous insular spaces in the romances that followed *Amadís*, from the new generations of the Amadisian family to other families of chivalric heroes—Belianís, Palmerín, Clarián—bear witness to the success of the change from forest to island as a site for the marvelous. Islands are multiplied in the Spanish book of chivalry in the most fabulous ways, sometimes finding a route to the New Continent, as in Montalvo's own *Sergas de Esplandián* (ca. 1496?).[34] The French translation of *Amadís* by Herberay des Essarts depicts this route to America as island in its woodcuts; the Spanish romances, beyond the direct reworkings of islands of the *Amadís*, such as the *Ínsula Peligrosa* and the *Ínsula del Sepulcro* of *Palmerín de Inglaterra* (1511),[35] elaborate spaces such as the *Ínsula Gigantea* and *Ínsula Salvajina* of *Lisuarte de Grecia* (1514), *Ínsula Despoblada* of

Figure 30. Cliffs and inaccessibility help frame islands that contain the most wonderful adventures for the knight. Folio 165v, from *Amadís de Gaula: Los quatro libros de Amadís d'Gaula nueuamente impressos et hystoriados* [Venice, 1533]. Houghton Library, Typ 525.33.138 F.

Amadís de Grecia (1530), the *Ínsula Solisticia* of *Belianís de Grecia* (1535), the *Ínsula Nublada* and *Ínsula No Hollada* of *Policisne de Boecia* (chapters 51 and 95, particularly plagued with marvelous beings such as dwarfs, unicorns, and giants; 1602), among scores of others. The toponyms reveal the insistent relationship between the insular and the marvelous, between books and cycles, as well as an emphasis on the Aegean Sea as setting, mirroring the genre of the *isolario* once again.[36]

In cartography, any new space would be initially designated as an island. Álvarez Cabral set out after Vasco da Gama but, extending his turn too far into the West, stumbled upon an island that he named Terra da Santa Cruz and which later became Brazil. Islands literally serve as excursus or stepping-stones in myriad places, as when Sebastián de Cobarruvias Orozco digresses, in his definition of *isla*, to point out that "in the navigation between Portugal and Eastern India, that is, five thousand water leagues, there is in the middle of the great Ocean (where they say no ground exists) an uninhabited islet called Saint Helen, provided with fresh water, fish, game, and fruits, which the same earth produces without effort, where sailors rest, fish, hunt, and supply themselves with water."[37] Among this incessant proliferation of islands in a variety of spatial meanings, Pantagruel's fourth book could be cited, with many others, as a comparative example, elegantly studied by Lestringant in his book. As literal middle grounds between the New and the Old Worlds, sailors, cartographers, and writers laid islands like paths. Columbus spent the last days before he set out on his trip in the monastery of Cartuja, upon an island, and sighted the New World for the first time as an island as well—much like ancient geographers would have. The islands drew itineraries to another *terra firma*.[38]

As I have argued, the genre of the *isolario*, anticipating the atlas in its gestures toward totality, presents the medieval practices of collecting and the idea of the encyclopedia that are accentuated in the Renaissance. It is not difficult to see how cartography would become a preferred medium for the compilation of "common places," from fantastic islands to the depiction of sea monsters and monstrous races or, as exploration pushed the latter off the map, the depiction of native peoples or the symbolic representation of places through the monuments that identified them. Literary works in the wake of romances of chivalry and early modern cartographic developments mirrored both the gesture toward totality and the collecting practice, at times connecting a marvelous and a geographical island through a historical reality, like Tasso; at other times turning islands into a discursive metaphor.

Bernal Díaz del Castillo, in a much quoted passage in his *Historia verdadera de la conquista de la Nueva España* (ca. 1568, printed 1632) writes, upon arriving at Tenochtitlan, that it all seemed a thing of enchantment as those of *Amadís*.[39] Stephen Gilman noted how Díaz's descriptions of these buildings in the water resemble constructions referred to in chivalric romances, quoting a very similar passage from *Amadís*. But beyond these similarities in the referent, the geographical subject matter, or even the landscape described, Gilman writes, "One of the fascinations of the *Historia verdadera de la conquista de la Nueva España* for the lover of Spanish literature is to encounter here and there along the slow broad current of the narrative familiar *islands of style and literary reference* . . . those familiar islands of style so refreshingly and expressively recreated amid the flow of exotic happenings, *islands which constitute a primordial anthology of Spanish letters*."[40] Two interesting points in Gilman's analysis bear on my purposes here. The first is his acknowledgment of the confusion between historical and fictional discourses in Bernal's writing, something that seems obvious but nevertheless needed to be pointed out. The second is his metaphorical use of the word *island* to refer to a discursive site for the enactment of a literary reference, or for the invocation of a literary theme. Gilman describes the sum of such references as a "primordial anthology of Spanish letters," thus making Díaz del Castillos's chronicle a sort of commonplace book or *isolario*, an archipelago of *fiction*.

"Islands of style" or of "literary reference" are commonplace in all literary writing, and may bear the name of *topoi* in their most codified forms, such as the recurrence of the inspirational landscape of the *locus amoenus* or the repetition of a certain behavioral pattern in the case of the hero. However, repetitions or representations that involve the work of a single author, or a particular use of a collective impulse are not usually codified as fixed themes, but their separateness remains functional to point to questions of poetics. In discussing the difficulty of pinning down Cervantes's autobiographical references or even a clearly personal note from the author, Mary Gaylord craftily terms Cervantine self-consciousness *"islands of concrete self-reference."*[41]

Cervantes's rewriting of the chivalric island in the *Ínsula Barataria* episode is not only the most famous of reworkings of book of chivalry's insular fictions, but also one that has been linked most personally to Cervantes's own disenchanted vision of politics. In this episode, Cervantes, through the prism of politics, highlights not only the multiple discourses that are at work in the chivalric motif but its structural role in the production of fiction.

BARATARIA, OR THE ISOLATION OF LANGUAGE

Indeed Cervantes, in many of his long prose fictions but particularly in *Don Quixote*, explores the potential of the "common place," which the book of chivalry as genre provides in hordes. In this, often labeled the first modern novel, it is possible to trace how the repetition of a setting as a motif, privileging certain contents, slowly metamorphoses into a fictional situation that in turn triggers a discussion on poetics, finally to become a metaphor for something else. That is, in Cervantes's representation of chivalric insularity, the island as setting becomes a literary reference, which in turn becomes a structure, a metaphor, and an island of style.

As an exemplar of its kind and as a model for Cervantes's protagonist, the *Amadís* is the privileged pretext for the writing of *Don Quixote*, but it is also a literary practice that flows through Cervantes's writing. Reference to other literary genres is made in many different ways in *Don Quixote*: interpolation of novellas, mention of a character and of either his name or his profession, a setting, or a place visited by the knight. Some of the latter, having to do with space, are also discussions on poetics, which Gaylord has studied as "simultaneously defining the space of poetry and poetics, and a poetics of space."[42] Gaylord concludes from her analyses of various episodes that simultaneous presence of literal and figurative spaces can be detected in almost all instances in Cervantes's work where aesthetic questions are addressed. These spaces are always plural and contradictory, but such oppositions are not to be understood as fixed binaries, but as the actualization of tensions, as an ambiguous presentation of the play between them.[43] Theresa Ann Sears reaches similar conclusions on the role of space in studying modernity in *Don Quixote* precisely from the question of space and place. Arguing from the conviction that Cervantes's narrative is more a continuation than a rejection of romance, this critic studies the duplication of spaces in *Don Quixote*. She focuses on how the Sierra Morena episodes, where Don Quixote and Sancho flee after freeing the galley slaves, work both as ideal and as real, as both chivalric site of adventure and the *despoblado* in which Roberto González Echevarría locates the absence of law.[44]

We have seen how the content of these spaces is not exclusive to a genre or a theme, but in fact cumulative, palimpsestic already within romance, that is, a *floresta* of the Spanish book of chivalry is both a space for the chivalric adventure *and* a *despoblado,* and it may also be a *locus amoenus* if the adventure is amorous, and it might be also reminiscent of a *hortus conclusus,* if the characterization of the space so allows. Moreover, these spaces might be located on an island, which would reinforce certain traits, such as isolation, an edenic idea, a distancing. These series of developed motifs and relocated contents emerge within a medieval system of space/place (with roots in classical oppositions) to produce the space of the forest as the site for adventure and, in the late Middle Ages, substituting it for the island in an atmosphere that proposes a new way of interrogating the real.

Sancho himself speaks of the chivalric as a style when he refers to the marvelous geography of *Amadís* and of books of chivalry in general as "errant writings" *(escrituras andantes).* Perhaps once again in imitation of *Amadís,* Don Quixote moves toward the Mediterranean; most of the interpolated stories will take place there, as is the case of the Tale of Foolish Curiosity and the Captive's Tale (even if in this last one there is a brother who is on his way to the Indies).[45] In this movement, the knight follows itineraries that resemble, to his mind, those of books of chivalry. These, of course, had to include islands. The specific elaboration of *Ínsula Firme* in *Don Quixote* as paradigm for the *Ínsula Barataria* episode, labeled by Augustin Redondo as the most important of the second part, is not the first reference to an Amadisian insular space.[46]

In the Sierra Morena episodes, Cervantes reelaborates an insular space related to *Amadís* for the first time. Fearful of the repercussions of liberating the galley slaves, Sancho leads the knight into the stark landscape of Sierra Morena.[47] As Don Quixote enters the mountains, he is excited by what the landscape suggests in terms of adventure/events. Don Quixote's heart rejoices, "for this seemed to him *a perfect place for the adventures* he was seeking" (I, 23, 128; my emphasis),[48] underscoring the relation between adventure and location, between wandering or erring into the site of a possible event that is characterized as coming from chivalric fiction (for to his mind come "all the miraculous things that had happened to knights errant in such solitary and rugged places" [I, 23]).

In the distance, they see a man jumping among rocks, half naked, wearing the "hairstyle" of the well-known character of the "wild man," whose story will be explained later on by a goatherd.[49] He is a young man named Cardenio, carrying out a "penance" for love in that landscape, alternating outbursts of raging love with those of a quiet melancholy. One of the many interpolated stories within *Quixote,* Cardenio's is specifically a parody of sentimental fiction, whose plot will be slowly developed over the next few chapters and picked up again in chapter 28 from a feminine perspective. In chapters 26 and 27, Don Quixote enacts his own penance, inspired by Cardenio's "real" model, which he has just witnessed. But not only on Cardenio's, of course.

Penance was one of the fixed motifs for the true, long-suffering lover, a protagonist shared by many genres and one that gave chivalry in Spain, through *Amadís,* a model. Entering chapter 25, and well into the depths of Sierra Morena, Sancho asks his master if it is good chivalric practice to be lost in the mountains, without a path or road, searching for a wild man. Don Quixote responds that he is not only in those mountains to search for a crazy man but also to achieve a feat that will earn him eternal name and renown. The feat consists in imitating a hero in his penance.[50]

Don Quixote hesitates, as we know, between imitating Amadís and imitating Orlando, between the lamenting and sentimentality of Montalvo's Amadís on the Poor Rock and the craziness and fury of Ariosto's Orlando: that is, Quixote hesitates between the book of chivalry and the epic.[51] Amadís's penance on the Poor Rock, part of the Amadisian archipelago, complements the hero's subjectivity through the construction of emotion, and was one of the most famous episodes of the book. As a result of a misunderstanding, Amadís loses his lady's favor and thus finds his chivalric drive missing. Symptomatically, it is not fortune that leads him to his next adventure, but arbitrariness, as he lets his horse err every other way, leading him to happen upon the hermit Andalod. Amadís's penance on the Poor Rock also registers the reconfiguration of the identity of the knight in the change of name, as the hermit rebaptizes Amadís as Beltenebros.[52] Sancho intervenes immediately, comparing model and imitation, by saying that these characters had a reason for their fury or their tears, unlike the *Caballero de la Triste Figura,* the Knight of the Sad Face. Don Quixote's answer is that therein, precisely, resides the subtlety of his imitation: there is neither pleasure nor merit in going mad *with* a reason, as madness is only to be expected in those occasions. If Don Quixote is to go mad *without* a reason, the intensity derives from asking what he would do if he actually had a reason. "Mad is what I am, and mad is what I have to be until you return" (I, 25, 144), he claims, and selects the foot of a mountain with a gentle stream and a lush green meadow to go mad for love.[53] A first setting, the Sierra Morena, triggers a discussion on imitation that sends the knight in search of the appropriate location for the subject of imitation he has chosen.

The place he chooses is a *locus amoenus,* laden with fixed meanings, where the *Caballero de la Triste Figura* begins his lament, as if he were out of his wits: "This is the spot, oh heavens, I choose and hereby take" (I, 25, 145) he cries, as he destines a *topos* to be the place for imitation, which is also the place for author and character to comment on literature and reality. It is an active selection that stems from the character's literary topographical culture, from his literary memory's commonplaces, and Cervantes *chooses* these places precisely for discussions on poetics.

Toward the end of the second part, there is a moment where different emphases on the uses of space and place come together, ciphering in a way the production of a new kind of space. This is the episode of *Ínsula Barataria,* told in alternate chapters from chapter 45 on, when Sancho sets out on his way to his governorship (even though the *ínsula* has been given to him in II, 32), and until chapter 54, when he leaves the *ínsula* to fall into the pit, and chapter 55, when Don Quixote finds him.

Sancho's common sense and popular wisdom are constantly opposed to Don Quixote's literary, cultivated, mad knowledge. Sancho's sensitivity to practical matters, his ability to point out contradictions, is gradually mediated by what is known as the "quixotification" of Sancho, which is corresponded to the "sanchification" of Don Quixote.[54] The progressive schizophrenic development of both protagonists culminates in the structural separation of the characters. In fact, the episode of *Ínsula Barataria* is the first time in *Don*

Quixote, as a technical innovation, that the narration of the adventures of one character will alternate with the narration of the adventures of the other, a reminder of interweaving in the book of chivalry as a way to tell stories occurring in different spaces.

Monique Joly and Avalle-Arce note that among the resources that Cervantes uses in order to underline the importance of this episode are two interventions by Cide Hamete Benengeli.[55] The first of these is a response to the criticism the first part had elicited on the use of interpolated stories.[56] The narrator relates that, in the original version, not translated exactly in the manner Cide Hamete had written it, in contrast with the use of interpolated novels in the first part, the Moor, "in this second volume, . . . had decided not to introduce any separate, artful tales, but only such narratives as, to his mind, emerged out of the strictly historical facts" (II, 44, 574). The topic had already been discussed in the 1616 *Quixote* (II, 3). Joly writes that "the development this theme receives, integrated into the supposed protests of Benengeli against the difficulty of keeping his narration to the events related with the main story" is particularly surprising: "It is of a certain importance that such a significantly theoretical fragment, regardless of its humorous tone, be located at the beginning of the chapter in which the technical innovation of alternating one chapter devoted to Don Quixote with another one referring Sancho's or his family's adventures is used for the first time."[57] The separation of the characters occurs in fact only twice before this episode, significantly in two moments of literary criticism: Sancho leaves Don Quixote in Sierra Morena to pine away for his lady, and they are separated again for the adventure of the Cave of Montesinos. In this case, the separation is accentuated by Don Quixote's sense of solitude: "We're told, then, that Sancho had hardly gone when Don Quixote became aware of pangs of loneliness" (II, 44, 576). It is also signaled structurally by a call to the reader just a paragraph before the one just cited: "And so, my dear reader, we will let our good Sancho make his departure in peace," anticipating the technical use of alternated episodes to narrate the adventures of the separated protagonists.

The arrival of Sancho at the *Ínsula Barataria* in chapter 45 is introduced by yet another intervention of Cide Hamete. An invocation of Apollo to illuminate the darkness of his wits is enriched by a subtle cartographic reference: "Oh You who regularly explore the opposite ends of the earth, light and torch of the world, eye of the heavens, You who make men run to the sweet, refreshing coolness of wine—You, known here as Thymbrius, there as Phoebus Apollo, in this place a bowman, in that a physician, father of Poetry, creator of Music—You who rise up forever and, appearances to the contrary notwithstanding, never set!" (II, 45, 581). Apollo's eye of heaven is, in fact, the metaphor for a godly or imperial perspective, an overarching view of the world, reinforced by a reference to Apollo as perpetual discoverer of the Antipodes, all of which seems to direct the reader to a geographical use of the insular setting.[58] Previously, in chapter 42, the duke has also described the island, in giving it to Sancho, as an "ínsula hecha y derecha, redonda y bien proporcionada" (a whole island, round and well made), adding to the sense that the *ínsula,* as much as we anticipate a parody, will be a place, an insular space. The reader, thus, is not clued in as to what sort of displacement will occur in spatial terms and might anticipate disruption at the level of plot in what will happen to the squire in his term as governor.

In chapter 42 Don Quixote states his first series of recommendations to Sancho in his new role as governor of the *Ínsula Barataria*. This first series consists precisely of a collection whose sources can be traced to biblical proverbs, to *sententiae* by Isocrates, and to Aristotle, Plutarch, Epictetus, Seneca, the Catos, and the medieval tradition of advice to princes, with Iberian examples in Alfonso X and Don Juan Manuel and even a chivalric one in the *Libro del cavallero Çifar,* along with other sixteenth-century authors such as Antonio de Guevara, Alfonso de Valdés, and Erasmus. Don Quixote's other personality comes to life in a second series of recommendations, in chapter 43. Here, the knight gives up rhetorical, spiritual, and political instructions in favor of advice on appearance, courtly behavior, and manners. This body of knowledge will be tested in the next chapters, as Sancho is made governor of *Ínsula Barataria*.[59]

The split between knight and squire occurs between chapters 44 and 45, one thread of discourse following Don Quixote to the palace, the other following Sancho to his island. Sancho proves to be an impeccable administrator, an insightful judge, and also very impatient with the jokes played on his stomach and his fears. He is ultimately defeated not as administrator or judge, but as soldier. The image of ideal governor comes to light in the triangle of justice, administration, and courage, when the false threat of a rebellion literally drives Sancho out of his wits, and he decides to give up the governorship.[60]

The arrival at *Ínsula Barataria* is framed by Sancho's use of popular sayings and proverbs. As soon as he is presented a series of matters, previously arranged to test his wit, Sancho changes his linguistic register. The first of these problems he solves in Solomonic form, a case whose source has been traced to Hispanic folklore. The other two cases belong to a written tradition and have their origin in *florilegia* of juridical *exempla*, or collections of such cases. Sancho's use of high-culture tradition and language contrasts with his use elsewhere of popular, traditional phrases. Later on, after finally having eaten, Sancho decides to make the rounds of his *gobierno*, underscoring the roundedness of his insular government, by walking his territory. His three encounters elaborate on popular tradition, except for the last one: Sancho encounters a beautiful girl dressed as a man, which is the usual cue for the beginning of a novelesque *excursus*, a motif amply used in sixteenth-century theater and prose fiction.[61] In this case, surprisingly, nothing happens. There is no story that follows the encounter.

What the language of Sancho frames and characterizes is a space, that of the Island of Barataria. The ambiguity of etymologies and Cervantes's movement between referents and their metaphors have led to the wildest geographical identifications of *Ínsula Barataria*, following leads toward a geographical image of the island. Eduardo Saavedra, for example, suggested that Cervantes had taken the word *baratario* from a diploma, called a *bara*, given to Christian merchants in Turkey to allow them to work. Fermín Caballero locates Sancho's governorship in the village of Alcalá del Ebro "which, if not an island, is almost completely surrounded by the river, which is why in the Succession War there was a project to isolate it completely, opening up a ditch in the isthmus," perhaps reminded of King Utopus.[62] Diego Clemencín, in his commentary on the episode, alludes to a series of hypotheses ranging from the reference to insular spaces in the chivalric romance to the identification of the village of Pedrola, to what is the common interpretation of Barataria, that is, a place associated with the idea of a fraud, a farce.[63]

The reference to romances of chivalry contained in Sancho's *ínsula* is immediate, as references to particular islands of *Amadís* throughout *Quixote*, such as the *Ínsula Firme* or the *Peña Pobre*, show. But this association is not limited to books reelaborating or explicitly referring to the chivalric romance, such as *Don Quixote* itself. The *Diccionario de Autoridades* obviates the relationship in its definition of *ínsula* by quoting book IV of *Amadís de Gaula*, as does Joan Corominas's *Breve diccionario etimológico de la lengua castellana*. Both of these, as well as the 1791 *Diccionario de la Real Academia*, note the persistence of an original meaning of the Latin *insula*, that is, as designating a block or group of houses on land, and sometimes even referring to a small area of land distinguished from the territory surrounding it, or a patch of trees in the middle of a meadow.[64] Going back in time to texts antedating *Quixote*, one finds references to *ínsula* mainly in two types of contexts: either legal ones, referring to government or prison, or in lapidaries, as places of origin for marvelous stones. One can also find documents using the term to refer to a discrete place on firm ground, in the sense of an isolated patch of land.[65]

As for *barataria*, many approximate definitions refer to deception, dissipation, dilapidation, or fraud; to a word used among sea merchants; and to barter or trade. The relationship between fraud and commerce is explained by Corominas: "Semantically we go from the idea of 'deceiving' to the idea of 'trapping with good words to do business' and from there to 'trade' or 'traffic, negotiate,'" which he compares then to the German *tausch* (trade) taken from *täuschen* (to deceive) and pointing to terms in Spanish with negative connotations such as *cambalache* (unfair trade), noted by Rubio García.[66] This meaning of "barata" as a trading trick or deception is consistent with the *Diccionario de Autoridades*, and Corominas explains in his article on *baratar* that the term, originally a verb common to all Hispanic, French, and Italian Romance languages, disappeared in the seventeenth century, leaving behind derivations such as our modern adverb *barato* (cheap) and the noun *barata* (sale).[67] The verb had a commercial referent from the beginning (*Libro de Alexandre, Kalila e Dimna*), and it could mean to win at chess, as in Alfonso X's *Tablas Alfonsíes;* but early on it acquired a shading of trickery, of abuse, documented in Wace and Chrétien de Troyes, in Dante, and in Alfonso X himself in his *Partidas* (VII, Tít. 16).

Ínsula, a term that was already old-fashioned at the time of Cervantes in the sense of "island," did not exclusively mean a geographical *island* as opposed to mainland, as I have noted before. Evidently, however, this use of the term *ínsula* already entails a transposition of meaning, a metaphorical use, basing its coincidences with the original term on a series of ideas, among them isolation, encirclement, delimitation, and, above all, distance, independence from what lies beyond that limit, beyond that isolating frontier.[68]

In all of the wondrous events that take place on literary islands, from Odysseus's Ithaca to Amadís's *Ínsula Firme,* the reference to a government, to a certain form of politics, is already present, as it is in Sancho's Barataria. Cervantes's ideas on power, framed by popular wisdom and regulated by linguistic practices, brought to misery by way of mockery, are here carefully framed in a particular space, and the episode is isolated, as it were, suggesting even its independent status.[69] Barataria occupies the place of a metaphorical island in the middle of an otherwise verifiable rural Spain, but suspiciously remains one of the few unmappable spaces in *Quixote.*

As the series of recommendations from the knight confirm, the episode is an invitation to reflect on the nature and the exercise of power and how it stands in contrast to eternal happiness, an antinomy referred to by both squire and knight in chapter 43. "In truth," writes Moner, "the idea that the exercise of power is not very compatible with the health of the soul constitutes a commonplace of political philosophy, which gave rise to many a controversy, notably after the publication of the theses of Machiavelli (*The Prince,* 1532), which we know to proclaim, precisely, the primacy of the Reason of State in relation to virtue." Virtue as a political value is then one of the main thematic threads that are at play in this episode, much in tune with the production of political space through the adventures of the *Ínsula Firme* in *Amadís.*[70]

References to islands throughout *Quixote* are numerous: there are in fact 118 cases of the word *ínsula* in the text, and the plural *ínsulas* occurs another 28. Of these references, relatively few are to particular, named islands. The more modern word *isla* is used only 6 times in the novel, 5 of these designating specific, existing islands.[71] The only instances where the word *isla* is used without a specific reference is by Sancho in part II, chapter 3, referring to his promised governorship, and Sansón Carrasco's reply to Sancho in the same chapter with the plural *islas.* This is the only time Sancho refers to the space of Barataria as an *isla.* Every other time that geography is invoked it is called *ínsula.* Of the 146 times the word *ínsula* or *ínsulas* occurs, only 5 refer to a specific, named island. The first occurrence is in part I, chapter 1, as Don Quixote imagines the giant Caraculiambro, lord of the *Ínsula Malandrania*; the third is the *ínsula* governed by the giant Pandafilando de la Fosca Vista (I, 30); the sixth is the *Ínsula Barataria* (II, 45). All of these places are Cervantes's inventions. The other 2 instances of named islands (I, 20; I, 50) are references to *Amadís de Gaula*'s *Ínsula Firme*. This calls, I believe, for a comparison between the two islands Firme and Barataria as figures of the same space, revisited from a Cervantine perspective.[72]

Comparison between Sancho's island and that of Amadís brings out immediate similarities and major differences. We have the infinite difference of the characters, of the governors: Amadís is the world's best knight, while Sancho is a dubious squire. In fact, it should be Don Quixote who obtains a territory, a kingdom; but he has been displaced to an activity more like that of Galaor, enacting love adventures in the duke's palace. Amadís is named king of his island, and has a governor, Isanjo, to take care of administrative matters. Sancho is the governor and must deal with all bureaucracy himself. Both characters must go through a certain initiation ritual in order to be accepted as rulers. In Amadís's case, it is a highly elaborate process (the *Arco de los leales amadores*), permeated with courtly meanings. Sancho's trial consists of a series of problems taken from popular tradition and solved with no sophistication but pure common sense.

The Island of Barataria, as the *Ínsula Firme*, is the production of a space for politics, though Cervantes collects a variety of genres and references through the various filters of the *mirror of princes*, carnival mockery of village ingenuity, philosophical reflection on the vicissitudes of power, and even a call for a debate on the worthiness of earthly power when compared to eternal happiness. Of those 146 occurrences of the word *ínsula/s*, 105 are situated very close to the words *gobierno, gobernador, gobernar*; only slightly enhanced by the change from *promise* to *possession*, which occurs around chapter 42 of the second part. *Ínsula* occurs in the same line with some word relative to *promesa* 17 times, and with *posesión* only twice, which offers some clues as to how this type of politics is emplaced in terms of time or possibility. *Gobierno* and *promesa* coincide with *ínsula* 5 times, all of them in the first ten chapters; from then on and up to part II, chapter 41, they are almost interchangeable. *Ínsulas* and *gobierno* coincide 14 times, the plural occurring only once in the first part, the other 13 throughout the episode of Barataria itself. To state the obvious, the word *gobierno* becomes so linked with the word *ínsula* that one cannot be understood without the other, but what is notable is the contamination of meaning. In this process of sharing of meaning, the geographical significance of *ínsula* is displaced to government, and government is locked in the time of promises.

Here one must note the imprecise ontological status of Sancho's Barataria, reminiscent of Urganda's *Ínsula No Fallada*. Sancho, in order to revive his master after the adventure with the goatherd and the penitents (I, 52), recalls the generosity of Don Quixote: "¡pues por solos ocho meses de servicio me tenías dada la mejor ínsula que el mar ciñe y rodea!" (for only eight months of service you would have given me the best *ínsula* the seas encircle and the waves wash upon!), where the squire reveals he *knows* what a geographical island is and establishes that he expects one like that. By 1615 the geography of this island is crumbling down. In part II, chapter 2, the meaning of *ínsula* is questioned. The knight's niece curses Sancho with the word and asks for a definition: "Malas ínsulas te ahoguen—respondió la sobrina—, Sancho maldito. Y ¿qué son ínsulas? ¿Es alguna cosa de comer, golosazo, comilón que tú eres?" ("Go choke on those damned *ínsulas*," answered Don Quixote's niece, "you good for nothing Sancho. And what are *ínsulas*? Something to eat, you greedy glutton?")[73] The play on genre, impossible since the island is geographical, seems to be pointing to an *ínsula* that is only a part of language and not part of a geography. Sancho responds that it is not a thing to eat but to govern.[74] Some lines later the word has become synonymous with a trick, mirroring the other part of the island's toponymy, contaminated by the "barataria," a deceit played on the squire (and his ambition), consciously or not, on the part of Don Quixote, when the barber claims to marvel at the simplicity of the squire, "que tan creído tiene aquello de la ínsula" (who has completely bought into that *ínsula* thing) anticipating the idea of disenchantment that we have discussed in terms of the lesson Sancho learns from the Barataria episode. All through the second part, there is an insistent recurrence of the word *ínsula* voided of a geographical meaning. The *ínsula* is delayed: "la dicha ínsula *se entretiene*, no sé dónde" (II, 3) (this *ínsula* is diverted, I don't know where); figured as an unforeseen obstacle: "alguna ínsula de las muchas que su merced dice que *se ha de topar*"

(II, 4) (one of the many *ínsulas* your grace says one shall stumble upon); as having equivalents: "me deparase el cielo alguna ínsula, *o otra cosa semejante*" (II, 4) (heaven might grant me an *ínsula*, or something like it), "se hallaban premiados con una ínsula o con *otra cosa equivalente*" (II, 7) (found themselves rewarded with an *ínsula* or something equivalent); as voided of all meaning: "ya ni habrá ínsula, ni ínsulos en el mundo que me conozcan" (II, 41) (there will not be neither *ínsula* nor *ínsulos* in the world that know me). Linguistic play destabilizes reference to the point where we read that the word is in fact empty of its geography, of what we usually think of as an island, of what Sancho himself in the beginning thought of as an island, that is, a land surrounded by water: "Y así, llevando adelante sus burlas, aquella tarde enviaron a Sancho con mucho acompañamiento al *lugar que para él había de ser ínsula*" (And so, furthering their mockery, that afternoon they sent Sancho with a great assembly to the place that for him was to be an *ínsula*), the place that was to be *for him* an island. Once again, as in many other moments in *Don Quixote*, language is perspectival, subjective. In the end, it doesn't really matter if it is an island or not, one of those situated in the Mediterranean or one of those already metaphorical *insulae*, groups of trees, or an isolated piece of land. Sancho's island is a linguistic one; it is one that exists in discourse, where its existence matters.[75] It is an island of style as well, in terms of the frames of linguistic registers it presents, and also in terms of the sources used for the legal cases Sancho is presented with. It is also generically something strange, as it seems to subvert the techniques previously used by the author, who sets out with the explicit purpose of not including interpolated stories in his text, exemplifying this effort in the refusal to elaborate the story of the girl dressed as a man. As a new island of discourse, however, the island has lost its fictional power with its geography, and cannot as space produce new fictions.

Following the idea that Cervantes's reelaboration of the insular episode constitutes a technical innovation, Avalle-Arce analyzes the episode of Barataria as a new form of *amplificatio, digressio,* and interweaving, which Cervantes takes from two models, Ariosto's *Orlando* and Montalvo's *Amadís*:

> His new masterful control of the technique of storytelling leads him to try to surpass the concept and use of *episode* as the romance had been doing. In 1605

the interventions had been *vertical*, falling from outside on the lives of the central characters, with whom they had no relation. Such is the case of the lovers of Sierra Morena, "El curioso impertinente" and "El capitán cautivo." Ten years later, in 1615, the novelist has matured a new concept of *episodio (digressio)*, and with it its intimate relatives *amplificatio* and *interweaving*.[76]

The episode in question is Barataria. This critic attributes the change to Cervantes's new interest in modifying his manner of elaborating the main thread of the story, but this elaboration depends strongly on the insular character of the Barataria episode in particular. In short, Cervantes would not have been able to make this innovation in technique had he not had the insular model—and the structural, technical blueprint that comes with it—provided by *Amadís*. The concern with the specific geography of that which is an island reflects concern with narrative technique and poetics, just as the prologue and Sierra Morena do. But this reflection on poetics occurs not at the level of characters or plot, but at the level of technique, of the structure of the novel itself. The introduction of interweaving—a technique characteristic of chivalric fiction—in the separation of the characters, coupled with Cide Hamete's intervention, marks such reflection at the technical level. *Ínsula Barataria* circumscribes a change in linguistic register, one that has served as the main characterizing trait of Sancho, the protagonist of this episode. The space of *Ínsula Barataria* provides the setting for a discussion on the nature of power and for a discussion of virtue against worldly ambition or eternity versus fame. Within the text itself, however, this *ínsula* is already a metaphor; it has already been displaced from geography to a space in discourse. As both a thematic island and an "island of style," the island serves as a figure for a new kind of episode, and for a complex kind of *amplificatio* that suggests a new form for the narration of fiction.

As the words *amplificatio* and *digressio* both suggest, this technical elaboration is a spatial one. *Amplificatio*, amplification, expansion; *digressio* means literally to set at a distance, to separate. The motif of the island, with the characteristics that I have enumerated, from limitation to reversibility, from imprisonment to paradisiacal isolation, is explored within Sancho's experience of his governorship. The uses of *ínsula* to designate a space are in fact limited to the episode in Barataria: "You, Your Lordship," replied the steward, "because the Panza now sitting on its throne is the only Panza who's ever come to this island" (II, 45); "and maybe here on this island you've got more gifts than rocks on the ground" (II, 45);[77] "after me there will not be a single doctor left on the island" (II, 47); "andáis de nones en esta ínsula" (II, 49) (no translation). In these instances, an *ínsula* is a lived space, a place.

Sancho's encounter with the *morisco* Ricote is eloquent testimony to the absolute emptying of geographical significance of the term *ínsula*: "And so it happened, before he'd traveled very far from the island where he'd been governor—though he'd never found out whether it was really an island, a city, a town, or a village he was governing—he saw coming toward him along the road a group of six pilgrims with staffs" (II, 54, 632–33). One of them is Ricote; and after much drinking and eating, Ricote tells his story and offers Sancho what, without knowing of the Barataria episode, seems to him to be a good deal. Sancho responds that he has just left his governorship on the island, and Ricote asks for the whereabouts of this island. After Sancho responds that it is two leagues from where they are, Ricote admonishes Sancho: "'Shut up, Sancho,' Ricote said, 'islands are out there in the ocean, not on dry land'" (II, 54, 636). As Ricote brings back the geographical meaning of the word *ínsula* and as Sancho emerges from his governorship, the world is restored to its ostensibly "proper," clear meanings. Knights travel with their squires at their sides and islands float happily, surrounded by water. Islands, now back in their proper domain, are available once again for future mappings.

CONCLUSION
Archipelagic Possibilities

> The question of fiction is first a question regarding
> the distribution of places.
>
> —JACQUES RANCIÈRE, *The Politics of Aesthetics*

Throughout this book I have been presenting different discourses that in the late Middle Ages and the early modern world led up to an intimate relation among insularity, fiction, and event: from voyages to maps to literature, from romance to book of chivalry to novel. The cultural atmosphere that in the late medieval period looks to insularity as a new way of interrogating the real with tools that draw from the encyclopedic and the singular, from bookish knowledge and humanist curiosity, allowed the emergence of genres in literature and cartography that focused on insularity as the space to explore those relations. In the book of chivalry and the *isolario*, island and fiction are articulated as a structure that comes to function as a stand-in for fiction itself, as the form of fiction where events will have taken place. This shape is taken from a geography in late medieval texts, as in *Amadís* and the *Liber insularum archipelagi*, then displaced to discourse in seventeenth-century elaborations, as in the late *isolarii* and Barataria.

In the Amadisian archipelago, fiction is the set of possible itineraries between islands, a probable constellation to be constituted by the relation among islands; it is a grouping process among them that might emphasize ontology, politics, or ethics. The relations are themselves underlined and linked through the figure of a subject that ties them together as itinerary, as narrative. Interestingly, *Amadís* does not point at any evolution in this itinerary of narrative: it does not present a development or progress (which is what many, even today, find "primitive" in the book of chivalry), but leaves it up to the reader to chart her own routes. Cervantes, by voiding the insular/the fictional from any particular geography, makes of *any* fiction that is framed, circumscribed by language, the possible site for the production of truths.

The status of truth within fiction in early modern Iberia has been studied from many points of view, particularly within the Renaissance debate in Italy surrounding Ariosto's *Orlando furioso* and the chivalric *romanzo* in general. In the Iberian Peninsula, the main attacks on chivalric literature were of a moral nature; that is, criticism centered not on the structure of romance but on its pretended moral implications and its effects on readers, with many critics taking this criticism as Cervantes's own. Among the zealous attackers in the fifteenth and sixteenth centuries were Luis Vives, Pedro Malón de Chaide, Pero Mexía, Alonso de Fuentes, Arias Montano, Gaspar de Astete, Gonzálo Fernández de Oviedo, and Miguel Sánchez de Lima, all cited by the influential critic Marcelino Menéndez Pelayo who, four centuries later, concurred that "the clamor of moralists against books of chivalry, which they saw as perpetual incentive of idleness and a plague of customs, were old and quite justified," establishing a national-critical continuity in the judgment of both the chivalric genre and its fictional core.[1] The two best-known Golden Age attacks on books of chivalry that argue for a structural reform based on morality and verisimilitude in such texts are Juan de Valdés's *Diálogo de la lengua* of 1535 and Alonso López Pinciano's *Philosophia antigua poetica* of 1596.

Valdés's criticism focuses on the way chivalric fictions fail to present their "lies"—which is the nature of every fiction, according to Valdés—as believable truths. The failure is due to the anachronisms that plague books of chivalry, exemplified by Valdés with passages taken from *Amadís de Gaula*. In this book, the critic argues, the problems with verisimilitude are worsened by the unbelievable immorality of characters belonging to the nobility (such as Elisena, Amadís's mother), a criterion intimately tied to Valdés's political emphasis on the respect of the customs and habits of a social hierarchy, on one hand, and to the use of "special effects," that is, unconvincing illumination or sound references in the narration of passages on which Valdés places a curious emphasis, on the other. In other words: Valdés's arguments lock together politics and poetics.

López Pinciano, on his part, elaborates on the concepts of imitation and verisimilitude to draw conclusions on genre:

> Assí que las descripciones de tiempos, lugares, palacios, bosques y semeja(n)tes, como sean con imitación y similitud, serán poemas, y no lo será(n) si de imitación carece(n); que el q(ue) descriuiese a Aranjuez o al Escurial assí como están, en metro, no haría poema, sino escriuir vna historia en metro, y assí no sería hazaña mucha; porque la obra principal no está en dezir la verdad de la cosa, sino en fingirla que sea verosímil y llegada a la razón.
>
> [So that the descriptions of time, places, palaces, forests, and such, if this is done with imitation and similitude, shall be poems, and they shall not be if they lack imitation, for he who were to describe Aranjuez or the Escorial such as they are, in verse, would not write a poem, but a history in verse, and that would be no great feat, because the main work is not in saying the truth of the thing but in pretending it verisimilar and close to reason.][2]

Books of chivalry do not comply with these rules of verisimilitude, according to López Pinciano. He remarks on the nature of art, dependent not on its proximity to truth but in its pretense of it. Because López Pinciano does not find the book of chivalry sufficiently artful in its *pretense* of truth, he characterizes chivalric romance not as fables but as *disparates,* absurdities or nonsense, similar to the immoral stories or fables he terms *fábulas Milesias,* written under the sign of entertainment and without any didactic purpose. Lope de Vega would use the same label, *disparates,* to characterize Columbus's cartographic fictions in *El Nuevo Mundo descubierto por Cristóbal Colón.*[3] Later in his poetic dialogue, López Pinciano will place chivalric fiction within the concept of fable, setting it apart as *pure fiction:* "There are three kinds of fables: ones that are pure fiction, and their ground and fabric is all imagination, such are Milesian tales and books of chivalry; others there are that ground a truth on lie and fiction, as Aesop's, called apologetic, which under a fable reveal fine and truthful advice; others there are that, ground upon a truth, fabricate a thousand fictions, as tragedies and epics, which always or almost always are founded upon some history."[4]

When turning to the concept of episode in order to distinguish it from the concept of fable and argument, López Pinciano provides a series of metaphors. The fable is compared to a "stomach," a *vientre*, a bodily metaphor that can be read in spatial terms, before turning to the metaphor of an open rose, and, finally, to space proper: "The episodes are the mountains, lakes, and groves that, as ornament and without need, painters pretend to surround that which is principal in their intention, as around a city, a castle, or a walking army."[5] Space as metaphor in this discussion on poetics is revealing, for here the fable resembles a collection of places, a map. López Pinciano will then turn again to the question of verisimilitude. When Ugo, one of the three characters in the poetic dialogue, argues that it is licit for the poet to alter History but not the fable, Fadrique responds that this license does not extend to Geography and Cosmography, or to Natural History. The history of time may be altered, but not that of space or nature: "Because past time is not evident to man's sight as is the place, for this remains and that vanishes."[6] Time's ephemerality makes it malleable, open to change, while space remains as evidence to the eye. The evidence of space is what constrains the imagination that wishes to imagine it, invent it, and change it in some way. The canon of Toledo in *Don Quixote* uses the same arguments to censure chivalric marvels and spatiality, in his diatribe against the genre in part I, chapter 47 (548): "Which brain, if not completely barbaric and ignorant can content itself reading that a great tower filled with knights goes into the sea, as a ship with favorable wind, and that night fall upon it in Lombardy and that tomorrow it dawns in the lands of Prester John in the Indies, or in others that Ptolemy did not describe nor did Marco Polo see?" And yet, just two paragraphs later, the canon revises his judgment and describes with pleasure the variety of good things he has found in the *largo y espacioso campo*, the "vast and spacious field" of which these fictions compose their worlds.[7]

Critics such as Juan de Valdés and Alonso López Pinciano establish a direct link between the book of chivalry and the notion of fiction as falsehood. This pejorative characterization affected the elements that were associated with of the book of chivalry, principally among them the island. To inquire then into the poetic contexts that made a place for the modern novel and the taxonomy of fiction contemporaneous to it places the chivalric genre and, particularly, its production of insular space at the center of the modern philosophical articulation of "truth." The separation of fiction from reality in early modern poetics severed the link between fiction and truth, since becoming a commonplace used sometimes for philosophical inquiry, but mostly as a tedious argument against fiction, and primarily, against literature. As a keyword in philosophy, however, the status of fiction, as I argued in the introduction, has recently undergone some revision. Characterized in terms of space, adventure, risk, self-denying language, but above all in relation to truth and event, this concept of fiction in modern thought has arresting parallels in the literary explorations of the book of chivalry and the *isolario*.

There are certain truths that are tied to the production of the chivalric archipelago, those tied to a politics and to an ethos. In the *Ínsula No Fallada*, however, one might also read, in its ontological oscillation, a theory of fiction in itself as pertaining to the entire archipelago. The archipelagic is crucial to this production of insular spaces, it is what constitutes what I have been calling the "insular turn," for it is in the relational structure that these events of fiction might be articulated through a subject. These island fictions supplement, as I argued in the introduction through Badiou's framework, the "real" situation by forcing onto it hypotheses of truth that in a future past, as adventure in its conjectural etymology suggests, change what is.

Books of chivalry and *isolarii* both stand in relation to the real political conditions of the Mediterranean, but the way in which they produce a political truth—for chivalry as class, for the humanist project, for the constitution of a modern subject—is in the production of spaces of fiction that have the shape of an island and that supplement the historical itinerary to provide it with a truth as if it were already part of history. This "as if" is important in the consideration of the genres that take up the insular, for it will be read as the linguistic marker for insularity, and thus contaminated by its paradigms, either in its enlarged metaphorical capabilities, containing all geography, or in its consideration as singular entity, devoid of any political possibility.

Badiou, as I summarized in the introduction, considers fiction in relation to truth through two variations, one called hypothetical reasoning, the other labeled reasoning through the absurd. The first relies on the assertion of an "unknown" to draw a conclusion about the truth of a relationship between two points, two statements. The passage through a fiction is that which makes possible the truth of the implication. The second variation is riskier, for it does not know what the second term of the implication is, therefore the assertion is over a void, and while the situation will be changed, it is not foreseeable in which way this will happen. After close reading of three insular adventures in *Amadís,* the parallels between the formulations of the book of chivalry and the formulations of philosophy are now clearly visible. Badiou himself describes fiction in the statements I have highlighted in spatial terms, which I read here to be those islands and their marvels that so enraged later moralists, and characterizes the movement of thought into these fictional spaces as adventurous and uncertain. Crucial to the reconsideration here of fiction in relation to truth is a positive evaluation of the absurd and the uncertain, of *disparates,* as necessary to change an existing situation. It is precisely here, in this ambiguity, in the undecidability of the fictional that moralists take a stand against the book of chivalry and rule in favor of fixed, established meanings.

Don Quixote's use of the family of words of *maravilla* is telling of how the idea of fiction has been displaced by the time Cervantes writes. Uses such as "And it would not be marvelous if it were so" (I, 27, 305) and "If I am not understood—answered Sancho—it is not a marvel that my sentences are taken for foolishness" (II, 19, 786) reveal that the marvelous here is defined by negation, noted in its absence, or, at best, characterized as a trick. The adventures at the palace of the dukes and specifically those having to do with Altisidora are all presented as trickery, and even the reference to technology in the "special effects" created by the dukes is tuned toward the idea of deception.

A few references, though, link the word *maravilla* to pleasure, particularly to the pleasure of reading: "any story of knights errant must provoke pleasure and marvel to anyone who reads it" (I, 50, 571). What is noteworthy here is that wonder has traveled from the book to the reader, and a sixteenth-century print culture reader to boot.[8] Related to that type of reading, which eloquently summarizes the tradition that goes from medieval chivalric romance to the printed novel, is the articulation of the marvelous and silence.[9] Quietness is described as marvelous in part I, chapter 16 (172), and the masculine adjective for marvel serves almost exclusively to qualify silence, the wonderful silence that holds in it knight, squire, and the two shepherdesses in the pretended Arcadia of part II, chapter 58, and that silence that Don Quixote and Sancho are forced into after their piggish adventure in chapter 69—this time not a trick but a misinterpretation of sounds that leads to the protagonists' painful and humiliating state.[10] Rather than to the well-known spectacularity of sixteenth-century courtly, magical elaborations of chivalric wonder, such transformations in the use of the marvelous lead us to a rhetorical, readerly construction of fiction.

The metaphorical use of insularity for the episode of Barataria in *Don Quixote* is radically different from any use of island spaces found before *Quixote* or afterward, in the many reformulations of the Amadisian chivalric paradigm. Tellingly, not a single time is the marvelous referred to during the episode of Barataria. The fictional, in this sense, has been displaced, just as the geographical meaning of insular has been relocated into metaphor. Fiction has become something else than the marvelous geographies of the knight. The debate on verisimilitude, present in Ricote's dismissal of Sancho's location of his insular government, affects not only spatiality, but also the very idea of fiction.

Fiction, built in as a structural space of the Spanish book of chivalry in the Amadisian archipelago, goes further, for it not only presents the possibility of apagogic reasoning (which includes both variations described above), which I read in the *Ínsula del Diablo* and the *Ínsula Firme* episodes, but also constructive reasoning. Constructive reasoning is for Badiou a statement that starts from the fiction of a situation, characterized as incoherent in the sense that it hazardously asserts itself as a contradiction of an established situation. This is, in my view, the *Ínsula No Fallada*'s central role in the archipelago, the direct consideration of a fiction as if it were already part of the situation, which in itself, in its sole consideration as such changes what is. This function of fiction as supplement, as mediation, as the detonator of torsion that transforms a situation, thus laying a claim on truth, is what Cervantes highlights in his use of the insular model of *Amadís:* it underscores only the function, translated as a metaphorization of the geography, but retaining all its power, baring the political thrust of such a function to its core, and rendering the subject of the event visible.

Quoting from George Simmel's essay "The Adventure," Stephen Gilman used to declare, on the first day of his seminar on *Don Quixote* at Harvard University: "Adventure is an island."[11] Simmel's essay seeks a definition of adventure through a series of approximations and nuances that capture its sense of time, its boundedness, and its intuition of the extraordinary from within. In looking for a way to express the affinity between artist and adventurer, Simmel finds in geography an especially appropriate analogy: "It [adventure] is like an island in life which determines its beginning and end according to its own formative powers and not—like the part of a continent—also according to those of adjacent territories... adventure does not end because something else begins; instead, its temporal form, its radical being-ended, is the precise expression of its inner sense."[12] It is telling but not altogether surprising that the notable Hispanist Gilman would find in adventure a parallel for the emergence of the novel in Cervantes's masterpiece. More remarkable is the fact that the island would figure in his discussion as the geography of adventure itself.

Atlas and novel use the structure of islands, of an archipelago—a structure that the book of chivalry and *isolario* produce and make work in a local manner—in order to organize in a colonial manner, in an imperial manner, all the geography and literature available for their assemblages.[13] If the atlas provides the stage of the world, the *theatrum mundi*, the novel provides all possible parliaments.

I have thus argued that fiction as crucial to the production of truth—at the core of Cervantine literary explorations—is tied in the *Ínsula Barataria* episodes to a particular production of space. For Cervantes has so carefully framed this episode to point to a question of poetics, but also to politics, subjectivity, and the articulation of truths, a possibility he finds in the spatial structure of the book of chivalry. In these "islands" in the middle of a continent, which are therefore unmappable, in islands of style, or foggy islands of truth, a situation can be a stake, supplemented by fiction, for a subject to articulate truths-to-come as being already there, in a future past that will have been an event. Fiction as such, as a site for the articulation of truths, is then not only at the core of literary investigation, but is precisely what, in the insular form of a conjecture, constitutes critical theory.

Space and fiction, the map and the marvel, cartography and literature are inextricably linked as tradition, technique, shared imaginary. Marvelous insular spaces continue to inhabit Hispanic literary cartographies mapping the poetical and the political, from Gracián on, coming home to America with Colón, Cortés, and Bernal, to the shorelines of Inca Garcilaso de la Vega. And they set anchor in the prose of Jorge Luis Borges, Julio Cortázar, Adolfo Bioy Casares, and Ricardo Piglia. If perhaps the Hispanic marvelous has changed its effects through history, one can still find it within the limit marked by the waves that ebb and flow around an island.

Notes

INTRODUCTION

1. See Romm, *The Edges of the Earth in Ancient Thought*, 5. The argument on generic overlaps with geography is developed throughout the book.

2. The single most important book to have addressed the relations between cartography and literature for the early modern period, on both sides of the colonial Hispanic Atlantic and focusing on the sixteenth century, is Padrón, *The Spacious Word*.

3. For the history of Homeric epic in Spain, from the Latin translations to the romance versions, see Serés, *La traducción en Italia y España durante el siglo XV*.

4. Certeau, *The Practice of Everyday Life*, 116.

5. Lefebvre, *The Production of Space*, 290.

6. Certeau, *The Practice of Everyday Life*, 123, 128–29.

7. Ibid., 79.

8. The subtlety of Certeau's reading of causal links between stories and space does not always make it easy for the reader to establish the limits of the parallel between them, for if one is to make synonyms of them, there would be no difference between architecture and literature, between urban planning and creative writing. And, while there are similarities, one cannot reduce them to equivalents.

9. Certeau, *The Practice of Everyday Life*, 115, 117.

10. Certeau draws from another critic to support his distinction between space and place: "Merleau-Ponty distinguished a 'geometrical' space ('a homogeneous and isotopic spatiality,' analogous to our 'place') from another 'spatiality' which he called an 'anthropological space,'" Certeau summarizes. "This distinction depended on a distinct problematic, which sought to distinguish from 'geometrical' univocity the experience of an 'outside' given in the form of space, and for which 'space is existential' and 'existence is spatial'" (117).

11. Lefebvre, *The Production of Space*, 68–85. The example he gives is that of maps. It is important to notice that here because cartography will inform our study of medieval practices of space later on. Considering the map here, as an illustration of Lefebvre's theory of space, will find a deeper articulation later on in this chapter.

12. Ibid., 17.
13. Zumthor, *La Mesure du monde*, 34.
14. See, for instance, how Oscar Martín analyzes this change in sentimental fiction in "Allegory and the Spaces of Love."
15. Slowly/spacedly duplicates in the translation the meanings contained in one word in the original. Translations are mine, unless otherwise noted.
16. Isidore, *Etimologías*, book 5, 29. "Time is divided in moments, hours, days, months, years, lusters, centuries and ages. Moment is the minimal and most reduced time, and has its name after the movement of the planets. . . . Hour is a limit of time, just as edge is the limit of a sea, a river, or dress." Admittedly, Isidore here confuses two terms, but the idea is that time is but a limited space.
17. See Le Goff, *La Naissance du purgatoire*; also Gourevitch, "Le Marchand," especially 267–313.
18. Zumthor, *La Mesure du monde*, 59. Zumthor's argument is here reminiscent of Greek perceptions of limits, especially those related to the ocean and its ambiguous denomination in ancient Greek, *pontos*, meaning, of course, bridge, passage, or path, but as Romm, recalling Benveniste warns, as a bridge that has been traced over an unstable medium, and therefore, more of a warning than a call to journey. See Romm, *The Edges of the Earth*, 16 n.22.
19. Zumthor, *La Mesure du monde*, 18–24.
20. Le Goff, *L'Imaginaire médiévale*, 123–126, 134.
21. Zumthor, *La Mesure du monde*, 22 and ss.
22. Le Goff, *L'Imaginaire médiévale*, 137.
23. Le Goff, *The Birth of Europe*, 47–56, 89–90.
24. Isidore, *Etimologías*, book 5, 27. "That is why those who return are called *postliminium*, for they return from exile where, ejected unjustly, they lived outside the limits of their homeland." *Exilio*, in Spanish, is taken from the Latin *exsilium*, derived from *exsilire*, which means "to jump outside," and appeared first in Spanish between 1220 and 1250, but was rare, eloquently, until 1939 (Corominas, *Breve diccionario etimológico*, s.v. *exilio*). Popular etymology takes us further: *ex-ilio*, "outside the island" or "outside, upon an island," "isolated."
25. Geremek, "Le Marginal," 384. Matvejevic, *Mediterranean*, mentions this as well: "Leafing through the writings of a little-known historian of the fourth century, Ammianus Mercellinus, I came upon the concept of *poena insularis* (island punishment, 15.7), which seems to have entered Roman legal terminology before the decadent period" (165), remarking on the popularity it has held up to our days, from Napoleon to Trotsky to Ellis Island or even Alcatraz. See also Sassoferrato's *De Insula*, a fourteenth-century precursor of international public law on "island" legislation and a renowned jurist linked to the discussion on nobility and virtue central to the political argument of books of chivalry (1979); for a discussion on Sassoferrato's

role in chivalric discourse, see Rodríguez Velasco, "Teoría de la fábula caballeresca," 343–58, and especially 354–57, with ample bibliography.

26. Geremek, "Le Marginal," 400–401, 409. Geremek has devoted much of his work to marginality, specifically in the area of Paris in the late Middle Ages. In this typology of the margins, Geremek writes, beggars presented a difficult case. Their functional role in the heart of society made them useful, necessary to the medieval concept of charity, almost a way of life; but it also associated them with poverty, with yet another ambiguous status in medieval society. From the thirteenth century on, beggars began to be assimilated into the marginal, and their exclusion from the community grew more visible. For an analysis of literary beggars in the frame of a political economy, see Bosteels, "Beggar's Banquet."

27. In Le Goff's words, *L'Homme médiévale*, 14.

28. Zumthor, *La Mesure du monde*, 184 and ss.

29. Zumthor, *La Mesure du monde*, 149. The spatialization of "Christianity" occurs in a process by which the term evolves from the dissolution of the concept of *Romania*, as in Orosius, through the ambiguity designating a community of believers, a faith, and the space inhabited by those believers, to the more geographical (and less religious, though it may seem contradictory) sense of a spatial limit. For more on Ocean as the outermost limit of the earth in ancient thought see Romm, *The Edges of the Earth in Ancient Thought*, esp. chap. 1, 9–44, in which he discusses variations on the idea of the encircling or open river Ocean from boundary to cosmological disorder, from Homer to Herodotus, Aristotle and Ptolemy.

30. Zumthor, *La Mesure du monde*, 207. He argues that even if errancy does not know where it will go, it however registers the space traveled as if in view of the "establishment of a cartographic survey" [*comme en vue de la rédaction d'une acte de proprieté ou de l'etablissement d'une relevé cartographique*], an idea that might be also elaborated through Deleuze or even Paul Virilio. The idea echoes the discussion in the introduction of the relation between site and event, or, between spatiality and "what happens," through the thought of Badiou.

31. Josiah Blackmore's articulation in *Manifest Perdition* of the import of nautical explorations not only in imperial imagination, but also as crucial to narrative development, in a close reading of these early modern Iberian texts (mainly Portuguese, but with close connections to a generally Iberian imperialist mind), is the obvious reference here, though he has argued elsewhere for a sort of rhetoric of navigation that runs along the lines of what I have argued via Certeau. His discussion of the genre as enabling and, in a way, destabilizing imperial notions reveals the intimate connections between science, writing, and politics, and his analysis of the production of imperial space through the genre of *historias trágico-maritimas* is parallel to the consequences my study bears on Spanish writing in the sixteenth century.

32. Zumthor, *La Mesure du monde*, 303.

33. Matvejevic, *Mediterranean*, 111.

34. Malkiel, "Old Spanish *maraviella* 'MARVEL,'" 509.

35. This ambiguity is what constitutes the eeriness, the *Unheimliche* that Todorov analyzed and which some critics take to be the marvelous in general. For an exhaustive theoretical analysis of the differences (and the inventory of instances in French medieval literature that follows) see Dubost's voluminous *Aspects fantastiques de la littérature narrative médiévale*. I disagree with him about the idea that the marvelous as such produces specifically and, seemingly in some other critics' opinions, exclusively, terror, or at least fear. The verb itself retains to this day, in Spanish, English, and French, its original undecidability: *maravillar*, to wonder, *s'emerveiller* does not imply the single effect of fear, even if fear can be part of a more complex set of effects.

36. Harf-Lancner, "Merveilleux et fantastique," 244.

37. For an extended discussion of this point, see Nykrog, *Chrétien de Troyes*.

38. Jordán Cólera, "The Etymology of *Insula*, *Aestus* and *Aestuarium*," 353. Jordán Cólera proposes a new etymology through a Paleo-European stem, meaning "to move fast, with impetus," in clear reference to the water, instead of the commonly accepted etymology I refer to above. Given that we are dealing with texts that probably shared Isidore's view, I use it as my etymology for *insula*.

39. Peyràs, "L'ile et le sacré dans l'Antiquité," 27.

40. That is, this study does not consider any kind of metaphorical island, nor geographic spaces that share some of the characteristics of the island (isolation or limitation) nor poetic realizations of the same traits, because, by inverting the phrase "no man is an island" one will inevitably arrive at the conclusion that *everything* can become an island. Thus I do not consider poems as islands (even if through Sonetti's *isolario* a sonnet does become such a precious territory), nor islands of texts (such as paragraphs or chapter titles or titles themselves), nor graphic islands (such as images inserted in the texts, woodcuts, typography, marginalia), but suggest how the genres move from geographic meaning to a metaphoric one.

41. I here summarize statements with slight variations, for example: "Thus Truth draws its guarantee from somewhere other than the Reality it concerns: it draws it from Speech. Just as it is from Speech that Truth receives the mark that instates it in a fictional structure" (Lacan, *Écrits*, 684); or, referring to Jeremy Bentham's theory, "'Fictitious' does not mean illusory or deceptive as such. It is far from being translatable into French by 'fictif,' although this is something that the man who was the key to his success on the continent, Étienne Dumont, did not fail to do—he was also responsible for popularizing Bentham's thought. 'Fictitious' means 'fictif' but, as I have already explained to you, in the sense that every truth has the structure of fiction" (Lacan, *The Ethics of Psychoanalysis*, 12).

42. See Gómez Redondo's didactic exposition of the use of *fiction* for medieval literature, *Historia de la prosa medieval castellana*, 2:1314–39.

43. Fuchs, *Romance*. Fuchs defines romance as a strategy that is used by genres across periods and cultures in varying degrees (see n.41).

44. Gómez Redondo, *Historia de la prosa medieval castellana*, 1:181–82, 235.

45. Fuchs uses and adds nuance to this definition of romance throughout her book, but specifies the technical definition on page 9: "The term describes a concatenation of both narratological elements and literary topoi, including idealization, the marvelous, narrative delay, wandering, and obscured identity."

46. Badiou, *Peut-on penser la politique?* 14. Compare with Badiou's paraphrasing or commenting on Mallarmé further in the book: "The fiction of the political is a funerary fiction, more so because it causes the true evaporation of politics. At its center, this fiction is that of community, of links, of rapport. It articulates sovereignty over community" (15), and so on, particularly in the section entitled "Liminaire" (9–21).

47. Ibid., 272, 273.

48. This vocabulary is obviously tied to Badiou's notion of the site and of the situation, which I do not address here since the emphasis I want to make is on fiction.

49. Badiou, *Peut-on penser la politique?* 273, 278.

50. Ibid., 279.

51. Ibid., 412–13.

52. It is interesting to note that Badiou's insistence in *Peut-on penser* on the fiction of the social bond, in order to delink the truth of politics from the bond itself so as to redirect it to the *out-place* of politics ("The truth of politics is in the point of that which is, and not in its link ... the space of politics as punctual *horlieu* of that place" [20–21]), is put in similar, chivalric, terms: "The political *errs* between civil society and the State. All sorts of concepts make up the metaphor of this hiatus" (15, emphasis mine).

53. Ibid., 437.

1. FOREST TO ISLAND

1. See Curtius, *European Literature and the Latin Middle Ages*.

2. On the relation between epic and romance see the classic studies by Köhler, "Quelques observations," and Jauss, "Chanson de geste et roman courtois."

3. Auerbach, *Mimesis*. The chapter in question is the famous "The Knight Sets Forth" (121–38), in which Auerbach demonstrates (in his way) the absolute lack of reality of the *roman courtois*, a "fictitiousness" and "lack of finality" he sees in the very motivation of the romance, its articulation on "adventure," the absence of "real" description and the general evasion from reality that courtly society instituted. His analysis is extremely interesting in that it shows how criticism on the romance has radically changed in just half a century. See also Zumthor, *Essai de poétique médiévale*, 352.

4. Quoted in Le Goff, *L'Imaginaire medieval*, 181.

5. Fuchs, *Romance*, 42. Quoting Segre, who opposes "glorious deeds" to love, Fuchs makes the opposition one between love and adventure, and later, one between eros and chivalry.

6. I do not consider here Classical romance, though in the chapter on *Amadís* several of the polemics between Byzantine and French romance influences will be noted. See Fuchs, *Romance*, 12–36, for an overview of Classical romance.

7. See Rodríguez Velasco's *Order and Chivalry*, which addresses a variety of chivalric discourses and practices, especially in relation to institutions, law, and juridical discourse.

8. Extant fragments of at least two fourteenth-century Catalan versions of *Lancelot* and one of a *Quête* (c. 1380) translated from the Vulgate indicate another way of entry of Arthurian material into Iberia. See Rubio Pacho, "Reflexiones sobre el desarrollo de la literatura artúrica castellana."

9. Gómez Redondo, *Historia de la prosa medieval castellana*, 2:1462; see also the itinerary of entry of Arthurian materials into the peninsula, 2:1459–78, with close analysis of the texts in ensuing pages.

10. This is what led Frye to characterize romance as an archetype. Frye, however, foregoes textual differences and offers this structure for all romance, avoiding the pitfalls of genre by labeling it a "mode." This approach, as Jameson noted, erases historicity and makes romance self-identical (comparison in Fuchs, *Romance*, 5–7). See Jameson, "Magical Narratives: Romance as Genre."

11. Auerbach studies adventure as central to Chretién de Troyes's *Yvain* and makes his analysis extensive to all of Arthurian romance, the "parent genre" of the book of chivalry. The quest for adventure is verified in narration as a series that thus constitutes a constant test of the virtues of the knight that come both from birth and from an adequate upbringing. Later, Auerbach remarkably refers to adventure as a peculiar form of "happening," as a sort of eventfulness that has nothing casual, peripheral, or disordered about it. See Auerbach, *Mimesis*.

12. Zumthor, *Essai de poétique médiévale*, 358. Nykrog also makes of this ambiguity a structural element of chivalric romance, if in a different key, arguing that the ambiguity surrounding many moments in the romance constitute, in fact, its own objective, as the romance is destined to be discussed, elucidated outside itself: "Disputable and not undetermined ... with the practical intention to provoke a discussion within the circle after the reading sessions. A court poet, he would have aimed to furnish an entertainment that would not end with the text presented." Thus, Nykrog continues, "the first romances seem to be conceived to pose, episode by episode, 'cases' of practical behaviors susceptible to evaluation and discussed on the field.... From Lancelot onwards and culminating in *Perceval*, another practice joins the first, one characterized by enigma. The cart is the first clear example of this, the

courtship of the Grail the most illustrious: the reader is mystified because the information he needs to form an opinion of what is being told is not given to him until much later—or never at all" (Nykrog, *Chrétien de Troyes,* 49, 50).

13. Auerbach's insistence on the "magical" and the "fabulous" as having a radical relationship with the earthly is curious, particularly in contrast with the emphasis on the "ideal" contents of the chivalric romance (Auerbach, *Mimesis*).

14. Jameson, "Magical Narratives: Romance as Genre," 143.

15. Resina, *La búsqueda del Grial,* 38–39.

16. This is Charles Méla's endeavor as he writes on *conjointure* to translate the *effects of reality* of the corpus, which he explains as follows: "What happens is that, in the Grail romances, the itinerary of the hero mimes for the reader the trajectory that the work makes him secretly accomplish on his own, that is, the trajectory that he must accomplish as subject" (Méla, *La Reine et le Graal,* 76).

17. Zumthor, *La Mesure du monde,* 202.

18. In a thorough study of chivalric romance in Spain, devoted in particular to presentation techinques relative to strategies of verisimilitude, Roubaud-Bénichou offers striking parallels between historiography and the romance: "Historical narration is, in fact, subjected in principle to a strict temporal division in years, but it is at the same time founded on the assemblage of undividable narrative units that imply the abandonment of the chronological frame; the King [Alfonso X] and his collaborators are thus forced from time to time to justify . . . their method" (Roubaud-Bénichou, *Le Roman de chevalerie en Espagne,* 120; see esp. chap. 10).

19. Alfonso el Sabio, *Las Siete Partidas,* Partida 1, Tít. 4, LXVIII, 45–46.

20. Ibid., 46.

21. See Romm, *The Edges of the Earth,* on *oikoumenē*, distant-world lore, and the politics of its presentation (37–40); Romm's characterization of the recurrence in a group of texts as the "island *oikoumenē*" concept (122); reflections especially related to India (83–84).

22. See Romm, *The Edges of the Earth,* 30–31, 31 n. 64, on catalogues of marvels or marvel-collection; related to India or wonders of the East, of particular importance to the medieval marvelous, see 91–108.

23. The monstrous also appears in the *Roman de Troie,* as resembling a man from the belly button up, but covered in hair everywhere else, like a beast, and in the shape of a horse, its flesh black as coal and gleaming, fiery eyes (quoted in Szkilnik, *L'Archipel du Graal,* 101).

24. Zumthor, *La Mesure du monde,* 258–72. See also Céard, *La Nature et ses prodiges,* esp. 292–316.

25. Park and Daston, *Wonder and the Order of Nature,* 11, 14.

26. Corominas, *Breve diccionario etimológico de la lengua castellana,* s.v. cura.

27. Park and Daston, *Wonder and the Order of Nature,* 16, 18–19.

28. Ibid., 125–26.

29. Le Goff (*L'Imaginaire médiéval*) notices a diversification in the vocabulary of the marvelous between the twelfth and the thirteenth centuries, which he classifies into three different domains: the *mirabilis,* the *magicus,* and the *miraculosis.* Since Christianity created relatively little in the domain of the marvelous, which has among its sources the Bible, Antiquity, Celtic traditions, Oriental heritages, and folkore, it is pertinent to think of the medieval marvelous as a series of appropriations from different fields. Only the *miraculosis* is proper to Christianity. The historian also establishes two other frontiers where the marvelous is appropriated; the "everyday" marvelous and the political marvelous as forms of appropriation within everyday life, as genealogy or origin.

30. See especially Daston and Park, *Wonder and the Order of Nature,* chaps. 2–4.

31. Le Goff, *L'Imaginaire médiéval,* 25–38.

32. In Münster's *Cosmography* of 1544, cited in Park and Daston, *Wonder and the Order of Nature,* 147.

33. Linehan, "The Beginnings of Santa María de Guadalupe," 299; Dodds, "Hunting in the Borderlands." For how these practices continue older ones, see Grabar, "Programmes iconographiques a l'usage," and Fernández Castro, *Villas romanas en España,* 52.

34. See the discussion of Curtius, *European Literature and the Latin Middle Ages,* in the next section.

35. In Le Goff, *L'Imaginaire médiéval,* 21, 24–25.

36. For a general theoretical discussion in narrative, see Zumthor, *La Mesure du monde,* 363–89, and *Essai de poétique médiévale,* 354.

37. Le Goff, *L'Imaginaire médiéval,* 231; see also "Lévi-Strauss en Brocéliande," a chapter in the same volume.

38. Zumthor, *La Mesure du monde,* 119, 139–40. See Gerli's articulation of Lefebvre's theory for Rojas's depiction of the city in "Precincts of Contention."

39. The medieval *descriptio urbis,* an elaboration on the Horatian *laus urbis,* was conditioned, above all, by the model established by the immensely popular eleventh-century *Mirabilia urbis Romae,* which had enormous influence into the Renaissance. Descriptions of cities in Iberian literature can be found as early as in the twelfth-century *Liber sancti Jacobi* (written by a French cleric, but about Spain), and from then onwards in almost every genre, from books of travel such as the *Libro del conoscimiento,* to romances, *cancionero* poetry, and so forth. See the brief but informative Crivat, "El género de la descriptio urbis."

40. Le Goff, *L'Imaginaire médiéval,* 229–40. The fourfold interpretive framework of the urban imaginary in the Middle Ages was based on the Bible. In the Old Testament, the city appears initially, in Genesis, as a cursed space: the work of Cain, the Tower of Babel, and Sodom and Gomorra. In the historical books, the image of the

city changes as Jerusalem becomes a more developed motif (introduced in Genesis, gaining real importance in the second book of Samuel and the first book of Kings). This positive presentation of the city is emblematized by David and Solomon, which give the city a double image as the seat for religious and royal power. The sapiential books but also the poetic and the prophetic ones continue this trend, particularly in the Psalms. It is Isaiah who introduces the popular opposition of Jerusalem to Babylon in chapter 13. In the New Testament, in typological fashion, the image of the city returns, particularly linked to preaching, as in the letters of Saint Paul, and in Saint John's Apocalypse, where the opposition is played out again, with Jerusalem triumphing in its celestial version. It is of special interest to my study to note that in Judeo-Christian tradition there is a displacement, a relocation of the image of Paradise from an ambigous time/place of origin or as golden age, to a decidedly spatial garden *(hortus conclusus)* and then to a city. This image of the eternal city is already in the Bible, and of the many who followed, Augustine sufficed to suggest its importance in the medieval urban imaginary.

41. Zumthor, *La Mesure du monde*, 147.

42. Le Goff, *L'Imaginaire médiéval*, 174.

43. Saunders, *The Forest of Medieval Romance*. For Spain, a study of the references to the forest in the many *fueros* (at the origin of the forest as a juridical dominion) would provide such documentation. See Zumthor's general remarks in *La Mesure du monde*, 66–68; see also Dodds, "Hunting in the Borderlands."

44. Menocal, "To Create an Empire"; Alfonso XI, *Libro de la Montería*. For a general perspective on the visual representation of hunting, see Cummins, *The Hound and the Hawk*.

45. See McGinn, "Ocean and Desert as Symbols," for a detailed account of these metaphors through the fourteenth century.

46. Guillaumont, "L'Enseignement spirituel des moines d'Égypte," 82. The bibliography is considerable, but see especially the classic study, Chitty, *The Desert a City*, and Gould's introduction to his *The Desert Fathers on Monastic Community*.

47. Numerous reflections on "wild men" or *salvajes* come to mind, from legal sources to literary characters to the type of the savage in popular festivities and its role in Spanish Golden Age theater. The *Primaleón* (Salmanca, 1512), a book of chivalry, articulates this idea of humanity at its limits in the figure of the Gran Patagón, when the hero, comforting his lady at the sight of the "monster," tells her she should not be afraid, for it is a "human man" ("es hombre umano") and will follow her orders, submitting to her if she chooses to approach and flatter him (336). See Bernheimer's classic, *Wild Men in the Middle Ages*; and López-Ríos's exhaustive catalogue of the figure in medieval Castile, with references to artistic representation, *Salvajes y razas monstruosas*. See also Pinet, "Walk on the Wild Side."

48. Le Goff, *L'Imaginaire médiéval*, 61.

49. Saunders, *The Forest of Medieval Romance*, 20.
50. See ibid., 19–24, for a detailed analysis of specific passages.
51. Curtius, *European Literature and the Latin Middle Ages*, 269.
52. Ibid., 275–76
53. Higounet, "Les Fôrets de l'Europe occidentale du Ve au XIe siècle," esp. 371–72, specific to Spain. See also various essays gathered by Corvol-Dessert in *Les Forêts d'occident du moyen âge à nos jours*.
54. Higounet, "Les Fôrets de l'Europe occidentale du Ve au XIe siècle," 324, 350.
55. Zumthor, *La Mesure du monde*, 62–67, esp. 62–63.
56. See Navarro González, *El mar en la literatura medieval castellana*, for a catalogue of scenes with seascapes in different genres up to the fifteenth century.
57. See the first chapter of Cátedra and Rodríguez Velasco, *Creación y difusión de "El baladro del sabio Merlín,"* for a concise introduction to filiations and chronology of Arthurian romance and its entry into the Iberian Peninsula.
58. Szkilnik, *L'Archipel du Graal*. I will refer to her work substantially in the next pages, but an interested reader should consult her book for a full analysis.
59. Such a silence, Szkilnik notes, reminds us of a similar one in the *Queste de Saint Graal*, when Galaad's and Lancelot's adventures of six months at sea and afterward on an island are left untold with the excuse that such a story would be too long.
60. Szkilnik, *L'Archipel du Graal*, 13–15.
61. Ibid., 17.
62. There are six islands in the *Estoire*: (1) the one where Mordrain is taken to and where the pirate Forcaire used to "repaire," (2) the Ile Tournoyante of Nascien, (3) the island where Chélidoine and also King Label and his men come to, (4) one where Nascien fights a giant using Salomon's sword, (5) where King Label and the messengers search for Nascien, and (6) the one in the interpolated story of Hippocrates upon the island of the giant.
63. Szkilnik, *L'Archipel du Graal*, 23.
64. Ibid., 85. One finds in the *Estoire* either divine or demonic ships. Demonic ones are all the same: black, full of earthly riches, often captained by a beautiful and dominating woman, surrounded by flames and lightning, provoking storms and whirlwinds in their wake, a motif that will be taken up in Spanish books of chivalry. For Spain, see Beltrán, "Urganda, Morgana y Sibila."
65. Szkilnik characterizes the islands of the *Estoire* alternatively as a "rediscovered firm land for the *Lancelot-Graal*," as a place where the character suffers "a confirmation of his excellence rather than a test," as an episode, as a ritual place, a theme, a metaphor of the narrative and as place of passage, and as an "archipelago." She also makes a very interesting observation on the inclusion of the island as a possibility for *excursus*, for a secondary narrative that will be relinked to the principal narrative but which retains a certain independence, serving as a counterpoint (Salomon and

Hippocrates) or as an illustration *(Ile Tournoyante)*. These observations are very close to my argument; however, the analysis of the island in Szkilnik's study seems to use "island" alternatively as a figure, a metaphor, a space, and a sign for something else. The role itself of the island in the *Estoire* is varied and, within that variation, contradictory (see Blumenfeld-Kosinski's review in *Speculum*). As an overarching argument, Szkilnik writes that the metaphor the *Estoire* "imposes" above all others is that of the archipelago, through the basic anecdote the *Estoire* tells: one of multiple ships traveling from island to island. She writes: "The image of the archipelago preserves the independence of each episode, suggesting their taking place in a geometrical or geographical configuration," offering a nice but contradictory image because the relationship between geometry and geography does not seem to settle so easily. A few lines afterward, Szkilnik argues that the characters' wish throughout the book will be to set foot on the firm ground of a continent, Great Britain. Further on, she writes, "Great Britain is to the seaworld, a harbor, a rediscovered mainland, what the *Estoire* is to the cycle of the *Lancelot-Graal*." This metaphor for the *Estoire* contradicts the previous one as an archipelago. The *Estoire* is conveyed ambiguously both as an archipelago and a continent, as an island and a mainland, opposing metaphors that, even beyond the literal, seem inaccurate, as they are forced to describe both a content and a structure in the same terms. It may well be the case that the structure is itself contradictory in the *Estoire*; I argue that the archipelago is cohesively explored as structure later, in the Spanish book of chivalry.

66. In this sense islands in the *Estoire* are linked to Augé's concept of the non-place (as one different from Deleuze's or Foucault's notion, or Certeau's heterotopias) in *Non-lieux*; for a comparative analysis of these conceptual differences, see Bosteels, "Nonplaces."

67. Gómez Redondo, *Historia de la prosa medieval castellana*, 2:1481.

68. Rubio García, "La Ínsula Barataria," 644–47.

69. Zumthor, *La Mesure du monde*, 72.

70. Bognolo, *La finzione rinnovata*.

71. García Piqueras, "Posibles estructuras literarias en *la Fazienda de Ultra Mar*," 361.

72. Ibid., 366–69. For a wide view of literary concerns with medieval travel narratives, see Beltrán's edition, *Maravillas, peregrinaciones y utopías*; for a very general account of medieval travel narratives, see Peebles and Zumthor, "The Medieval Travel Narrative."

73. Pérez Priego, "Maravillas en los libros de viajes medievales," Popeanga, "Lectura e investigación de los libros de viajes medievales," and Beltrán, "Los libros de viajes medievales castellanos," complement one another for a survey of texts and problems of the genre in the peninsula.

74. Reprinted as *Repertorios de caminos*.

75. Braudel, *El Mediterráneo y el mundo mediterráneo en la época de Felipe II*, 12.
76. Ibid., 48; Tony Campbell, "Portolan Charts from the Late Thirteenth Century to 1500," 415.
77. Olschki, *Storia letteraria delle scoperte geografiche*, 39.
78. See Piehler, *The Visionary Landscape*, 82 n.24, with bibliography.
79. See Olschki, *Storia letteraria delle scoperte geografiche*, especially 34–35, 39, 48.
80. Compare with Olschki's summary: "Japan is imagined as a large island, located near the sea of China in which another seven thousand, four hundred and fifty islands are laid out, all rich in spices, pearls, precious stones, and gold, so abundant that it could not be valued" (Olschki, *Storia letteraria delle scoperte geografiche*, 39).
81. Ibid., 48.
82. Pérez Priego, "Estudio literario de los libros de viajes medievales," 235, 237.
83. Salvador Miguel, "Descripción de islas en textos castellanos medievales."
84. The passage of the *Çifar* corresponds to the "Ínsulas dotadas." The passage from the *Laberinto* corresponds to the coplas 51–52, in which the protagonist is taken to the abode of Fortune, where he can contemplate an allegorical vision of the universe, which besides the traditional Isidorian tripartite world presents a vision of the "islas particulares" (the description is inspired directly from chapters 34–36 of the *De imagine mundi*; see Lida de Malkiel, *Juan de Mena*, 34ff). Pero Tafur's text contains insular descriptions of his periplus through the Adriatic, while in Breidennbach's text Salvador Miguel stresses a description of Crete, already referred to above. Salvador Miguel notes the differences between the texts: one is the first chivalric text in the peninsula, another is a politico-moral poem, another is a travelogue, and the last is an itinerary or pilgrimage guide. Salvador Miguel uses as well the *Libro del conoscimiento* (mid-fourteenth century) to compile a list of mythological data in insular descriptions, for which Mena is particularly prolific (and precise in the definition by Salvador Miguel).
85. Salvador Miguel, "Descripción de islas en textos castellanos medievales," 48.
86. Ibid., 54. The concept of the perfect island would be picked up by Saint Anselm in the famous ontological problem known as the "Lost Island" debate—a logical argument following the idea of the existence of a perfect island in the middle of the ocean but never seen by anyone. This argument would be refuted, notably by Gaunilon de Marmoutiers in his *Liber pro insipiente adversus Anselmum in Prosologio ratiocinantem* (section 6 in Migne, *Patrologia Latina*, vol. 158, col. 246). See Back, "Anselm on Perfect Islands," and the discussion in chapter 3 on the *Ínsula No Fallada*.
87. The milestone interpretation of the episode is Wagner's, who pointed out the correspondences with the *matière de Bretagne* (in consonance with Gracia's analysis of the Sulphuring Lake episode, "Varios apuntes sobre el 'Cuento del Caballero Atrevido,'" see esp. 24n.; see also Mullen, "The Role of the Supernatural in *El libro del Cavallero Çifar*," who emphasizes the Spanish Christian origin of these

episodes). Krappe ("Le Lac enchanté dans le *Chevalier Çifar*") denounces what he calls "Celtic mirage" as determining Wagner's interpretation, in detriment to an Oriental tradition whose motifs he grounds in the episode through an Arabic transmission. Finally, Burke ("The Meaning of the Islas Dotadas Episode") analyzes the episode following a general interpretational scheme based on the struggle between *caritas* and *cupiditas*. See as well Toledano Molina, "El elemento maravilloso en las aventuras," which attempts to establish, in consonance with Mullen, cited above, the existence of a "native marvelous" of Spanish literature, revealed through the "folkloric fantastic." It should be noted that these terms are defined following Todorov, whose pertinence for the study of medieval texts has been much debated. For this debate, see Dubost, *Aspects fantastiques*. For a general bibliography for *Çifar*, see Cristina González, *El Cavallero Zifar y el Reino Lejano*, chap. 1, which can be supplemented with Harney, "The *Libro del Caballero Zifar*."

88. See Burke, "The Meaning of the Islas Dotadas Episode," 57–58, for the list of motifs. Burke ends by arguing that the episode is an allegory—following French use in the twelfth century—of the Augustinian "*Caritas-Cupiditas* conflict." His radical polarization of Fortuna and Christianity (Providence) is problematic, along with analyses that evince a too-literal reading, such as in the parallel with the classic figure of Venus in Virgil and Ovid; of the confusion between terms, such as *lujuria* for *codicia, codicia* for ambition, desire for savagery.

89. Cristina González, *El Cavallero Zifar y el Reino Lejano*, 95–110.

90. Gracia analyzes the episode of the *Caballero Atrevido* and the traditon of the Sulphuring Lake in terms that can be related to these three characteristics. As sources for the lake motif, she goes back to the *Aeneid*, where Lake Averno is located in a deep cave, with rivers that boil and are inhabited by monsters and marvelous beings, a motif that is taken up by Dante and that crosses over to Arthurian texts in relation to the Beste Glatissant, a motif that would permeate the Spanish and Portuguese *Demandas* and into chivalric peninsular material: "Echoes of this motif reach the *Amadís de Gaula*: in the boiling lake where the giant Famangomadán, before leaving, must always decapitate a damsel in front of his idol" ("Varios apuntes sobre el 'Cuento del Caballero Atrevido,'" 31 n.25). The lake, as was suggested before, is a mirror image of the island, and in this sense its meaning, its *sens*, is likewise inverted, even if most of the characteristics (limitation, exuberance, special sexuality, lust versus chastity) are shared.

91. These are, evidently, related through the presence of water, which Ayerbe-Chaux sees as a symbol of the travel to "an imaginary, extraterrestrial" space, however inappropriate ("Las islas dotadas," 31).

92. Ayerbe-Chaux, "Las islas dotadas," 37.

93. Ibid., 48. Numerous enigmatic aspects of this text remain unsolved, such as the symbolism of the dog and the hawk, the still-problematic symbol of the horse as

lust or willfulness, which still does not go well with the laughter of both emperor and Roboán at the end of the episode. Ayerbe-Chaux analyzes this last element as an indication that they accept the loss of a utopian ideal, that is, the idea of courtly love, as opposed to love in the real world (ibid., 35–37).

94. For these and the texts in which they appear, see Alvar, *Diccionario de mitología artúrica*, s.v. *reino de las islas, isla de la alegría, isla de oro, isla giratoria, isla perdida*.

2. Islands and Maps

1. Lefebvre, *The Production of Space*, 14.
2. Braudel, *El Mediterráneo*, 44.
3. For an analysis of the fear of drowning and shipwreck, from Greece and Rome to romanticism, see Blumenberg, *Shipwreck with Spectator*.
4. Braudel, *El Mediterráneo*, 46–47.
5. In Jacob, *The Sovereign Map*, 307.
6. Romm, *The Edges of the Earth*.
7. Jacob, *The Sovereign Map*, 134, partly summarizing Lewis, "The Origins of Cartography."
8. Jacob, *The Sovereign Map*, 100.
9. Strabo, *Geography*, II, 5.5, C 112–13, Plutarch, *Parallel Lives, Life of Theseus*, paraphrased in Jacob, *The Sovereign Map*, 137.
10. In Jacob, *The Sovereign Map*, 50.
11. Romm, *The Edges of the Earth*, 27.
12. Ibid., 29–41.
13. In Dilke, "Itineraries and Geographical Maps," 244.
14. Romm goes back several times to belabor the discussion in ancient thought around this concept, but his focus is much more on the nature of the boundary, on the character of the circumscription and the conceptual delimitation than on the geography or metaphor of the island in itself.
15. Romm, *The Edges of the Earth*, 31.
16. Bouloux notes that Strabo and Ptolemy, and even Pomponius Mela, had already given islands separate treatment, but other authors, better known throughout the Middle Ages, such as Pliny and Solinus, discuss islands merely on the way of describing seas or littorals (Bouloux, "Les Îles dans les descriptions géographiques," 48–50).
17. An obvious exception is Ptolemy. He was mostly unknown throughout the Middle Ages, and his rediscovery in the late Middle Ages led to the acceleration in the development of what we know as modern cartography. For a summary of existing scholarship and the cultural reception of Ptolemy, see Gautier-Dalché, "The Reception of Ptolemy's *Geography*."

18. "Indenting the edge of the circular world are the prominent gulfs of the Red Sea and the Mediterranean; the Caspian Sea is also often shown as a small gulf in the northeast. The Gulf of Azov—the Palus Maeotis of Classical times, which becomes Meotides Paludes on the mappamundi—also sometimes appears as a small gulf of the surrounding ocean, as on the Corpus Christi College, Oxford, version of Higden's map of the world map of Guido de Pisa (1119)" (Woodward, "Medieval Mappaemundi," 328).
19. In Woodward, "Medieval *Mappaemundi*," 328 n.210.
20. Edson, *Mapping Time and Space*, 4–5.
21. See the classic studies by Yates, *The Art of Memory*, and Carruthers, *The Book of Memory*. See also Jacob, *The Sovereign Map*, esp. 178–80.
22. Jacob, *The Sovereign Map*, 132. Edson elaborates this idea structural to Isidore's thought in chapter 3 of *Mapping Time and Space*, entitled "The Nature of Things." She also succinctly expounds these ideas in the introduction and chapter 4 in the book coauthored with Savage-Smith, *Medieval Views of the Cosmos*. For a discussion of the subject of macro/microcosm specific to Iberia with examples in a variety of texts, see Rico, *El pequeño mundo del hombre*.
23. See the detailed discussion of the representation of Paradise in medieval cartography in Scafi, *Mapping Paradise*, esp. 84–124.
24. Jacob, *The Sovereign Map*, 136.
25. Edson, *Mapping Time and Space*, 100, 116. The expression "geographical framework" is taken from Woodward, "Medieval *Mappamundi*," 326. Romm makes a similar argument for ancient thought through the notions of limit and origin in *The Edges of the Earth*, 20–26.
26. Tony Campbell, "Portolan Charts from the Late Thirteenth Century to 1500," 372.
27. In chapter 4 of his *European Expansion in the Later Middle Ages*, "Columbus and the American Islands" (143–97), Chaunu draws a quick if careful itinerary of Columbus's cartographic imagination in the development of the project to search a route to the East by sailing west. The relevance of an insular imaginary, in particular of the island of Saint Brendan and its juridical implications, and of the island of Antillia as hypothetical horizon that would make the enterprise thinkable for Columbus, is emphasized in this chapter. Mary Baine Campbell also writes, "The 'island' [note the potentially metaphorical use of the word, signaled by quotation marks] was, as we have seen, the landform that functioned as a *king of master tropes* of New World topography, and that characterized the focus of classic voyage literature, especially where it spoke most directly to private desire: Columbus finds islands, as do André Thévet and Thomas More" (*Wonder and Science*, 135, my emphasis). Lestringant discusses insularity in the context of conquest and mapping of the Americas in *Le Livre des îles*, especially chapters 3–6 of part 1. Padrón studies the

island as master trope in Gómara in chapter 4, "Charting an Insular Empire," of *The Spacious Word*, 137–84.

28. Bouloux, "Les Îles dans les descriptions cartographiques," 57.

29. Lestringant, "La Voie des îles," 16. For information on islands in Roman cartography, see Dilke, "Roman Large-Scale Mapping in the Early Empire," esp. 217–23, where he talks of Roman plans depicting islands. For the most comprehensive work on floating islands, see van Duzer's *Floating Islands, a Global Bibliography*.

30. Jacob, *The Sovereign Map*, 149. Jacob uses the Miller Atlas throughout his book but devotes particularly pages 149–53 to the description of islands in the atlas.

31. See Romm, *The Edges of the Earth*, 106–9.

32. Jacob, *The Sovereign Map*, 150.

33. See Finazzi-Agrò, *A invençao da ilha*.

34. Tony Campbell, "Portolan Charts from the Late Thirteenth Century to 1500," 415.

35. Lestringant, "La Voie des îles," 18.

36. Contrast Jacob's chapter 2 (especially the sections entitled "Figures of *deixis*" and "Hic sunt leones"; also the section "I Am Here" in *The Sovereign Map*, chapter 4) with Émile Benveniste's "Subjectivity in Language" for a common grammar between language and cartography.

37. Zumthor, *Essai de poétique médiévale*, 340–41.

38. Karamustafa, "Introduction to Islamic Maps," 7.

39. Bearman et al., "Djazīra."

40. I have left out passages from the *Arabian Nights*, and specifically those that refer the travels of Sinbad, which refer to islands, as they are better known, and they represent an oral tradition shared by the Islamic world. The islands and wonders referred there appear as well in the texts compiled by Arioli; I merely present a general inventory of their variety and some obvious links with the Christian insular imaginary.

41. California is an island kingdom ruled by Calafia, queen of Amazons in the *Sergas*, book V of *Amadís*, located to the right of India and near Paradise. See Cacho Blecua and Lacarra, *Lo imaginario en la conquista de América*, and Javier González, "Libros de caballerías en América," with ample bibliography.

42. See van Duzer, *Floating Islands*, on this particular topic, with numerous examples.

43. Arioli, *Le isole mirabili*, 31.

44. See Arioli, *Le isole mirabili*, 122–23, and Platts, *A Dictionary of Urdu, Classical Hindi, and English*, 650.

45. See Hunsberger, "Marvels."

46. See Oman, "Al-Idrīsī." This is a very general sketch; for a detailed introductory article with bibliography, see Maqbul and Taeschner, "Djughrāfiyā" [geography].

47. Arioli, *Le isole mirabili*, 87, 90–91, 181–82. For a detailed account of continuation of Latin geography into Arabic, see Vallvé Bermejo, "Fuentes latinas de los geógrafos árabes," and Molina, "Orosio y los geógrafos hispanomusulmanes." For an overview of Islamic cartography, see Maqbul, *A History of Arab-Islamic Geography*.

48. See Lewicki, "Ibn 'Abd al-Munìm al-Ḥimyarī."

49. Ibn Wasif Sah and Al-Ḥimyarī in Arioli, *Le isole mirabili*, 70–72. See A. Scobie, "The Battle of the Pygmies and the Cranes."

50. Reproduced in Harley and Woodward, *The History of Cartography*, vol. 2, *Cartography in the Traditional Islamic and South Asian Societies*, part 1, 391.

51. I present selected interpretations from a very complicated tradition summarized in Viré, "Wāḵwāḵ, Waḵwāḵ, Wāḵ Wāḵ, Wāḵ al- Wāḵ, al- Wāḵwāḵ (a.)." See also Toorawa, "Wâq al-wâq."

52. See Maqbul, "Cartography of al-Sharīf al-Idrīsī."

53. Arioli, *Le isole mirabili*, 201.

54. Arioli writes: "One of the many flexions of this root, the word *hadath*, means at the same time 'novelty' and 'event.' Yet another flexion of the same root, reduplicating the second radical, gives us the verb *haddatha*, which means 'to narrate'; an ulterior flexion produces the homograph and homophone *hadith*, from then on one word, distinguishable only in their respective and different plurals, with the meaning of 'new' and 'narration'" (201n).

55. Clutton, "Isolarios." This anthropological gaze is precisely what will begin to dominate the *isolario* in later versions, such as in the writings of Sonetti, Bordone, and particularly Thévet. Conley writes, "The perspectival distance that goes with self-detachment becomes, thanks to the ethnographic matrix offered by the island-book format, a space for anthropology" (*The Self-Made Map*, 178), a perspective that would be progressively shared by writing in general. I would argue that, even if Buondelmonti, whom I am about to discuss, does not make this perspective a general one, he certainly anticipates it, making it part of the beginning and, maybe the nature itself, of the *isolario*.

56. Tolias, "*Isolarii*, Fifteenth to Eighteenth Century," 264, 265.

57. For the manuscripts of the *Liber*, see Almagià, *Monumenta cartographica Vaticana*.

58. Clutton, "Isolarios," 482. Tolias writes: "There is nothing particularly remarkable about the conception of *isolario* as a genre, for the practice of organizing knowledge in thematic compartments is widely found in medieval and Renaissance learned literature. Lengthy lists in chronicles, books of wisdom, bestiaries, books of miracles, and later, collections of views of towns, harbors, costumes, battles, or military formations had accustomed people to the thematic encyclopedic approach" ("*Isolarii*, Fifteenth to Eighteenth Century," 281). What was original was the focus on islands.

59. Clutton, "Isolarios," 483; Weiss, "Un umanista antiquario."

60. The multiple redactions have been determined to be as follows: a first written at Rhodes before 1420; a second also written at Rhodes, appearing in 1420; a shorter version written in Constantinople in 1422; and a fourth around 1430, with additional maps and information (Tolias, "*Isolarii*, Fifteenth to Eighteenth Century," 266n).

61. Legrand, preface, xxiv, xxv; but his list is incomplete. See Weiss, "Un umanista antiquario," esp. 110–11. There are only two editions of Christophoro Buondelmonti's most famous work, the *Liber insularum archipelagi*. The first was Ludovicus von Sinner's edition of 1824; the second, by Émile Legrand, was originally published in Paris in 1897.

62. Legrand, preface, xiii.

63. In Tolias, "*Isolarii*, Fifteenth to Eighteenth Century," 266.

64. Buondelmonti, *Description des îles de l'Archipel grec*, 159.

65. Three copies I have seen follow these instructions quite closely: the Biblioteca Nacional de España, Madrid, MS 18246; MS Latin 4825 in the Bibliothèque Nationale de France (reproduced in Buondelmonti, *Description des îles de l'Archipel grec*); and the one reproduced in *History of Cartography*, 1:483. The alternation between text and map is the first trait of the *isolario*, a physical, visual one, which will underscore the island-hopping nature of the genre. A fourth manuscript I have consulted, Escorial f.II.17, begins by following these instructions for five islands, but then puts them in an appendix.

66. Turner, "Christopher Buondelmonti and the Isolario." See also Montesdeoca, "Del enciclopedismo al isolario humanist" and *Los islarios de la época del humanismo*.

67. Turner, "Christopher Buondelmonti and the Isolario," 13. Among owners of copies of the *Liber* were merchants, doctors of law and medicine, and a bishop. A shared bourgeois ideology with his readers might thus explain the incredible success Buondelmonti had. See ibid., 24 n.29.

68. Though Conley writes about Bordone's *isolario*, I think it appropriate for Buondelmonti's as well: "Equal importance is ascribed to text and illustration. A sensible balance of verbal and visual material dictates the form of the book, each element intended to complement the other. The map offers a *spatial* order of figures that suspends the discursive itinerary.... The layout of language and image implies that the one may be unlike but is also a necessary part of the other; that, too, each can be figured as what defines its surrounding border or what it encompasses; that heterogeneity is the basis of the genre; that as system of alterity is literally 'written' or 'mapped' into the relation between the island and the sea, between the illustration and the text.... Serving to produce totality and a mirror of matter familiar and bizarre, or an archipelago of things, places and oddities, the *isolario* heralds a diagrammatic arrangement of knowledge. A sense of something 'other' is held in its

logic and execution and reveals its latent attraction to ethnography" (*The Self-Made Map*, 179–80).

69. Buondelmonti, *Description des îles de l'Archipel grec*, 192.
70. This is the case of Samos (ibid., 227).
71. Buondelmonti in Turner, "Christopher Buondelmonti and the Isolario," 19.
72. Buondelmonti, *Description des îles de l'Archipel grec*, 236.
73. Ibid., 180, 197, 212. For a full analysis of Buondelmonti as archaeologist, see Weiss, "Un umanista antiquario."
74. Cachey, "Print Culture and the Literature of Travel," 14. Page numbers correspond to my copy of this lecture, kindly provided by Prof. Cachey.
75. Ibid., 15.
76. Ibid.
77. Conley, *The Self-Made Map*, especially the chapter "An Insular Moment: From Cosmography to Ethnography." See also "Virtual Reality and the *Isolario*."
78. Lestringant, "L'Insulaire des Lumières," 89, and also "Fortunes de la singularité à la Renaissance."
79. Cachey, "Print Culture and the Literature of Travel," 6.
80. Jacob, *The Sovereign Map*, 67.
81. Tolias, "*Isolarii*, Fifteenth to Eighteenth Century," 271.
82. Comprising 111 maps, drawn ca. 1540, this *isolario*'s maps are more functional than aesthetic, including scales of latitude and some of longitude. The book is divided into four parts (North Atlantic, Mediterranean, Africa and India, and the New World) and preceded by a brief cosmographical treatise. A historian and builder of navigational instruments, royal cosmographer Santa Cruz probably intended this work to be part of a Universal Geography that he never completed. The *Islario* is kept at the Biblioteca Nacional de España (Res 38) and has been digitized: http://bibliotecadigitalhispanica.bne.es:1801/. Among some traits of this *isolario* are that it is a manuscript written on paper (a first, for these types of charts were typically drawn on parchment), and that it follows the map–text alternation but considerably expands the text, perhaps as a result of its author's historiographic interests. See also Cuesta, *Alonso de Santa Cruz y su obra cosmográfica*.
83. It is curious that of the eleven compilations that constitute the genre (in Lestringant's exhaustive study), there is a Portuguese author (Valentim Fernandes, *De Insulis et peregrinatione Lusitanorum*), a German (Henricus Martellus Germanus, *Insularium illustratum Henrici Martelli Germani*—produced in northern Italy), a Dutch (Olfert Dapper, *Naukeurige Beschryving der Eilanden, in de Archipel del Middelantsche Aee, en ontrent dezelve, gelegen: Waer onder de voornaemste Cyprus, Rhodus, Kandien, Samos, Scio, Negroponte, Lemnos, Paros, Delos, Patmos, en andere, in groten getale . . . Door Dr. O. Dapper*), a French (André Thévet, *Le Grand Insulaire et Pilotage*), and a Spanish one (Alonso Fernandez de Santa Cruz, *Islario general de*

todas las Islas del Mundo por Alonso de Santa Cruz Cosmógrafo mayor de Carlos I de España, which was dedicated to the monarch but never published). The remaining six *isolarii* are by Italians.

84. Cachey, "Print Culture and the Literature of Travel," 22.
85. Jacob, *The Sovereign Map*, 127.
86. Conley, *The Self-Made Map*, 195, 196.
87. Tolias, "*Isolarii*, Fifteenth to Eighteenth Century," 283–94.
88. Jacob, *The Sovereign Map*, 76.
89. Conley, *The Self-Made Map*, 197.
90. Braudel, *El Mediterráneo*, 37.
91. Ibid., 38.
92. Jacob, *The Sovereign Map*, 286.
93. Conley, *The Self-Made Map*, 169.
94. Jacob, *The Sovereign Map*, 297, esp. the section entitled "Cartographic Fictions" in chap. 4.
95. This can be exemplified in the image of insularity conveyed in the *Imago mundi*, which, particularly in its French version, was disseminated from 1250 on. See Dubost, "Insularités imaginaires et récit médiéval," 49.
96. Examples are legion, from *marginalia*—both literary and cartographic—to bestiaries and travelogues.
97. Avalon submitted to the authority of fairies is the best example anteceding the Spanish book of chivalry. Mixed with the ideas of strangeness and the other world, the supernatural presence of evil on an island can be attested in the Arabic imaginary in the island of The Evil One, or in the *Roman d'Alexandre*, where the hero imprisons the Devil on the deserted island of Urion.
98. Another, among many, important example of islands associated with the other world is the Island of Saint Brendan, which I have referred to before. In the Iberian Peninsula, related to the Celtic *imram* to which the *Voyage de Saint Brandan* relates, we can refer to the *Conto de Amaro* (fourteenth century), a tale of a journey through a series of islands, populated by beasts, hermits, and marvels, culminating with the arrival onto the island of Paradise. See Lida de Malkiel, "La visión de trasmundo en las literaturas hispánicas," esp. 377–78. Indeed, the insular other world makes reference not only to the world of the dead, Hades or the Elyseum Fields, but to Purgatory and, of course, Paradise. While there seems to be a general impression that the medieval insular imaginary has more negative connotations (as opposed to a more "utopian" or positive modern archipelago, see Dubost, "Insularités imaginaires et récit médiéval") in the Islamic insular imaginary briefly reviewed above, in cartography, in the recuperation of versions of the other world and in their Christianized forms of paradise, utopian and even "robinsonesque" islands can be found. See Le Goff's history of Purgatory, *La Naissance du Purgatoire*, and Lida de Malkiel,

"La visión del trasmundo en las literaturas hispánicas" (she provides specific bibliography on the Spanish versions of the *Tractatus de Purgatorio* on page 377). For a general account of the medieval imaginary of the other world, see Patch's classic work on the subject, *The Other World*. The best known Spanish examples are probably the Exemplo 49 of *El conde Lucanor* ("De lo que contesçió al que echaron en la ysla desnuyo quándol tomaron el señorío que tenié") and the "Insolas Dotadas" episode of *Libro del caballero Zifar*, which has been discussed in chapter 1.

99. See Peyràs, "L'Île et le sacré dans l'Antiquité," esp. 27–32. Mysterious and prominent births in medieval literature are also often staged on islands, such as Clinevent's in the *Chanson de Gaydon*, and Bayar's, the horse of the "quatre fils Aymon," in the *Chanson de Maugis* (Dubost, "Insularités imaginaires et récit médiéval," 50).

100. Dubost writes that "the devil appears as the figure of insularization par excellence, whether in terms of doctrine or as a structure of representation. In a series of encirclements, the islands of evil, of temptation, of perversion, of Morganian imprisonment surround the devil and the traps of desire. All these arrangements, all these plays of insularity are in conformity with the theological, Augustinian idea that evil does not exist in itself. It is perceived as a lack in ontological space, as an island of non-being, an obsession that can be captured only in the image of *an island that does not exist*"("Insularités imaginaires et récit médiéval," 57).

101. Peyràs, "L'Île et le sacré dans l'Antiquité," 32.

102. Lestringant, "L'Insulaire des Lumières," 90.

103. Ibid., 91. For a politically and philosophically informed, if opaque, study on the archipelago as figure, see Cacciari, *L'Arcipelago*.

104. Minerva distinguishes two types of island: the atoll-island and the island-island. The first she relates to the idea of monstrosity, sterility, desert, stasis, and solitude; the second to notions of center, refuge, paradise, and happiness (Minerva, "Le Cercle magique," 152, 153, 156).

105. On the subject of utopia, one can conjecture that for postmodernity the utopian island cannot be drawn on a map anymore, and it is not even imagined in its possibility. For these texts, the most beautiful island will be that which cannot be found or may not exist, the island of nowhere (or of the day before), the truly fantastic island. Dystopia consists thus in this receding of a floating or mobile island, in the impossibility of fixing it to specific coordinates, in the chase after a mirage. See Minerva, "Le Cercle magique," 157.

106. Jacob, *The Sovereign Map*, 201. I will look closely at two examples of insular toponymy in the next two chapters. For more on naming in the Renaissance, see Greenblatt, *Marvelous Possessions*, especially 52–85. For intelligent criticism of Greenblatt's use of the term wonder see González Echevarría's review, "Europeans in Wonderland."

107. In considering the toponymy of islands, it is particularly important to remember that "one of the paradoxes of toponymical nomenclature, and, for that matter, all inscriptions contained on the surface of a map, means occupying a portion—even infinitesimal—of the space that it claims to name. We might then consider the letters of the toponym as elements integrated into the cartographic design (that is, as geographical sites, islands, set out in a linear archipelago), that can generate meaning when one follows the other" (Jacob, *The Sovereign Map*, 202–3). Jacob emphasizes the relationship between a name and a geography as elements of cartography, but one can also emphasize here the particular equivalence between language and insularity, between letters and islands that can lead to a syntax, the idea of a structure and a grammar.

108. Lestringant, "L'Insulaire des Lumières," 91.

109. Jacob, *The Sovereign Map*, 286.

110. Lestringant, "L'Insulaire des Lumières," 95. It is in this sense, in the oppositions singularity/diversity and purity/hybridity, that Peyràs opposes the Greek and the Roman insular imaginary. In Greek mythology the island is not only a reconquering of self, or the search for a home, that is, the return to a form of singularity, of a "personal autarchy," but neither is it a site of passage, nor only a refuge: "it is also the deepening of an ethnic and cultural méttisage.... The island constitutes in Greek culture a privileged space of experiences that pose and seek to solve the problem of the human condition.... Romans, on the contrary, due to their religious ideology in the time of empire, conceived only of a politically closed group in which each was subjected to his place. The island, inasmuch as it represented the possibility of alterity, did not have a reason for being" (Peyràs, "L'Île et le sacré dans l'Antiquité," 32, 35).

111. Buondelmonti, *Description des îles de l'Archipel grec*, 241. Buondelmonti also briefly describes another city, Gallipoli, stating that that description obviously anticipates the longer one of Constantinople. For more on Buondelmonti's description of Constantinople, see Gerola, "Le vedute di Constantinopoli di Cristofor Buondelmonti."

112. Turner, "Christopher Buondelmonti and the Isolario," 22.

113. Braudel in *El Mediterráneo en la época de Felipe II* writes of the role the construction of wood boats had in the destruction of the Mediterranean forests. Thickets and bushes take the place of pinewoods, leaving extensive spaces nude. Victim of its own exploitation, the ship suffered due to the difficulty of obtaining wood, and to the high prices that had to be paid for it. Braudel reminds us that Carmelo Traselli, historian of Sicily, attributed to this, among many other reasons, the decadence of the Mediterranean in the sixteenth century, which intensified in the seventeenth: Venetian sailors bought their ships then from Holland. The Venetian crisis coincided with a similar one in the Islamic world that had been occurring

since the eleventh century, surrendering the control of the inner sea to English and Dutch sailors.
114. Tolias, "*Isolarii*, Fifteenth to Eighteenth Century," 272.
115. Ibid., 279.
116. Braudel, *El Mediterráneo*, 264.

3. ADVENTURE AND ARCHIPELAGO

1. Two recent publications, not available to me when I wrote this book, gather the latest lines of thought on chivalric literature and evaluate the considerable attention the genre has garnered in the last few years: *Amadís de Gaula, 500 años después: Homenaje a Juan Manuel Cacho Blecua*, and the catalogue of the exhibit in the Biblioteca Nacional, *Amadís de Gaula: 1508 (quinientos años de libros de caballerías)*.
2. See Gómez Redondo, "La literatura caballeresca castellana medieval."
3. See Infantes, López, and Borrel, *Historia de la edición y de la lectura en España*. I will refer to Garci Rodríguez de Montalvo as Montalvo.
4. See Roubaud-Bénichou, *Le Roman de chevalerie en Espagne*, 73–84, for an overview. I will not enter debate on the "Amadís question." Portuguese and French theories for the original *Amadís* were silenced by Rodríguez Moñino's mid-twentieth century discovery of fragments of a primitive *Amadís*, dated 1420, in Spanish. Within the complex set of references to *Amadís* in Spain and hypotheses on the structure of the "primitive" version in three books, this discovery placed *Amadís* firmly in the Spanish literary tradition. For a concise summary of the debate, see the chapter devoted to it by Pierce, *Amadís de Gaula*, 39ff; for an exhaustive and up-to-date study presenting the *estado de la cuestión* see Roubaud-Bénichou's "Annexe" in *Le Roman*, 237–305. On the matter of the primitive *Amadís*, see Lida de Malkiel, "El desenlace del *Amadís* primitivo," and Avalle-Arce's controversial monograph, *"Amadís de Gaula."*
5. Williams, "The Amadis Question"; Lida de Malkiel, "El desenlace del *Amadís* primitivo."
6. One proposal is the equation of Vindilisora to Windsor. For other cases, see González, "Realismo y simbolismo en la geografía del *Amadís de Gaula*," and an extreme in Suárez Pallasá, "La ínsula Firme del Amadís de Gaula."
7. Place, "*Amadis of Gaul*, Wales or What?" 106–7. I summarize here Place's careful tracing of the debate around the term "Gaul," part of the "*Amadís* question" debate: "Bernardo Tasso's equation of *Gaula* with French *Gaule* (English *Gaul*, Spanish *Galia*) as evidenced by the title, *Amadigi di Francia*" in his versified redaction (1560) of the *Amadís*, caused J. C. Dunlop (1814) to identify the two without question. Only later, in 1849, would George Ticknor state that "Amadís is the son of a merely imaginary king of the imaginary kingdom of Gaula," while suggesting a connection between Gaula and Wales. Baret identified Gaula and Wales in 1853. Place notes that it is interesting that it should be a French Hispanist who would

categorically deny the claim of Herberay des Essarts, translator of the *Amadís* into French, that Gaula meant France and that *Amadís* was a redaction of a Picard original. Marcelino Menéndez y Pelayo in *Orígenes de la novela* followed the identification with Wales. Grace S. Williams in 1909, in her "The *Amadís* Question," wrote that "in the beginning Gaula is undoubtedly France or a part of it, later, on the same kind of evidence, it is Wales, and then in the third book we have a return to France . . . and finally, when Amadís sets out for Germany, the inference would be the same." Place notes Williams also relates the mingling of geographic fact and fancy in the *Amadís* with Arthurian romance in general (100–101). Place further examines the use of the term in Geoffrey of Monmouth's *Historia Regum Britanniae* and Wace's *Brut,* and its absence in the *Tristan* versions, recalling that "in the second half of the twelfth century *France* usually meant merely the Ile de France area around Paris plus the French Vexin and French Gâtinais" (103). He continues his search through Chrétien, Robert de Boron, and the prose Vulgate, finding interesting parallels with *Amadís*'s Roman episodes (105). He extends this all the way to the *Perlesvaus,* to conclude that "the *Vulgate* 'Gaule' is a fictional region on the continent not far removed from Brittany. Furthermore, it can be established that according to the *Vulgate,* in the two regions, *la petite Bretagne* and *Gaule,* were four so-called petty kingdoms—fictional of course—of which one, *Benoic* or *Benoich,* was originally ruled by Lancelot's father, King Ban, who was later deprived of his territory by a certain Claudas described variously as 'king of the Deserted Land' and 'a liege man of the king of Gaul, nowadays called France'" (105–6).

8. Avalle-Arce, "El arco de los leales amadores en el *Amadís*," tries to establish an influence of the *Tirant lo Blanc* on the *Amadís* in terms of space, and of the Orientalism denoted by the Constantinople episodes. Sea travel, however, was already present in French romance, as we have seen, and the reference to Constantinople is there a *topos,* as will be discussed later.

9. For López Estrada the sea is simply another dimension of adventure, and he writes that while the island appears "occasionally" as a setting for combat, the preferred space of the author of *Amadís* is the mainland. López Estrada also claims the islands of *Amadís* are not "islands": they are *ínsulas,* he insists, a term that for him stresses the "utopian depth" of these spaces in the Spanish romance ("El *Tirante* castellano de 1511," 457). I devote a long discussion to this aspect of insularity in the book later on.

10. See Lastra Paz, "Tipología espacial," 189, who studies these spaces in terms of their "trial" quality.

11. Olschki, *Storia letteraria delle scoperte geografiche,* 51–52.

12. Cacho Blecua, introduction, 158.

13. Lastra Paz ("Tipología espacial") rationalizes the spaces of the *Amadís* in thirteen categories, while Fogelquist summarizes the book into events. See Fogelquist,

El Amadís y el género de la historia fingida. Another term commonly used to describe these events is as *rite of passage* (Cacho Blecua, *Amadís*), or what Maier considers the "forging of a reputation . . . of structural importance in the work" ("Golden Age Imagery," 58).

14. Lastra Paz's essay is useful, but has theoretical and terminological flaws. For example, the definition of *area (ámbitos)* is confusing, and within the classification itself, the systematization shows inconsistencies: the difference between feminine *areas* and masculine *space* calls for an elaboration that is not present in the article, and the difference within the classification between spaces and areas is not explained. A footnote explains that by area she means the *locus*: a space characterized by its permanence, while space is to her "space proper," *spatium*. Even within this frame, the distinction is unclear (Lastra Paz, "Tipología espacial," 174, 172 n.1).

15. "In this way, one of these places may be tinged with violence and be an area appropriate for adventure (Castle of Dardán the Proud, *Ínsula Triste* of the giant Madarque, the *Malaventurada* glade, etc.), and it can also be a place of refuge and happy encounters" (Lastra Paz, "Tipología espacial," 180).

16. Sieber, "The Romance of Chivalry in Spain," 209.

17. Lastra Paz, "Tipología espacial,"188.

18. Fogelquist, *El Amadís y el género de la historia fingida*, 128.

19. Cacho Blecua, *Amadís,* 240. See Fogelquist, *El Amadís y el género de la historia fingida,* esp. 113–23, where he summarizes and disagrees with Durán's analysis. Fogelquist relates Weber de Kurlat's study ("Estructura novelesca del Amadís de Gaula") on the structure of *Amadís* to techniques of medieval historiography that constitute the core of his hypothesis. This argument is extended in Roubaud-Bénichou, *Le Roman de chevalerie.* Cacho Blecua takes Weber de Kurlat's references and refines her terminology; his is the most exhaustive look at *Amadís* from a formal point of view.

20. Of the latter kind, "in the *Amadís,* especially in book IV and in the *Sergas,* the syntagm 'dexa la historia' predominates over 'dexa el cuento,' used more in Arthurian tradition. This might imply a connection with historiography, as Alfonso's *Primera Crónica General de España* uses similar links to resolve space-time problems," bearing witness to the shared motifs of these two genres. See Roubaud-Bénichou, "La *General Estoria,*" in *Le Roman de chevalerie,* 115–28.

21. Cacho Blecua identifies ten diverse techniques of interweaving in the *Amadís,* four of them dealing with questions of space specifically (*Amadís,* 250–56).

22. Cacho Blecua, *Amadís,* 258–59.

23. See Avalle-Arce's synopsis of book II in *Amadís de Gaula,* 185–92.

24. Whenever possible, quotations from *Amadís* include book numbers in Roman numerals, followed in Arabic numerals by chapter and page number of the Spanish edition, Rodríguez de Montalvo, *Amadís de Gaula.* For example, "IV, 129" refers to

the 129th chapter of book IV; and "II, Prol, 658; 420" indicates the prologue to book II, on page 658 in the modern Spanish edition and page 420 in the English translation. English translations refer to page numbers in the Place and Behm translation.

25. See Cacho Blecua's "name index" at the end of the second volume to his edition of Rodríguez de Montalvo, *Amadís*.

26. Here, fiction is considered generally as that which is outside the "real," in its possibility suggested through the recurrent presence of the marvelous rather than in specific content. Specific instances of marvelous events in *Amadís* have been studied in detail by Mérida Jiménez *("Fuera de la orden de natura")*, in the variations of the marvelous, the magical, the supernatural, and the miraculous. This exceptional study does not, however, give any particular attention to spatial configuration.

27. See Morreale, "Sobre algunas acepciones de 'extraño' y su valor ponderativo."

28. See Mérida Jiménez, "Fuera de la orden de natura," 129–136.

29. See ibid., esp. 146–59 and 165–70 for Arcaláus; and Bognolo, *La finzione rinnovata*, for complementary analyses. See Neri, "Lo maraviloso arquitectónico," for an overview of architectural marvels.

30. The Ínsula Gravisanda is introduced in chapter 41 of the first book, along with Galaor, Amadís, and Agrajes himself. By the end of chapter 40 Amadís and Agrajes leave Galaor to search for this valorous knight by himself, as they continue on to fulfill Amadís's promise given to Briolanja a year before. At the beginning of chapter 41 we meet Galaor being led by a damsel. Galaor finds a series of adventures, marked by his moodiness and his sexual volubility, until he confronts a most valorous knight who turns out to be his brother, Florestán. Insular spaces also stage amorous and sexual encounters, at times constituting adventures, others merely providing the possibility for genealogy to continue, as heroes of later cycles are conceived as result of these encounters.

31. Authorship is the first of the many issues debated around the Ínsula Firme episodes. Many critics coincide in believing that this prologue, along with the fourth book and as confirmed by the related events in the fifth book, written entirely by Montalvo, the *Sergas de Esplandián*, are products of Montalvo's pen. I refer the reader to the "Amadís question" and register my agreement with Cacho Blecua who, correcting a radical affirmation made in his doctoral dissertation, the classic *Amadís*, declares it is practically impossible to discern which paragraphs or words have been revised by Montalvo and which are products of his own invention. The opposite position is represented by Avalle-Arce's *Amadís de Gaula*, in which he dissects the *Amadís* and finds evidence of four different redactions prior to Montalvo's version.

32. Maier, "Golden Age Imagery," 61. "Psychoanalytic interpretations," such as those by Mircea Eliade, Joseph Campbell, Otto Rank, are common in this type of approach, in formulations that lead to predictable analogies and repetitiveness.

Mérida Jiménez analyzes the episodes in terms of the specific nuances the marvelous receives in the various elements that configure the episode (Mérida Jiménez, *"Fuera de la orden de natura,"* esp. 175–276).

33. The particular name of the island is interpreted by Avalle-Arce to be evidence of the episode's late addition to the romance. That is, it would not have been a part of the primitive *Amadís* for a cartographic reason: "because *terra firme* is a name set in circulation by Rodrigo de Bastidas in 1502 to designate the American coastline from Margarita Island to the Darien River, in contrast with the Caribbean islands, where the Spanish had first arrived." For Avalle-Arce the name would remit to geography and the discoveries in particular. The syntagm "Islas y Tierra Firme," characteristic of the Spanish Golden Age, was formed, and the term was most often used to distinguish the coast from adjacent islands; the term might also be used to designate large islands. For Avalle-Arce, both the *Ínsula Firme* of *Amadís* and the island of California in the *Sergas de Esplandián* are a definite sign of the influence of the discovery of the Americas on Montalvo's refurbishing of the romance (Avalle-Arce, *"Amadís de Gaula,"* 195–96). Emilio José Sales Dasí, however, has demonstrated that the syntagm was in use already in the last third of the fourteenth century (in Mérida Jiménez, *"Fuera de la orden de natura,"* 187). Javier González summarizes the many aspects in which books of chivalry conditioned, filtered, and responded to the Americas in "Libros de caballerías en América," 369. See also the classics Leonard, *Books of the Brave;* Rodríguez Prampolini, *Amadises de América;* and Cacho Blecua and Lacarra, *Lo imaginario en la conquista de América.*

34. Maier, "Golden Age Imagery," 66–67. This political reading assumes a reordering of the material corresponding to the *Ínsula Firme* episode with the goal of effecting a comparison between Apolidón and Grimanesa on the one hand and Amadís and Oriana on the other: "In this manner, Montalvo draws a direct analogy between the past and the future of the *Ínsula,* on the one hand, and establishes a dialectical relationship between the *Ínsula* and the court at London, on the other" (60).

35. Ibid., 63.
36. Ibid., 60. See also Romm, *The Edges of the Earth,* 51.
37. Harney, "Economy and Utopia," 395.
38. Ibid., 396.
39. Ibid., 399.
40. Ibid., 397.
41. Rodríguez Velasco, "Para una periodización de las ideas sobre la caballería en Castilla," 1336.
42. See Fuchs, *Romance,* 40.
43. I refer the reader to Rodríguez Velasco, "Para una periodización de las ideas sobre la caballería en Castilla," for a full discussion of these periods, 1338–42;

compare with Gómez Redondo's periodization of chivalric literature in *Historia de la prosa medieval castellana*.

44. In Sieber, "The Romance of Chivalry in Spain," 205–6.
45. Ibid., 216.
46. Harney, "Economy and Utopia," 393. Harney quotes Marin.
47. Ibid., 394.
48. Maier, "Golden Age Imagery," 54.
49. Harney, "Economy and Utopia," 388. Harney continues to analyze this historical incongruity of the economy represented in the romances through Bourdieu's concept of the *habitus*, and concludes that this incongruity only creates an effect when "the practices generated by the habitus appear as ill adapted because they are attuned to an earlier state of the objective conditions," something that the romance will defer until Cervantes. Then, this incongruity will become apparent in what Bourdieu himself terms the "Don Quijote effect" (388–89).
50. See ibid., 383–84, which quotes Weber for this argument.
51. See Pleij, *Dreaming of Cockaigne*, and Claeys and Sargent, *The Utopia Reader*, among many others.
52. The striking differences between these adventures and Lancelot's *val des faux amants* or *val sans retour* make their kinship remote, both in nature and meaning, though there is a similarity in their being trials of love even when Paris and later Williams identified the arch as an imitation of French romance (Paris's edition of the *Romans de la Table Ronde*, Williams in "The *Amadís* Question"). Avalle-Arce details these differences, for the Arch of Loyal Lovers goes further into a complex process of trial, reward, and punishment for both ladies and knights, and identified the arch as an imitation of French romance. In the same article in which Avalle-Arce discusses these differences ("El arco de los leales amadores en el *Amadís*"), he suggests we consider the influence of the Byzantine novel in this particular episode, for the trial of chastity and/or fidelity is commonplace in this genre. Menéndez Pelayo, recalls Avalle-Arce, wrote of the similarity of the Arch of Loyal Lovers to an episode in *La historia de Leucipe y Clifonte*, by Achilles Tatius (Menéndez Pelayo, *Orígenes de la novela*, via Avalle-Arce, "El arco de los leales amadores en el *Amadís*," 151–54), and Avalle-Arce takes on the task of reviewing numerous texts to prove the similarity of the Amadisian episode with the same motif in the Byzantine novel. While a series of elements from the episode in the romance can be found in the Byzantine novel (such as the palace or temple, the statues, the musical element, the smoke and flames, the inscriptions, the punishment, and the permanence of the enchantment), their direct relationship with the *Amadís* remains to be traced. The Arthurian model as a general one had itself absorbed elements from many traditions, which were given special attention in the *Amadís* and developed in its peninsular context. See Fuchs, *Romance*, 12–36.

53. Campos Rojas, "Centros geográficos," 10, points out the *hortus conclusus* aspect of the garden. For him, it is not only that the place itself is linked to the topos of the garden and its relations to a *locus amoenus*, but also that the arch suggests a rite of passage into a sacred place. His take on the character of the place, labeling it "sacred," seems exaggerated, as it is simply a space for an elite. He further associates the arch with the Roman triumphal arch, which is much more suggestive.

54. See Piehler, *The Visionary Landscape*, 99, for a summary of traits related to the *hortus conclusus*.

55. Ibid.

56. Ibid., 79. For a study of architectonic marvels in other romances, see Campos Rojas, "El Mediterráneo como representación de un imperio," 7–8. See also Neri, "Lo maravilloso arquitectónico."

57. This cycle, defined as the possibility of recurrently establishing a parallel hierarchy, is what Harney considers the chivalric utopia ("Economy and Utopia," 399).

58. For an analysis of the episode as one of the most gratuitous and fantastic of the entire romance, see Cacho Blecua, *Amadís*, 281. For the contrary argument in terms of its conception as a key episode in Montalvo's recantation, see Avalle-Arce, "*Amadís de Gaula*," chap. 7, esp. 290–95.

59. See Blumenberg, *Shipwreck with Spectator*, and also my "Where One Stands," where I analyze the figure of shipwreck in *Claribalte* as central to the changing role of fiction in sixteenth-century writing.

60. See Cuesta Torre, "Las ínsolas del Zifar y el Amadís," and Lucía Megías, "Sobre torres levantadas, palacios destruidos, ínsulas encantadas y doncellas seducidas." Cuesta Torre is especially interesting, as she periodizes the use of islands in books of chivalry; however, consideration of space is subordinated to the types of characters that inhabit them.

61. For the Castilian *Tristan* as a source for the *Ínsula Triste*, see Riquer, "Agora lo veredes, dixo Agrajes." See also Ramos, "El *Amadís* de Juan de Dueñas," which argues that the *Ínsula Firme* "pudo tener en algun momento de su ajetreada vida textual el nombre de ínsola del Ploro" (852), based on the analysis of Juan de Dueñas's verses.

62. I write on giants and the Tower of Babel in the Spanish tradition in "Babel historiada."

63. For wild men, see Bernheimer, *Wild Men in the Middle Ages: Study in Art, Sentiment, and Demonology*; also Deyermond, "El hombre salvaje en la novela sentimental."

64. Cacho Blecua, "La génesis del monstruo," in *Amadís*, 31–37; Delpech, "Fragments hispaniques d'un discours incestueux"; and Gracia, "La bestia ladradora," put the Endriago in relation to the Arthurian motif of the Barking Beast, the *Beste*

Glattisant from the *Suite du Merlin* to the Castilian *Baladro del sabio Merlín* and the Castilian and Portuguese *Demandas*.

65. Cited in Goldberg, "The Several Faces," 81.
66. Ibid., 84; Gracia, "El 'Palacio Tornante,'" 92.
67. Quoted in Gracia, "El 'Palacio Tornante,'" 75.
68. Ibid., 93–94.
69. Goldberg, "The Several Faces," 82.
70. The title for chapter 74 remarks how it is through honor and service to the emperor that Amadís can free this island, previously lost, restoring it to the emperor. The historical mirrorings with conflicts in the eastern Mediterranean and, in the other direction, with the conquest of the Americas emphasize how *Amadís* brings together the edges of the map to coincide at the center of the Mediterranean world.
71. Dubost, "Insularités imaginaires et récit médiéval," 57.
72. Ibid., 47.
73. See Back, "Anselm on Perfect Islands."
74. See chapter 1 for a discussion of portolan charts. The survey of representations I present here is not an exhaustive inventory of cartographic representations of the Canary Islands. I have selected those materials of special interest to the theme of the marvelous and for the depiction of Saint Brendan's island.
75. Lemarchand, introduction, xv.
76. "Indeed, the charts themselves were to play an important part in broadcasting knowledge, or theories, about the Atlantic archipelagoes and the western coast of Africa. Because the islands depicted on the charts were stepping-stones for later voyages to America or have been treated as evidence of pre-Columbian discoveries of the new continent itself, this aspect of the subject has attracted more comment than any other. It would require an entire volume to summarize the complex and contradictory arguments about the apparently imaginary islands of Man, Brazil, Antilia, and others" (Tony Campbell, "Portolan Charts from the Late Thirteenth Century to 1500," 410). See chapter 2.
77. Ibid.
78. Ibid., 372.
79. Quoted in Tous Meliá, *El Plan de las Afortunadas Islas*, 12.
80. Ibid., 13, 18.
81. Contrary to what Cro argues in "Las fuentes clásicas de la utopía moderna."
82. Benedeit, *El viaje de San Brandán*, 58.
83. Quoted in Tous Meliá, *El Plan de las Afortunadas Islas*, 18.
84. Ibid., 22.
85. Covarrubias remarks in parentheses, under "isla," still another version of the story: "En la navegación que ay de Portugal a la India Oriental, que son cinco mil leguas de agua, está en medio del gran Occéano (donde dizen no hallarse suelo) una

isleta despoblada llamada Santa Elena, abastada de dulces aguas, de pescados, de caça y frutas, que la misma tierra sin labor alguna produce, donde los navegantes descansan, pescan caçan y se proveen de agua."

86. The island cannot be found unless Urganda allows it, it is in fact not described but merely alluded to in the first five books of *Amadís,* though Juan Díaz describes it in chapter 7 of *Lisuarte de Grecia* (1514), the eighth book of *Amadís,* and Francisco de Morais, in *Palmeirim de Inglaterra,* a different cycle, also finds the island again and names it Isla Peligrosa (Marín Pina, "Palmerín de Inglaterra," 82–84).

87. Foucault, "Of Other Spaces."

88. Olschki, *Storia letteraria delle scoperte geografiche,* 42. He writes: "One is reminded that Columbus followed the example of the sovereign, in a more positive way, conceding as territories to his navigation companions certain islands of the Antilles. In one of these ceremonies (if it is true) Michele da Cuneo took purely theoretica possession of one of them which, to remember his homeland, he baptized 'La Bella Saonese'" (42 n.60).

89. See Marín Pina, "Palmerín de Inglaterra," for an account of the rewriting (and devoiding of this fiction's structural/political function) of the *Ínsula No Fallada* into the *isla peligrosa,* thus "finding it," and for a revisiting of other insular spaces of *Amadís* in other texts.

4. Shores of Fiction

1. Cachey, "Print Culture and the Literature of Travel," 10–11.
2. Gautier Dalché, "The Reception of Ptolemy's *Geography,*" 297.
3. Cachey, "Maps and Literature in Renaissance Italy," 456. My argument here derives from Cachey's conclusions on this topic.
4. See Baranda, "El *Guarino Mezquino* [1527]" and La *"Corónica del noble cavallero Guarino Mezquino."*
5. Amozurrutia Nava, *Guía de lectura del Guarino Mezquino,* 7–12.
6. Nebrija specifically states his admiration for Ptolemy in terms of the precision his method allows for the location of places, even if, Gautier Dalché notes, like many of his contemporaries, Nebrija considered Ptolemy needed supplementation and correction through the information provided by navigation (342). See also Rico, "El nuevo mundo de Nebrija y Colón."
7. Cachey, "Maps and Literature in Renaissance Italy," 456, 458.
8. For an elaboration of these tensions in Italian literature in relation to the origins of the novel, see Quint, "The Boat of Renaissance Epic." See also chapter 5 of Padrón, *The Spacious Word,* on Ercilla's epic poem *La Araucana,* and particularly 225ff, for use of chivalric language within epic. For books of chivalry and courtly spectacle, see the panorama by del Río Nogueras, "Libros de caballerías y fiesta nobiliaria," and Cátedra, "Fiestas caballerescas en tiempos de Carlos V."

9. Santana Paixão, "Ficção e realidade," 1422.

10. Ibid., 1421. Santana Paixão develops this idea not only for *Amadís*, but also for the book of chivalry as a genre, looking especially closely at the prologues. Her ideas support my argument on subjectivity and, through it, the idea of an ethical utopia argued above (1424).

11. Marín Pina summarizes the process, which highlights an emphasis on the East and particularly related to Greek islands, as follows: "If the fourth book of *Amadís de Gaula* and the *Sergas* were found in a tomb in a hermitage near Constantinople, the rest are found in the most unusual places. Feliciano de Silva discovers the whereabouts of the second part of *Amadís de Grecia* (1530) dreaming of a cave called the palaces of Hercules; Páez de Ribera claims *Florisando* (1510) as a book from Petrarch; and Juan Díaz locates *Lisuarte de Grecia* among the possessions of the master of the order of Saint John, on the island of Rhodes. Gonzalo Fernández de Oviedo confesses to finding the *Claribalte* (1519) during a trip to Tartary, and Beatriz Bernal finds the *Cristalián de España* (1545) through prayer. On almost all occasions the discovery is a marvelous adventure in itself meriting admiration and wonder" (Marín Pina, "El tópico de la falsa traducción en los libros de caballerías españoles," 544).

12. Other authors of *isolarii* followed this singular mode of self-inscription, emphasizing the trip as heroic trial. Such inscriptions are almost a motif in chivalric literature, from Ariosto's heroes to Don Quixote himself.

13. Cachey, "Print Culture and the Literature of Travel," 12.

14. See ibid., 12–13. Gaylord has pointed out a parallel in Lucian's *Vera Storia*, where inscription is carved on a tree. Gaylord studies Lucian's influence in Renaissance writing, particularly in relation to *Don Quixote*'s engagement with historiography: "Cervantes incorporates many of the same tricks into the *Quixote* [self-references of a first-person author–witness, geographic detail, physical description, etc.], largely through such surrogate authorial figures as Cide Hamete Benengeli and the 'second author.' The last ploy finds its way into the episode in which the novel has its closest brush with historical reality: the interpolated tale of the *Capitán cautivo*. . . . In the *Araucana* Ercilla, too, appropriates the Lucianesque motif of writing on trees to certify his presence in the South American places he describes" (Gaylord, "The True History of Early Modern Writing in Spanish," 90–91).

15. Lina Bolzoni in Cachey, "Print Culture and the Literature of Travel," 5–6.

16. Ibid., 6.

17. See Diez Borque, "Edición e ilustración," for a list of these "traditionalist" characteristics of the printed book of chivalry, in imitation of the manuscript.

18. Ibid., 37–38.

19. Rothstein, "The Commemorative Images of *Amadís de Gaula*," 101. Gilman remarks on another version of this commemorative use of the *Amadís* in a well-known

article, when he writes on the influence of our romance in the writing of Bernal Díaz del Castillo: "The *Amadís* in those days was . . . as it was for its most celebrated reader, intensely perused and intensely present, *sharply visual.* Hence, its suitability to this particular moment. The first long-awaited sight of lake and city—after the unsatisfactory descriptions of the Tlaxcalans and the *distant glimpse* that Diego de Ordaz and his comrades had of it from the summit of Popocatépetl—is *the apogee of marvel and so of memory, visual memory*: 'Agora que lo estoy escribiendo *se me representa todo delante de mis ojos* como si ayer fuera cuando esto pasó'" (Gilman, "Bernal Díaz del Castillo and *Amadís de Gaula,*" 112, my emphasis) (and now that I am writing about it, it all comes before my eyes as if it had happened but yesterday).

20. Rothstein, "The Commemorative Images," 100. On *Amadís*'s normative role, see Baret, *De l'Amadís de Gaule et de son influence sur les mœurs et sur la littérature au XVIe et au XVIIe siècles.*

21. See Lacarra Ducay, *Aportación al estudio de la pintura mural gótica en Navarra,* 92–93. The desire for the representation of simultaneous events, related by Cacho Blecua to the technique of interweaving, is not frequent, however. Nevertheless, painting generally makes free use of time and place order, juxtaposing the events, as Francastel points out in *La figura y el lugar,* 141.

22. See *Les "Amadis" en France au XVIe siècle.*

23. The plan follows that of the palace–castle of Chambord, which was first drafted in 1519 and redrawn in 1526 on the return of François I to France from his imprisonment after being defeated by the Spaniards in the battle of Pavia.

24. This was suggested by Foulché Delbosc, "Sergas."

25. See Desprechins de Gaesebeke, "À la gloire d'Amadís" and "Une Tenture d'Amadis de Gaule," and Buijs, "Works Related to the Princeton Tapestry."

26. The catalogue of the 2001 Metropolitan Museum of Art exhibit contains articles by several authors, among them the curator, summarizing the scant work on the tapestries, reduced to the cited article by Rothstein (and another, repeating most of the information, by the same author) and unpublished material by Hans Buijs, curator of the small exhibit at Princeton in June of 2001, when the tapestry was exhibited. The articles in the catalogue lack information on the romance or misread it, and do not establish an interpretive comparison between text and textile.

27. Jacob, *The Sovereign Map,* 42.

28. Ibid., 338.

29. Ibid., 42. I summarize the latest information on the tapestries in "Los tapices de la *Historia de Amadís de Gaula,*" and develop the ideas on the Princeton tapestry in "The Knight, the Kings, and the Tapestries" and earlier, in "La traducción de lo visible."

30. Jacob, *The Sovereign Map,* 150.

31. López Estrada, "El *Tirante* castellano de 1511," 450.

32. In this sense, Avalle-Arce *("Tirant lo Blanc, Amadís")* has said that the Constantinopolitan phase of the romance is due to Montalvo, as a way of anticipating his own novel, the *Sergas de Esplandián*. His argument is, however, that the episode is inspired by *Tirant lo Blanc*. See Paloma Gracia, in "El 'Palacio Tornante,'" based on an analysis of the Turning Castle, one of the buildings of Apolidón on the *Ínsula Firme*. Regardless of the numerous Oriental elements and precisely because of them, Gracia concludes that the Orientalism of the *Amadís* is nothing but a reflection of the Orient in the various mirrors of Western literature, particularly texts from the *matière de Bretagne*, which had previously incorporated Oriental elements in their constructions. Thus, Gracia concludes, once again, that the *Ínsula Firme* episode is a "reading" of the valley of false lovers, the dangerous valley or forest of French Arthurian romance, while the arch and the chamber are just reworkings of the perilous castle motif, contradicting Avalle-Arce's theories, particularly his arguments around the Arch of the Loyal Lovers: "The difference is that *Amadís* refashions the adventure in Byzantine dress, which does not imply neither a rupture nor a radical change in model, for the Byzantine universe was present in Romance literatures at its beginnings, as much as the Celtic atmosphere had become a distinct trait of the matter of Britain" (453). Gracia explains the gradual displacement of the Celtic landscape in favor of an Oriental one as a consequence of history, as the fight against the infidel substituting for the shady evil forces of the Celtic world, in short, a "realness" that took over the ambiguous Arthurian marvels, for which the *Tirant lo Blanc* is a case in point (453–54).

33. See Foulché-Delbosc, "Sergas." Cacho Blecua remarks that for Montalvo's "linguistic awareness" the term means feats, moving from the *representation* to the *events represented* in his interpretation of the term (see Rodríguez de Montalvo, *Amadís de Gaula*, 1171 n.64).

34. See Javier R. González, "Libros de caballerías en América."

35. Marín Pina specifically discusses how the rewriting of this space—Urganda's *Ínsula No Fallada*—both creates an important genealogical link between books, and at the same time undoes the marvelous that characterizes the space by "finding" it and locating it, which explains the need to rename it ("Palmerín de Inglaterra," 83–84).

36. The first "catalogue" of islands in chivalric romance is Diego Clemencín's footnote to his edition of Cervantes, *El ingenioso hidalgo* (part 2, chapter 45, n.7); see another in Cuesta Torre, "Las ínsolas del Zifar y el Amadís."

37. Covarrubias Orozco, *Tesoro de la lengua castellana*, s.v. *isla*.

38. Vergès remarks on the ambiguous pause between discovery and posession: "If at the very moment of this discovery the tropical island has not yet acquired its full phantasm composition as a paradisiacal place in Western discourse, the story of Columbus and those who will follow him announces this representation. In this

process of mastering that which seems foreign but at the same time familiar—because in these voyages, it is also the similar which is discovered—close to the Freudian *Unheimlich*, this disquieting strangeness, Columbus and his successors build a discourse that seeks to inscribe again this reality in a codified discourse. The discourse of the marvelous will integrate these spaces, tropical islands, into the familiar confines of European imagination" ("Merveilles de la prise de posession," 213).

39. "Y otro día por la mañana llegamos a la calzada ancha y vamos camino de Estapalapa. Y desde que vimo tantas ciudades y villas pobladas en el agua, y en tierra firme otras grandes poblazones, y aquella calzada tan derecha y por nivel cómo iva a México, nos quedamos admirados, y decíamos que parecía a las cosas de encantamiento que cuentan en el libro de Amadís, por las grandes torres y *cúes* y edificios que tenían dentro en el agua, y todos de calicanto, y aun algunos de nuestros soldados decían que si aquello que veían si era entre sueños, y no es de maravillar que yo escriba aquí de esta manera, porque hay mucho que ponderar en ello que no sé como lo cuente: ver cosas nunca oídas, ni aun soñadas, como veíamos" (Díaz del Castillo, *Historia verdadera de la conquista,* chap. 87, p. 159). (During the morning we arrived at a broad Causeway and continued our march toward Iztapalapa, and when we saw so many cities and villages built in the water and other great towns on dry land and that straight and level Causeway going toward Mexico, we were amazed and said that is was like the enchantments they tell of in the legend of Amadís, on account of the great towers and cues and buildings rising from the water, and all built of masonry. And some of our soldiers even asked whether the things that we saw were not a dream. It is not to be wondered at that I here write it down in this manner, for there is so much to think over that I do not know how to describe it, seeing things as we did that had never been heard of or seen before, not even dreamed about [Díaz del Castillo, *The History of the Conquest,* 156].)

40. Gilman, "Bernal Díaz del Castillo and *Amadís de Gaula,*" 99, 100, emphasis mine.

41. Gaylord, "Cervantes' Portrait of the Artist," 93, emphasis mine.

42. Gaylord, "Los espacios de la poética cervantina," 358. Cervantine poetics in *Don Quixote* has been the focus of a number of studies. For an analysis concerned with space, see Hutchinson, *Cervantine Journeys,* which studies different spaces in Cervantine writing and devotes the chapter entitled "Cervantine Worlds" to the chronotope and the experience of different realms. Spatial analysis is, as I advanced in the introduction, subordinated to time (as in the chronotope) or other considerations. Martínez-Bonati, *Don Quixote and the Poetics of the Novel,* also considers space in an opposition of idealism to realism and in the juxtaposition and hybridization of fictive realms in terms of poetics. Casalduero establishes a spatial opposition between the first and the second parts, concerned with "roads" and "houses" respectively that emphasize the static nature of the social order in contrast with the

dynamism of the knight's activity (*Sentido y forma*, esp. 218–22). María Caterina Ruta, "La descripción de ambientes," continues this analysis, but excludes the Barataria episode. See also Selig, "*Don Quijote* and the Exploration of (Literary) Geography," esp. 341–57. Gaylord summarizes debates on theory and poetics in *Don Quixote*, writing that "the acknowledgement of a well-read Cervantes has not revealed in him a rare inventor of literary precepts but a knowledgeable man, a sort of used-book dealer who limits himself to quoting—or to having his characters quote—other thinkers more concerned with theory and more original in their exposition of it" ("Los espacios de la poética cervantina," 358). Her analysis of space *as* poetics looks at the 1605 prologue, where the space of the prison works as a negative, as an implicit contrary to the space of literary creation, an inspirational commonplace of lyrical and pastoral poetry. The spaces simultaneously overlap and contradict each other, ciphering in a way the poetics of Cervantine composition (358). Moreover, these spaces are invoked by way of an entirely different space. As the narrator tells us of his efforts to write a proper prologue, that is, one that includes an endless succession of sonnets, epigrams, eulogies, marginalia, endnotes, maxims, and *sententiae,* he does so from a literal, if poetic, common place, the writing studio. In chapters 47–50 of the first part, Gaylord shows how the closed space of the prison not only overlaps or coincides once again with that of the *locus amoenus* but actually coexists physically as part of the plot: the knight, caged, is carried across the same green meadows where the Priest and the Canon of Toledo reflect on the poetic values of the chivalric romance (359–64).

43. Gaylord writes: "Cervantes' work cultivates a more ambivalent representation of the play between open space and limitation" ("Los espacios de la poética cervantina," 361).

44. Sears, "'Lighting Out'"; González Echevarría, in *Love and the Law in Cervantes,* looks at legal institutions and practices as a discourse that invades and shapes the novel.

45. References to a geography of empire are not to be overlooked especially through the presence of America in the text, elegantly studied by Diana de Armas Wilson in *Cervantes, the Novel, and the New World.* The implicit mediation of cartography is interesting because of its near absence in *Quixote:* the word "map" appears only twice. The Indies themselves, to be exact, are referred to directly only on nine occasions. So the America of maps is there, and it is not: its value seems to be a sign of something else, as metaphor.

46. Redondo, *Otra manera de leer el Quijote,* 192.

47. Interpretations of these episodes are numerous. Herrero ("Sierra Morena as Labyrinth") explores the biblical subtexts and analyzes the space as labyrinth both topographic and psychic. On labyrinths see also Fajardo, "The Sierra Morena as Labyrinth in *DQ,* I."

48. Quotations from *Don Quixote* are from Rico's edition and are marked by part and chapter number only; for English versions, modified to reveal what I am emphasizing in the original Spanish, I have consulted both Raffel's and Grossman's translations.

49. See Bernheimer, *Wild Men in the Middle Ages,* for a general study of the figure of the wild man.

50. The concept of *mimesis* in Cervantes has received considerable attention; for a philosophically informed study, see Cascardi's differentiation of imitation and representation in "Genre Definition and Multiplicity in *Don Quixote*."

51. Numerous critics have commented on this debate. See de Armas, "Cervantes and the Italian Renaissance," esp. 43–56, for a discussion of epic versus romance in terms of mimesis and genre. For Amadís's penance as model for Don Quixote, see Burton, "Peña Pobre to Sierra Morena"; Márquez Villanueva, *Personajes y temas del "Quijote,"* esp. 35–51; Gregorio C. Martín, "Don Quijote imitador de Amadís"; and Riley, "Don Quixote and the Imitation of Models."

52. See Avalle-Arce, "La penitencia de Amadís en la Peña Pobre," and the more general Aguilar Perdomo, "La penitencia de amor caballeresca."

53. Adrienne Martín underscores the links between fiction and a marvelous power at stake in the gratuitousness of imitation: "Don Quixote's poetic madness, as funny as it may be, ultimately illustrates the enchantment of the written word, the power of literature and its capacity to move us" ("Humor and Violence in Cervantes," 167).

54. Madariaga first elaborated this idea in chapters 7 and 8 of his *Guía del lector del Quijote*.

55. Joly, commentary to pt. II, chap. 44, pp. 185–87, of the second volume of Rico's edition (Cervantes, *Don Quijote de la Mancha*); Avalle-Arce, "La Ínsula Barataria: la forma de su relato," notes that, besides the "authorial intervention," the presence of a letter from Sancho to his wife is the beginning of a series of letters that also serve to characterize the episode and that set it generically aside not only within the second part, but also from the use of letters in general in the first part.

56. The second intervention refers to Don Quixote, which is why I do not look at it here.

57. Joly, commentary to pt. II, chap. 44, pp. 185–86.

58. See Cosgrove, *Apollo's Eye,* esp. 1–28.

59. On Quixote's advice, see Percas de Ponseti, "Los consejos de Don Quijote a Sancho." Sources for this advice appear in Cervantes, *El ingenioso hidalgo,* ed. Rodríguez Marín, 6:229–65, 7:149–61.

60. Critical interpretations of Sancho's governorship range from the idea of a triumph of the utopia of natural reason to the emphasis on the carnival scenes to political and social criticism to parody and mere mockery of the ambitious squire. For the *topos* of arms and letters in the episode, see Pelorson, "Le Discours des

armes et lettres et l'épisode de Barataria." For an interpretation related to carnival, see Durán, "El *Quijote* a través del prisma de Mikhail Bakhtine"; Joly, "D'Alberto Naseli, dit Ganasse"; and Redondo, "Tradición carnavalesca y creación literaria" and "El *Quijote* y la tradición carnavalesca."

61. For folkloric motifs and stories in the novel, see Barrick, "The Form and Function of the Folktales in *Don Quixote*."

62. Cervantes, *El ingenioso hidalgo*, ed. Rodríguez Marín, vol. 7, chap. 45, pp. 8–9 n.8; Fermín Caballero discussed in Rubio García, "La Ínsula Barataria."

63. In Cervantes, *El ingenioso hidalgo*, ed. Diego Clemencín, 404–6.

64. Rubio García, "La Ínsula Barataria," 644–45.

65. Ibid., 644–47, cites the following: "Ínsulas nascen à las vegadas en los rios, et contienden los homes sobre el señorío dellas" (*Partidas* III, tit. 28) (Islands sometimes appear in rivers, and men fight for lordship over them); "E cuemo quier que lo aquel dixiesse por losenía, cuydo el que assy orauan por su muerte los que él desterrara, et fizo los todos atar por las ínsulas o estauan" (*Primera Crónica General de España*) (And even though he said so because of his youth, he saw that those he had exiled prayed for his death, and had them tied in the places they were); "La ínsula de Topaza engendra piedra desse mismo nombre" ("Lapidario," ed. Vollmöller) (The island of Topaz engenders stone of the same name); "Habitatores qui sumus de villa que vocant Ínsula Langovardi, id est, Malagneigo, Argeleva, Odorico, Loba Teudemiro, Elisabeth, Martino, etc, etc." (Archivo Condal de Barcelona, IX–X centuries) (We inhabitants of the town called Island of the Langobars, that is, Malagneigo, Argeleva, Odorico, Loba Teudemiro, Elisabeth, Martino, etc., etc.).

66. Ibid., 649–50.

67. The verbs *abaratar* ("to cheapen") and *malbaratar* ("to sell for a cheap price") are in common use in Latin America, which Corominas does not note.

68. López Estrada draws the links toward political criticism through More's influence in the peninsula, in *Tomás Moro y España*, esp. 75–79; the main reference to the concept of utopia in Cervantes is Maravall, *Utopía y contrautopía en el Quijote*; see also Montero Reguera, *El "Quijote" y la crítica contemporánea*, esp. 35–38.

69. Eisenberg judges it a probable independent novella through a number of linguistic markers in "'Sancho Gobernador.'"

70. Moner, "Sancho à Barataria," 90, 89. Moner argues that, in addition to the tradition of Saturnalia and the concept of carnival as a satire of village ingenuity and old Christian prejudice, there are also obvious references to the *menosprecio de corte y alabanza de aldea* theme, as well as to the idea of dissipating the illusions of the simple man rather than chastising the vanities of power. Chiong Rivero studies the political ideas of the episode as a "palimpsest" of Guevarian political thought, detailed in "Ínsula de buen gobierno," with ample discussion of other political analyses of the episode.

71. *Isla Trapobana* (I, 18), *isla de Chipre* (I, 39), *isla de Modón* (I, 39), *isla de Malta* (II, 1), *isla de Sicilia* (II, 1).

72. In order to transition from the model of knight to the model of conquistador, de Armas Wilson reads the episode of Barataria in tune with a *historical* cession of islands by conquistadors to vassals: "The gift of a governorship . . . serves needless to say as a literary parody of the books of chivalry, in which knights occasionally dispense islands as gifts to their squires" ("Cervantes and the New World," 217–18). Reference to books of chivalry, however, is direct, while the allusion to the imperial project in the Americas is phantasmatic.

73. The passage cannot be fully translated. In Spanish, the joke is played on the niece's inability to understand the meaning of an uncommon word such as *ínsula*. She shows this misunderstanding through a play on the word by giving it the possibility of gender differentiation, masculine and feminine, which the word in its geographical meaning does not allow for, *ínsulas* and *ínsulos*.

74. The play with *ínsulas* and *ínsulos* occurs three times, in I, 26, II, 2, and II, 41.

75. These conclusions from space are related to Lezra's analysis of *Don Quixote* as the laying bare of language's failure to reconcile act and representation. His discussion of naming and representation, shape, form, and body is interesting as parallel to this discussion of insularity (*Unspeakable Subjects,* see esp. chap. 3).

76. Avalle-Arce, "La Ínsula Barataria," 42.

77. The play here is on *dones,* which means gifts or talents but also plays on Don, as a title.

CONCLUSION

1. Menéndez Pelayo, *Orígenes de la novela,* 1:440. For the relationship between quixotic poetics and the romance of chivalry, see Mancing, *The Chivalric World of Don Quijote,* among many others. The change in evaluation of books of chivalry can be easily assessed in the many publications devoted to the genre, some devoted to links with Cervantine writing, but most now independent of it. See Eisenberg and Marín Pina's *Bibliografía de los libros de caballerías castellanos,* and the ongoing and expanding editorial project of the *Centro de Estudios Cervantinos,* especially the editions of books of chivalry and the "guías de lectura" (reading guides).

2. López Pinciano, *Philosophia antigua poetica,* 1:265.

3. See my "Literature and Cartography in Spain."

4. López Pinciano, *Philosophia antigua poetica,* 2:12.

5. Ibid., 2:12. For the metaphor of the body in López Pinciano and in Cervantes, see Orozco Díaz, "Sobre los elementos o 'miembros'"; and Gaylord, "The Whole Body of Fable." For a general Golden Age perspective see Redondo, ed., *Le Corps comme métaphore dans l'Espagne des XVIe et XVIIe siècles.* For a theoretically

tuned reading of bodily metaphors in relation to language, see Lezra, *Unspeakable Subjects*, esp. chap. 4, "Cervantes's Hand."

6. López Pinciano, *Philosophia antigua poética*, 2:80.

7. For a rigorous study on poetics and space in *Don Quixote*, see Martínez-Bonati, *Don Quijote and the Poetics of the Novel*. For López Pinciano as a source (later debated) for Cervantes's theory of the novel, see Canavaggio, "Alonso López Pinciano y la estética literaria de Cervantes en el *Quijote*." For the Aristotelian arguments in these chapters in *Quijote*, see Forcione, *Cervantes, Aristotle, and the Persiles*, esp. 91–130.

8. Reading practices in *Don Quixote* include reading out loud as well. For the transitions, see Frenk, *Entre la voz y el silencio*.

9. Egido has looked at the role of silence in both *La Galatea* and the *Persiles*: "El sosegado y maravilloso silencio de *La Galatea*" and "Los silencios del *Persiles*." For *Don Quixote*, see Trueblood, "El silencio en el *Quixote*."

10. Other cases are: "all the others there kept a marvelous silence" (I, 13, 144), "so quiet, that to declare us the excellence of its marvelous silence, only once its name is named in that as great as truthful story" (I, 20, 221), "all the damsels watching him serve, keeping a wonderful silence" (I, 50, 571), and "what pleased Don Quixote the most was the marvelous silence that there was in the entire house" (II, 18, 776).

11. Gregory Hutcheson kindly allowed me to use this anecdote from his life as a graduate student and provided a copy of the handout Gilman circulated in this seminar.

12. Simmel, "Das Abenteuer," 4.

13. For an insightful overview of generic appropriation and reelaboration as theory of the novel in Cervantes, see Cascardi, "*Don Quixote* and the Invention of the Novel."

Bibliography

Aguilar Perdomo, María del Rosario. "La penitencia de amor caballeresca: Lisuarte, Florambel, Felixmarte y otros enfermos de amores." In *Fechos antiguos que los cavalleros en armas passaron: Estudios sobre la ficción caballeresca*. Edited by Julián Acebrón Ruiz. Lleida: Edicions de la Universitat de Lleida, 2001. 125–50.

Alfonso X. *Las Siete Partidas: The Medieval Church: The World of Clerics and Laymen*. Translated by Samuel Parsons Scott. Philadelphia: University of Pennsylvania Press, 2001.

Alfonso XI. *Libro de la Montería: Based on Escorial MS Y.II.19*. Edited and translated by Dennis P. Seniff. Madison, Wis.: Hispanic Seminary of Medieval Studies, 1983.

Almagià, Roberto. *Monumenta cartographica Vaticana*. 4 vols. Rome: Biblioteca Apostolica Vaticana, 1944–45.

Alvar, Carlos. *Diccionario de mitología artúrica*. Madrid: Alianza, 1985.

Amadís de Gaula: 1508 (quinientos años de libros de caballerías). Madrid: Biblioteca Nacional de España/Sociedad Estatal de Conmemoraciones Culturales, 2008.

Amadís de Gaula, 500 años después: Homenaje a Juan Manuel Cacho Blecua. Edited by José Manuel Lucía Megías and María Carmen Marín Pina. Alcalá de Henares, Spain: Centro de Estudios Cervantinos, 2008.

Les "Amadis" en France au XVIe siècle. Paris: Éditions rue d'Ulm, 2000.

Amozurrutia Nava, Karla P. *Guía de lectura de Guarino Mezquino*. Alcalá de Henares: Centro de Estudios Cervantinos, 2008.

Arioli, Angelo. *Le isole mirabili: Periplo arabe medievale*. Turin: G. Einaudi, 1989.

Auerbach, Erich. *Mimesis: The Representation of Reality in Western Literature*. Translated by Willard R. Trask. Princeton: Princeton University Press, 1974.

Augé, Marc. *Non-lieux. Introduction à une anthropologie de la surmodernité*. Paris: Seuil, 1992.

Avalle-Arce, Juan Bautista. *"Amadís de Gaula": El primitivo y el de Montalvo*. Mexico City: Fondo de Cultura Económica, 1990.

———. "El arco de los leales amadores en el *Amadís*." *Nueva Revista de Filología Hispánica* 6 (1984): 149–56.

———. "La Ínsula Barataria: La forma de su relato." *Anales de Literatura Española* 6 (1988): 33–44.

———. "La penitencia de Amadís en la Peña Pobre." In *Josep María Solà-Solé: Homage, Homenaje, Homenatge (Miscelánea de estudios de amigos y discípulos).* Edited by A. Torres-Alcalá et al. Barcelona: Puvill, 1984. 2:159–70.

———. "*Tirant lo Blanc, Amadís de Gaula* y la caballeresca medieval." In *Studies in Honor of Sumner M. Greenfield.* Edited by Harold L. Boudreau and Luis T. González del Valle. Lincoln, Neb.: Society of Spanish and Spanish-American Studies, 1985. 17–31.

Ayerbe-Chaux, Reinaldo. "Las islas dotadas: Texto y miniaturas del manuscrito de París, clave para su interpretación." In *Hispanic Studies in Honor of Alan D. Deyermond: A North American Tribute.* Edited by John S. Miletich. Madison, Wis.: Hispanic Seminary of Medieval Studies, 1986. 31–50.

Back, Allan. "Anselm on Perfect Islands." *Franciscan Studies* 43 (1983): 188–204.

Badiou, Alain. *L'Etre et l'événement.* Paris: Seuil, 1988.

———. *Peut-on penser la politique?* Paris: Seuil, 1985.

Baranda, Nieves. *La "Corónica del noble cavallero Guarino Mezquino."* Critical study and edition. Madrid: Universidad Nacional de Educación a Distancia, 1992 (microfiche).

———. "El *Guarino Mezquino* [1527]." *Edad de oro* 21 (2002): 289–304.

Baret, Eugène. *De l'Amadis de Gaule et de son influence sur les mœurs et sur la littérature au XVIe et au XVIIe siècle.* Paris: A. Durand, 1853; Geneva: Slatkine Reprints, 1970.

Barrick, Mac E. "The Form and Function of the Folktales in *Don Quixote.*" *Journal of Medieval and Renaissance Studies* 6 (1976): 101–38.

Bearman, P., et al. "Djazīra." *Encyclopaedia of Islam.* Edited by P. Bearman et al. 2nd ed. Leiden: Brill, 2009. Brill Online. http://www.brillonline.nl/.

Beltrán, Rafael. "Los libros de viajes medievales castellanos: Introducción al panorama crítico actual: ¿Cuántos libros de viajes medievales castellanos?" *Revista de filología románica* 1 (1991): 121–64.

———. "Urganda, Morgana y Sibila: El espectáculo de la nave profética en la literatura de caballerías." In *The Medieval Mind: Studies in Honour of Alan Deyermond.* Edited by Ian Macpherson and Ralph Penny. London: Tamesis, 1997. 21–47.

———, ed. *Maravillas, peregrinaciones y utopías: Literatura de viajes en el mundo románico.* Valencia: Publicacions de la Universitat de València, Departament de filologia espanyola, 2002.

Benedeit. *El viaje de San Brandán.* Madrid: Siruela, 1986.

Benveniste, Émile. "Subjectivity in Language." In *Problems in General Linguistics.* Translated by Mary Elizabeth Meek. Coral Gables, Fla.: University of Miami Press, 1971. 223–30.

Bernheimer, Richard. *Wild Men in the Middle Ages: A Study in Art, Sentiment, and Demonology.* New York: Octagon Books, 1970.

Blackmore, Josiah. *Manifest Perdition: Shipwreck Narrative and the Disruption of Empire*. Minneapolis: University of Minnesota Press, 2002.
Blumenberg, Hans. *Shipwreck with Spectator*. Cambridge, Mass.: MIT Press, 1997.
Blumenfeld-Kosinski, Renate. Review of Michelle Szkilnik, *L'Archipel du Graal: Etude de l'"Estoire del Saint Graal*." *Speculum* 68.4 (1993): 1223–25.
Bognolo, Anna. *La finzione rinnovata: Meraviglioso, corte e avventura nel romanzo cavalleresco del primo Cinquecento spagnolo*. Pisa: ETS, 1997.
Bosteels, Bruno. "Beggar's Banquet: For a Critique of the Political Economy of the Sign in Borges." *Variaciones Borges* 29 (2010): 3–52.
———. "Nonplaces: An Anecdoted Topography of Contemporary French Theory." In *New Coordinates: Spatial Mappings, National Trajectories*. Edited by Bob Davidson and Joan Ramon Resina. Special issue, *diacritics* 33.3–4 (2003): 117–39.
Bouloux, Nathalie. "Les Îles dans les descriptions géographiques et les cartes du moyen âge." In *Îles du moyen âge*. Edited by Antoine Franzini and Nathalie Bouloux. Special issue, *Médiévales* 47 (2004): 47–62.
Braudel, Fernand. *El Mediterráneo*. Madrid: Espasa-Calpe, 1987.
———. *El Mediterráneo y el mundo mediterráneo en la época de Felipe II*. Translated by Mario Monteforte Toledo and Wenceslao Roces. 2 vols. Mexico City: Fondo de Cultura Económica, 1953.
Buijs, Hans. "Works Related to the Princeton Tapestry: A Tapestry Designed by Karel van Mander." *Brochures from the Princeton Exhibit*. March 6–June 10, 2001.
Buondelmonti, Christoforo. *Description des îles de l'Archipel grec*. Edited and translated by Émile Legrand. Amsterdam: Philo Press, 1974.
———. *Liber insularum archipelagi (1420)*. Biblioteca Nacional de España, Madrid, MS 18246.
Burke, James. "The Meaning of the Islas Dotadas Episode in the *Libro del Cavallero Çifar*." *Hispanic Review* 38 (1970): 56–68.
Burton, David G. "Peña Pobre to Sierra Morena: Cervantes' Inversion of a Model." *Romance Languages Annual* 2 (1990): 353–61.
Cacciari, Massimo. *L'Arcipelago*. Milan: Adelphi, 1997.
Cachey, Theodore. "Maps and Literature in Renaissance Italy." In *The History of Cartography*. Vol. 3, *Cartography in the European Renaissance*, part 1. Edited by David Woodward. Chicago: University of Chicago Press, 2007. 450–60.
———. "Print Culture and the Literature of Travel: The Case of the *Isolario*." Paper presented at "Narratives and Maps: Historical Studies of Cartographic Storytelling," the Thirteenth Kenneth Nebenzahl Jr. Lectures in the History of Cartography. Newberry Library, Chicago, October 1999.
Cacho Blecua, Juan Manuel. *Amadís: Heroísmo mítico cortesano*. Madrid: Universidad de Zaragoza, 1979.

———. Introduction to Garci Rodríguez de Montalvo, *Amadís de Gaula*. Edited by Juan Manuel Cacho Blecua. Madrid: Cátedra, 1987–88. 1:19–216.

———, and María Jesús Lacarra. *Lo imaginario en la conquista de América*. Zaragoza: Comisión Aragonesa Quinto Centenario, 1990.

Campbell, Mary Baine. *Wonder and Science: Imagining Worlds in Early Modern Europe*. Ithaca: Cornell University Press, 1999.

Campbell, Tony. "Portolan Charts from the Late Thirteenth Century to 1500." In *The History of Cartography*. Vol. 1, *Cartography in Prehistoric, Ancient, and Medieval Europe and the Mediterranean*. Edited by J. B. Harley and David Woodward. Chicago: University of Chicago Press, 1987. 371–463.

Campos Rojas, Axayácatl. "Centros geográficos y movimiento del héroe de la Ínsola Firme a la Peña Pobre en el *Amadís de Gaula*." *Voz y letra: Revista de Literatura* 11.2 (2000): 3–20.

———. "El Mediterráneo como representación de un imperio: Moros, corsarios y gigantes paganos en *Tristán el Joven*." In *Actas del II Congreso Internacional de Estudios Históricos: El mediterráneo: Un mar de piratas y corsarios*. Coordinated by Ana Sánchez Fernández. Alicante: Ajuntament de Santa Pola, Regidora de Cultura, 2002. 295–91.

Canavaggio, Jean. "Alonso López Pinciano y la estética literaria de Cervantes en el *Quijote*." *Anales Cervantinos* 7 (1958): 13–108.

Carruthers, Mary. *The Book of Memory: A Study of Memory in Medieval Culture*. Cambridge: Cambridge University Press, 1992.

Casalduero, Joaquín. *Sentido y forma del Quijote*. Madrid: Insula, 1966.

Cascardi, Anthony J. "*Don Quixote* and the Invention of the Novel." In *The Cambridge Companion to Cervantes*. Edited by Anthony J. Cascardi. Cambridge: Cambridge University Press, 2002. 58–79.

———. "Genre Definition and Multiplicity in *Don Quixote*." *Cervantes: Bulletin of the Cervantes Society of America* 6.1 (1986): 39–49.

Cátedra, Pedro M. "Fiestas caballerescas en tiempos de Carlos V." In *La fiesta en la Europa de Carlos V: Real Alcázar de Sevilla*. Sevilla: Sociedad Estatal para la Conmemoración de los centenarios de Felipe II y Carlos V, 2000. 93–117.

———, and Jesús D. Rodríguez Velasco. *Creación y difusión de "El baladro del sabio Merlín*." Salamanca: Publicaciones del SEMYR, 2000.

Céard, Jean. *La Nature et ses prodiges. L'Insolite au XVIe siécle*. Geneva: Droz, 1996.

Certeau, Michel de. *The Practice of Everyday Life*. Translated by Steven Rendall. Berkeley: University of California Press, 1984.

Cervantes, Miguel de. *Don Quijote de la Mancha*. Edition coordinated by Francisco Rico. 2 vols. Madrid: Crítica, 1998.

———. *The History of That Ingenious Gentleman Don Quijote de la Mancha*. Translated by Burton Raffel. New York: Norton, 1995.

———. *Don Quixote*. Translated by Edith Grossman. Introduction by Harold Bloom. New York: Ecco/Harper Collins, 2003.
———. *El ingenioso hidalgo don Quijote de la Mancha*. Commentary by Diego Clemencín. 4 vols. Madrid: Castilla, 1966.
———. *El ingenioso hidalgo Don Quijote de la Mancha, de Miguel de Cervantes Saavedra*. Edited by Francisco Rodríguez Marín. 7 vols. Madrid: Tip. de la "Revista de archivos, bibliotecas y museos," 1927–28.
Chaunu, Pierre. *European Expansion in the Later Middle Ages*. Amsterdam: North Holland, 1979.
Chiong Rivero, Horacio. "Ínsula de buen gobierno: El palimpsesto guevariano en 'Las Constituciones del gran gobernador Sancho Panza.'" *Cervantes: Bulletin of the Cervantes Society of America* 28.1 (2008): 135–65.
Chitty, Derwas. *The Desert a City*. Crestwood, N.Y.: St. Vladimir's Seminary Press, 1966.
Claeys, Gregory, and Lyman Tower Sargent, eds. *The Utopia Reader*. New York: New York University Press, 1999.
Clemencín, Diego. *El ingenioso hidalgo Don Quijote de la Mancha*. Edited by Justo García Morales. Madrid: Castalia, 1966.
Clutton, Elizabeth. "Isolarios." In *The History of Cartography*. Vol. 1, *Cartography in Pre-Historic, Ancient, and Medieval Europe and the Mediterranean*. Edited by J. B. Harley and David Woodward. Chicago: University of Chicago Press, 1997. 482–84.
Conley, Tom. *The Self-Made Map: Cartographic Writing in Early Modern France*. Minneapolis: University of Minnesota Press, 1997.
———. "Virtual Reality and the *Isolario*." In *L'odeporica/Hodoeporics*. Edited by Luigi Monga. Special issue, *Annali d'italianistica* 14 (1996): 121–30.
Corominas, Joan. *Breve diccionario etimológico de la lengua castellana*. Madrid: Gredos, 1973.
Corvol-Dessert, J. Andrée, ed. *Les Forêts d'occident du moyen âge à nos jours: Actes des XXIVes Journées internationales d'histoire de l'Abbaye de Flaran*. Toulouse: Presses Universitaires du Mirail, 2004.
Cosgrove, Denis. *Apollo's Eye: A Cartographic Genealogy of the Earth in the Western Imagination*. Baltimore: Johns Hopkins University Press, 2001.
Covarrubias Orozco, Sebastián de. *Tesoro de la lengua castellana o española*. Madrid: Turner, 1979.
Crivat, Anca. "La descriptio urbis." In *Los libros de viajes de la Edad Media española*. Bucarest: Universitatea din Bucuresti, 2003 (section V.2.a). http://www.unibuc.ro/eBooks/filologie/AncaCrivat/cap52.
Cro, Stelio. "Las fuentes clásicas de la utopía moderna: El 'buen salvaje' y las 'islas felices' en la historiografía indiana." *Anales de Literatura Hispanoamericana* 6 (1977): 39–51.

Cuesta, Mariano. *Alonso de Santa Cruz y su obra cosmográfica*. 2 vols. Madrid: Consejo Superior de Investigaciones Científicas, 1984.

Cuesta Torre, Luzdivina. "Las ínsolas del Zifar y el Amadís, y otras islas de hadas y gigantes." In *Fechos antiguos que los cavalleros en armas passaron. Estudios sobre la ficción caballeresca*. Edited by Julián Acebrón Ruiz. Lleida: Edicions de la Universitat de Lleida, 2001. 11–39.

Cummins, John. *The Hound and the Hawk: The Art of Medieval Hunting*. London: Phoenix Press, 2001.

Curtius, Ernst Robert. *European Literature and the Latin Middle Ages*. Translated by Willard R. Trask. Princeton: Princeton University Press, 1990.

De Armas, Frederick A. "Cervantes and the Italian Renaissance." In *The Cambridge Companion to Cervantes*. Edited by Anthony J. Cascardi. Cambridge: Cambridge University Press, 2002. 32–57.

De Armas Wilson, Diana. "Cervantes and the New World." In *The Cambridge Companion to Cervantes*. Edited by Anthony J. Cascardi. Cambridge: Cambridge University Press, 2002. 206–25.

———. *Cervantes, the Novel, and the New World*. Oxford: Oxford University Press, 2000.

Delpech, François. "Fragments hispaniques d'un discours incestueux." In *Autour des parentés en Espagne au XVIe et XVIIe siècles: Histoire, mythe et littérature*. Edited by A. Redondo. Paris: Publications de la Sorbonne, 1987. 77–128.

Desprechins De Gaesebeke, Anne. "À la gloire d'Amadís: Tapisseries de Delft d'après Karel van Mander." *Gazette des Beaux-Arts* 28 (1996): 253–63.

———. "Une Tenture d'Amadis de Gaule tissée à Delft d'aprés les cartons de Karel van Mander." *Gentse bijdragen* 31 (1996): 81–96.

Deyermond, Alan. "El hombre salvaje en la novela sentimental." In *Actas del Segundo Congreso Internacional de Hispanistas*. Edited by Jaime Sánchez Romeralo and Norbert Poulussen. Nijmegen: Instituto de la Universidad de Nimega, 1967.

Díaz del Castillo, Bernal. *Historia verdadera de la conquista de la Nueva España*. Mexico City: Porrúa, 1992.

———. *The History of the Conquest of New Spain by Bernal Diaz del Castillo*. Edited by David Carrasco. Albuquerque: University of New Mexico Press, 2008.

Diccionario de Autoridades. Madrid: Gredos, 1964.

Diez Borque, José María. "Edición e ilustración de las novelas de caballerías castellanas en el siglo XVI." *Synthesis: Bulletin du Comité National Roumain de Littérature Comparée et de l'Institut d'Histoire* 8 (1981): 21–58.

Dilke, O. A. W. "Itineraries and Geographical Maps in the Early and Late Roman Empires." In *The History of Cartography*. Vol. 1, *Cartography in Pre-Historic, Ancient, and Medieval Europe and the Mediterranean*. Edited by J. B. Harley and David Woodward. Chicago: University of Chicago Press, 1997. 234–57.

———. "Roman Large-Scale Mapping in the Early Empire." In *The History of Cartography*. Vol. 1, *Cartography in Pre-Historic, Ancient, and Medieval Europe and the Mediterranean*. Edited by J. B. Harley and David Woodward. Chicago: University of Chicago Press, 1997. 212–33.

Dodds, Jerrilyn. "Hunting in the Borderlands." In *Courting the Alhambra: Cross-Disciplinary Approaches to the Hall of Justice*. Edited by Simone Pinet and Cynthia Robinson. Special issue, *Medieval Encounters* 14.2–3 (2008): 267–302.

Dubost, Francis. *Aspects fantastiques de la littérature narrative médiévale: L'Autre, l'ailleurs, l'autrefois*. Geneva: Slatkine, 1991.

———. "Insularités imaginaires et récit médiéval: 'L'Insularisation.'" In *L'Insularité: Thématique et représentations*. Edited by Jean-Claude Carpanin Marimoutou and Jean-Michel Racault. Paris: L'Harmattan, 1995. 47–57.

Durán, Manuel. "El *Quijote* a través del prisma de Mikhail Bakhtine: Carnaval, disfraces, escatología y locura." In *Cervantes and the Renaissance*. Edited by M. D. McGaha. Easton, Pa.: Juan de la Cuesta, 1980. 71–86.

Edson, Evelyn. *Mapping Time and Space: How Medieval Mapmakers Viewed Their World*. London: British Library, 1997.

———, and E. Savage-Smith. *Medieval Views of the Cosmos*. Oxford: Bodleian Library, 2004.

Egido, Aurora. "El sosegado y maravilloso silencio de *La Galatea*." *Anthropos* 98–99 (1989): 85–89.

———. "Los silencios del *Persiles*." In *On Cervantes: Essays for L. A. Murillo*. Edited by J. A. Parr. Newark: Juan de la Cuesta, 1991. 21–46.

Eisenberg, Daniel. "'Sancho Gobernador': ¿Una novela cervantina?" *Cervantes: Bulletin of the Cervantes Society of America* 21 (2001): 3–4.

———, and María Carmen Marín Pina. *Bibliografía de los libros de caballerías castellanos*. Zaragoza: Prensas Universitarias de Zaragoza, 2000.

Fajardo, Salvador J. "The Sierra Morena as Labyrinth in *DQ*, I." *Modern Language Notes* 99 (1984): 214–34.

Fernández Castro, María Cruz. *Villas romanas en España*. Madrid: Editora Nacional, 1982.

Finazzi-Agrò, Ettore. *A invençao da ilha: Topica literaria e topologia imaginaria na descoberta do Brasil*. Rio de Janeiro: PUC-Rio Historia, 1993.

Fogelquist, James D. *El Amadís y el género de la historia fingida*. Madrid: José Porrúa Turanzas, 1982.

Forcione, Alban K. *Cervantes, Aristotle, and the Persiles*. Princeton: Princeton University Press, 1970.

Foucault, Michel. "Of Other Spaces." *diacritics* 16.1 (1986): 22–27.

Foulché-Delbosc, R. "Sergas." *Revue Hispanique* 23 (1910): 591–93.

Francastel, Pierre. *La figura y el lugar: El orden visual del Quattrocento*. Caracas: Monte Ávila, 1967.
Frenk, Margit. *Entre la voz y el silencio: La lectura en tiempos de Cervantes*. Alcalá de Henares: Centro de Estudios Cervantinos, 1997.
Frye, Northrop. *Anatomy of Criticism*. Princeton: Princeton University Press, 1957.
———. *The Secular Scripture*. Cambridge, Mass.: Harvard University Press, 1978.
Fuchs, Barbara. *Romance*. New York: Routledge, 2004.
García Piqueras, Isabel. "Posibles estructuras literarias en la *Fazienda de Ultra Mar*." In *Medioevoy literatura*. Edited by Juan Paredes. Granada: Universidad de Granada, 1995. 2:359–69.
Gautier Dalché, Patrick. "The Reception of Ptolemy's *Geography* (End of the Fourteenth to Beginning of the Sixteenth Century)." In *The History of Cartography*. Vol. 3, *Cartography in the European Renaissance*, part 1. Edited by David Woodward. Chicago: University of Chicago Press, 2007. 285–360.
Gaylord, Mary M. "Cervantes' Portrait of the Artist." *Cervantes* 3 (1983): 83–102.
———. "Los espacios de la poética cervantina." In *Actas del Primer Coloquio Internacional de la Asociación de Cervantistas*. Barcelona: Anthropos, 1990. 357–68.
———. "The True History of Early Modern Writing in Spanish: Some American Reflections." In *The Places of History: Regionalism Revisited in Latin America*. Edited by Doris Sommer. Durham: Duke University Press, 1999. 81–93.
———. "The Whole Body of Fable with All of Its Members: Cervantes, Pinciano, Freud." In *Quixotic Desire*. Edited by Ruth A. El Saffar. Ithaca: Cornell University Press, 1993. 117–34.
Geremek, Bronislaw. "Le Marginal." In *L'Homme médiéval*. Edited by Jacques Le Goff. Paris: Seuil, 1989. 381–413.
Gerli, Michael. "Precincts of Contention: Urban Places and the Ideology of Space in Celestina." *Celestinesca* 21.1–2 (1997): 65–77.
Gerola, G. "Le vedute di Constantinopoli di Cristofor Buondelmonti." *Studi bizantini e neoellenici* 3 (1931): 249–79.
Gilman, Stephen. "Bernal Díaz del Castillo and *Amadís de Gaula*." In *Studia philologica: Homenaje ofrecido a Dámaso Alonso*. Madrid: Gredos, 1960. 2:99–114.
Goldberg, Harriet. "The Several Faces of Ugliness in Medieval Castilian Literature." *La Corónica: Spanish Medieval Language and Literature Newsletter* 7 (1979): 80–92.
Gómez Redondo, Fernando. *Historia de la prosa medieval castellana*. 3 vols. Madrid: Cátedra, 1999.
———. "La literatura caballeresca castellana medieval: El *Amadís de Gaula* primitivo." In *Amadís de Gaula: 1508 (quinientos años de libros de caballerías)*. Madrid: Biblioteca Nacional de España/Sociedad estatal de conmemoraciones culturales, 2008. 53–79.
González, Cristina. *El caballero Zifar y el Reino Lejano*. Madrid: Gredos, 1984.

González, Javier R. "Libros de caballerías en América." In *Amadís de Gaula: 1508 (quinientos años de libros de caballerías)*. Madrid: Biblioteca Nacional de España/ Sociedad estatal de conmemoraciones culturales, 2008. 369–82.

———. "Realismo y simbolismo en la geografía del Amadís de Gaula." *Letras* 27–28 (1993): 15–30.

González Echevarría, Roberto. "Europeans in Wonderland." Review of Stephen Greenblatt, *Marvelous Posessions*. *New York Times*, February 16, 1992.

———. *Love and the Law in Cervantes*. New Haven: Yale University Press, 2005.

Gould, Graham E. *The Desert Fathers on Monastic Community*. New York: Oxford University Press, 1993.

Gourevitch, Aron. 1989. "Le Marchand." In *L'Homme médiéval*. Edited by Jacques Le Goff. Paris: Gallimard, 1989. 267–343.

Grabar, André. "Programmes iconographiques a l'usage des propiétaires des latifundia romains." *Cahiers Archeologiques* 12 (1962): 394–95.

Gracia, Paloma. "La Bestia ladradora, la Beste Glatissant y el pecado del rey Arturo." *Anuario Medieval* II (1990): 91–101.

———. "El 'Palacio Tornante' y el bizantinismo del *Amadís de Gaula*." In *Medioevo y literatura*. Edited by Juan Paredes. Granada: Universidad de Granada, 1995. 2:443–55.

———. "Varios apuntes sobre el 'Cuento del Caballero Atrevido': La tradición del 'lago solfáreo' y una propuesta de lectura." *Cuadernos para investigación de la literatura hispánica* 15 (1992): 23–44.

Greenblatt, Stephen. *Marvelous Possessions: The Wonder of the New World*. Chicago: University of Chicago Press, 1991.

Guillaumont, Antoine. "L'Enseignement spirituel des moines d'Égypte: La Formation d'une tradition." In *Études sur la spiritualité de l'Orient chrétien*. Bégrolles-en-Mauges: Abbaye de Bellefontaine, 1996. 81–92.

Harf-Lancner, Laurence. "Merveilleux et fantastique dans la littérature du Moyen Age: Une catégorie mentale et un jeu littéraire." In *Actes du Colloque International et Interdisciplinaire sur les Dimensions du merveilleux*. Edited by Juliette Frølich. Oslo: Universitet i Oslo, Romansk Institut, 1987. 1:243–56.

Harley, J. B., and David Woodward, eds. *The History of Cartography*. Vol. 2, *Cartography in the Traditional Islamic and South Asian Societies*, part 1. Chicago: University of Chicago Press, 1992.

Harney, Michael. "Economy and Utopia in the Medieval Hispanic Chivalric Romance." *Hispanic Review* 62 (1994): 381–403.

———. "The *Libro del Caballero Zifar*: Recent Editions and a Recent Monograph." *Romance Philology* 42 (1990): 569–601.

Herrero, Javier. "Sierra Morena as Labyrinth: From Wilderness to Christian Knighthood." *Forum for Modern Language Studies* 17 (1981): 55–67.

Higounet, Charles. "Les Fôrets de l'Europe occidentale du Ve au XIe siècle." In *Agricoltore e mondo rurale in Occidente nell'alto medioevo, XIII Settimana di studio, 1965*. Spoleto: Centro italiano di studi sull'alto Medioevo, 1966. 343–98.
Hunsberger, Alice C. "Marvels." *Encyclopaedia of the Qur'ān*. Jane Dammen McAuliffe, general editor. Leiden: Brill, 2009. Brill Online. http://www.brillonline.nl/.
Hutchinson, Steve. *Cervantine Journeys*. Madison: University of Wisconsin Press, 1992.
Infantes, Víctor, François Lopéz, and Jean-François Borrel. *Historia de la edición y de la lectura en España (1472–1914)*. Madrid: Fundación Germán Sánchez Ruipérez, 2003.
Isidore of Seville. *Etimologías*. Bilingual edition. 2 vols. Edited and translated by José Oroz Reta and Manuel A. Marcos Casquero. Madrid: Biblioteca de Autores Cristianos, 1992.
Jacob, Christian. *The Sovereign Map*. Translated by Tom Conley. Chicago: University of Chicago Press, 2006.
Jameson, Fredric. "Magical Narratives: Romance as Genre." *New Literary History* 7.1 (1975): 135–63.
Jauss, H. R. "Chanson de geste et roman courtois au XIIe siècle (Analyse comparative du *Fierabras* et du *Bel Inconnu*)." In *Chanson de geste und höfischer Roman*. Edited by Pierre Le Gentil. Heidelberg: C. Winter, 1963. 61–77.
Joly, Monique. "D'Alberto Naseli, dit Ganasse, au comte de Benavente: Deux notes cervantines." *Bulletin Hispanique* 78 (1976): 240–53.
Jordán Cólera, Carlos. "The Etymology of *Insula, Aestus* and *Aestuarium*." *Journal of Indo-european Studies* 25 (1997): 353–60.
Karamustafa, Ahmet T. "Introduction to Islamic Maps." In *The History of Cartography*. Vol. 2, *Cartography in the Traditional Islamic and South Asian Societies*, part 1. Edited by J. B. Harley and David Woodward. Chicago: University of Chicago Press, 1992. 3–11.
Köhler, Erich. "Quelques observations d'ordre historico-sociologique sur les rapports entre la chanson de geste et le roman courtois." In *Chanson de geste und höfischer Roman*. Edited by Pierre Le Gentil. Heidelberg: C. Winter, 1963. 21–36.
Krappe, Alexander H. "Le 'Lac enchanté' dans le *Chevalier Cifar*." *Bulletin Hispanique* 35 (1933): 107–25.
Lacan, Jacques. *Écrits*. Translated by Bruce Fink. New York: Norton, 2006.
———. *The Ethics of Psychoanalysis, 1959–1960 (Seminar of Jacques Lacan)*. Edited by Jacques Alain-Miller. Translated by Dennis Porter. New York: Norton, 1997.
Lacarra Ducay, M. C. *Aportación al estudio de la pintura mural gótica en Navarra*. Pamplona: Institución Príncipe de Viana, 1974.
Lastra Paz, Silvia Cristina. "Tipología espacial en el *Amadís de Gaula*." *Incipit* 14 (1994): 173–92.

Lefebvre, Henri. *The Production of Space*. Translated by Donald Nicholson-Smith. Cambridge, Mass.: Blackwell, 1991.
Le Goff, Jacques. *The Birth of Europe*. Oxford: Blackwell, 2005.
———. *L'Imaginaire médiéval*. Paris: Gallimard, 1985.
———. *La Naissance du purgatoire*. Paris: Gallimard, 1981.
———, ed. *L'Homme médiéval*. Paris: Gallimard, 1989.
Legrand, Émile. Preface to Christoforo Buondelmonti, *Description des îles de l'Archipel grec*. Amsterdam: Philo Press, 1974.
Lemarchand, Marie José. Introduction to Benedeit, *El viaje de San Brandán*. Madrid: Siruela, 1986. 1–39.
Leonard, Irving A. *Books of the Brave: Being an Account of Books and of Men in the Spanish Conquest and Settlement of the Sixteenth-Century New World*. Cambridge, Mass.: Harvard University Press, 1949.
Lestringant, Frank. "Fortunes de la singularité à la Renaissance: Le genre de l'isolario." *Studi francesi* 84 (1984): 415–36.
———. "Les Îles creuses de l'Archipel (*L'Insulaire* d'André Thevet)." In *L'Île, territoire mythique*. Edited by François Moureau. Paris: Aux amateurs de livres, 1989. 19–26.
———. "L'Insulaire des Lumières: Esquisse introductive." In *L'Insularité: Thématique et représentations*. Edited by Jean-Claude Carpanin Marimoutou and Jean-Michel Racault. Paris: L'Harmattan, 1995. 89–96.
———. *Le Livre des îles: Atlas et récits insulaires de la Genèse à Jules Verne*. Geneva: Droz, 2002.
———. "La Voie des îles." In *Îles*. Paris: Gallimard, 1987.
Lewicki, T. "Ibn ʿAbd al-Munìm al-Ḥimyarī. (or rather al-<u>shaykh</u> al-fakīh al-àdl Abū ʿAbd Allāh Muḥammad b. Abī ʿAbd Allāh Muḥammad b. Abī Muḥammad ʿAbd Allāh Ibn ʿAbd al-Munìm b. ʿAbd al-Nūr al-Ḥimyarī." In *Encyclopaedia of Islam*. Edited by P. Bearman et al. 2nd ed. Leiden: Brill, 2009. Brill Online. http://www.brillonline.nl/.
Lewis, G. Malcolm. "The Origins of Cartography." In *The History of Cartography*. Vol. 1, *Cartography in Prehistoric, Ancient, and Medieval Europe and the Mediterranean*. Edited by J. B. Harley and David Woodward. Chicago: University of Chicago Press, 1987. 50–53.
Lezra, Jacques. *Unspeakable Subjects: The Genealogy of the Event in Early Modern Europe*. Stanford: Stanford University Press, 1997.
Lida de Malkiel, María Rosa. "El desenlace del *Amadís* primitivo." *Romance Philology* 6 (1952–53): 283–89.
———. *Juan de Mena, poeta del prerrenacimiento español*. Mexico City: Centro de Estudios Lingüísticos y Literarios, El Colegio de México, 1984 [1950].
———. "La visión de trasmundo en las literaturas hispánicas." Supplement to the Spanish translation of Patch, *El otro mundo en la literatura medieval*. Mexico City: Fondo de Cultura Económica, 1983. 369–449.

Linehan, Peter. "The Beginnings of Santa María de Guadalupe and the Direction of Fourteenth-Century Castile." In *Past and Present in Medieval Spain*. Aldershot: Variorum, 1992.

López Estrada, Francisco. "El *Tirante* castellano de 1511 y los libros de viajes." In *Actes del symposion Tirant lo Blanc*. Barcelona: Quaderns Crema, 1993. 441–70.

———. *Tomás Moro y España: Sus relaciones hasta el siglo XVIII*. Madrid: Universidad Complutense, 1980.

López Pinciano, Alonso. *Philosophia antigua poética*. 3 vols. Edited by A. Carballo Picazo. Madrid: Consejo Superior de Investigaciones Científicas, 1953 [1596].

López-Ríos, Santiago. *Salvajes y razas monstruosas en la literatura castellana medieval*. Madrid: Fundación Universitaria Española, 1999.

Lucía Megías, José Manuel. "Sobre torres levantadas, palacios destruidos, ínsulas encantadas y doncellas seducidas: De los gigantes de los libros de caballerías al Quijote." *Artifara* 2 (2003). http://www.artifara.com/rivista2/testi/gigantes.asp.

Madariaga, Salvador de. *Guía del lector del Quijote*. Buenos Aires: Editorial Sudamericana, 1972 [1926].

Maier, John R. "Golden Age Imagery in the *Amadís de Gaula*." *Hispanic Journal* 6 (1984): 53–70.

Malkiel, Yakov. "Old Spanish *maraviella* 'MARVEL,' Late Old Spanish *Sierta* 'SYRTIS.'" *Romance Philology* 33, no. 4 (1980): 509–10.

Mancing, Howard. *The Chivalric World of Don Quijote: Style, Structure, and Narrative Technique*. Columbia: University of Missouri Press, 1982.

Maqbul, Ahmad, S. "Cartography of al-Sharīf al-Idrīsī." In *The History of Cartography*. Vol. 2, *Cartography in the Traditional Islamic and South Asian Societies*, part 1. Edited by J. B. Harley and David Woodward. Chicago: University of Chicago Press, 1992. 156–74.

———. *A History of Arab-Islamic Geography (9th–16th Century A.D.)*. Amman: Āl al-Bayt University, 1995.

———, and F. Taeschner. "Djughrāfiyā." *Encyclopaedia of Islam*. Edited by P. Bearman et al. 2nd ed. Leiden: Brill, 2009. Brill Online. http://www.brillonline.nl/.

Maravall, José Antonio. *Utopía y contrautopía en el Quijote*. Santiago de Compostela: Pico Sacro, 1976.

Marín Pina, María Carmen. "Palmerín de Inglaterra: Una encrucijada intertextual." *Península: Revista de Estudios Ibéricos* 4 (2007): 79–94.

———. "El tópico de la falsa traducción en los libros de caballerías españoles." In *Actas del III Congreso de la Asociación Hispánica de Literatura Medieval (Salamanca, 3 al 6 de octubre de 1989)*. Edited by María Isabel Toro Pascua. Salamanca: Universidad de Salamanca, Departamento de Literatura Española e Hispanoamericana, 1994. 1:541–48.

Márquez Villanueva, Francisco. *Personajes y temas del "Quijote."* Madrid: Taurus, 1975.
Martín, Adrienne L. "Humor and Violence in Cervantes." In *The Cambridge Companion to Cervantes.* Edited by Anthony J. Cascardi. Cambridge: Cambridge University Press, 2002. 160–85.
Martín, Gregorio C. "Don Quijote imitador de Amadís." *Revista de estudios Iberoamericanos* 1 (1975): 139–47.
Martín, Oscar. "Allegory and the Spaces of Love." In *Theories of Medieval Iberia.* Edited by Oscar Martín and Simone Pinet. Special issue, *diacritics* 36.3–4 (2006): 132–46.
Martínez-Bonati, Félix. *Don Quixote and the Poetics of the Novel.* Ithaca: Cornell University Press, 1992.
Matvejevic, Predrag. *Mediterranean: A Cultural Landscape.* Translated by Michael Henry Heim. Berkeley: University of California Press, 1999.
McGinn, Bernard. "Ocean and Desert as Symbols of Mystical Absorption in the Christian Tradition." *Journal of Religion* 74.2 (1994): 155–81.
Méla, Charles. *La Reine et le Graal: La Conjointure dans les romans du Graal de Chrétien de Troyes au Livre de Lancelot.* Paris: Seuil, 1984.
Menéndez Pelayo, Marcelino. *Orígenes de la novela.* 4 vols. Madrid: Bailly-Ballière e hijos, 1905–15.
Meneses, Alonso de. *Repertorio de caminos.* Madrid: Ministerio de Educación y Ciencia, Dirección General del Patrimonio Artístico y Cultural, D. L., 1976.
Menocal, María Rosa. "To Create an Empire: Adab and the Creation of Castilian Culture." *Maghreb Review* 31.3–4 (2006): 194–202.
Migne, Jacques Paul. *Patrologia Latina.* 1844–65. Full-text database. http://pld.chadwyck.co.uk/.
Mérida Jiménez, Rafael M. *"Fuera de la orden de natura": Magias, milagros y maravillas en el Amadís de Gaula.* Kassel: Edition Reichenberger, 2001.
Minerva, Nadia. "Le Cercle magique: Strategies de protection du milieu insulaire dans le mythe et en utopie." In *L'Insularité: Thématiques et représentations.* Edited by Jean-Claude Carpanin Marimoutou and Jean-Michel Racault. Paris: L'Harmattan, 1995. 151–59.
Molina, Luis. "Orosio y los geógrafos hispanomusulmanes." *Al-Qantara* 5 (1984): 63–92.
Moner, Michel. "Sancho à Barataria: Les incommodités de la grandeur; et les vicissitudes du pouvoir." *Cahiers d'Études Romanes* 14 (1989): 85–91.
Montero Reguera, José. *El "Quijote" y la crítica contemporánea.* Alcalá de Henares: Centro de estudios cervantinos, 1997.
Montesdeoca, J. M. "Del enciclopedismo grecolatino a los islarios humanistas: Breve historia de un género." *Revista de filología* 19 (2001): 229–53.

———, ed. and trans. *Los islarios de la época del humanismo: El De Insulis de Domenico Silvestri*. La Laguna: Servicio de Publicaciones Universidad de La Laguna, 2004.

Morreale, Margarita. "Sobre algunas acepciones de 'extraño' y su valor ponderativo." *Revista de filología española* 36 (1952): 310–17.

Mullen, Edward J. "The Role of the Supernatural in *El libro del Cavallero Zifar*." *Revista de estudios hispánicos* 5 (1971): 257–68, 383–94.

Navarro González, Alberto. *El mar en la literatura medieval castellana*. La Laguna: Universidad de La Laguna, 1962.

Neri, Stefano. "Lo maravilloso arquitectónico en los libros de caballerías." In *De la literatura caballeresca al Quijote*. Edited by Juan Manuel Cacho Blecua. Zaragoza: Prensas Universitarias de Zaragoza, 2007. 383–94.

Nykrog, Per. *Chrétien de Troyes: Romancier discutable*. Geneva: Droz, 1990.

Olschki, Leonardo. *Storia letteraria delle scoperte geografiche: Studi e ricerche*. Florence: L. S. Olschki, 1937.

Oman, G. "Al- Idrīsī , Abū 'Abd Allāh Muḥammad b. Muḥammad b. 'Abd Allāh b. Idrīs al-'Ālī bi-amr Allāh, called also al-S͟harīf al-Idrīsī." In *Encyclopaedia of Islam*. Edited by P. Bearman et al. 2nd ed. Leiden: Brill, 2009. Brill Online. http://www.brillonline.nl/.

Orozco Díaz, Emilio. "Sobre los elementos o 'miembros' que integran el 'cuerpo' de la composición del *Quijote* de 1605." In *Serta Philologica F. Lázaro Carreter*. Madrid: Cátedra, 1983. 2:365–78.

Padrón, Ricardo. *The Spacious Word*. Chicago: University of Chicago Press, 2004.

Paris, Paulin, ed. *Romans de la Table Ronde*. Paris: L. Techener, 1868–77.

Park, Katharine, and Lorraine Daston. *Wonder and the Order of Nature*. New York: Zone Books, 2000.

Patch, Howard R. *The Other World, according to Descriptions in Medieval Literature*. New York: Octagon Books, 1970.

Peebles, Catherine, and Paul Zumthor. "The Medieval Travel Narrative." *New Literary History* 25.4 (1994): 809–24.

Pelorson, Jean-Marc. "Le Discours des armes et lettres et l'épisode de Barataria." *Les Langues Néo-Latines* 212 (1975): 41–58.

Percas de Ponseti, Helena. "Los consejos de Don Quijote a Sancho." In *Cervantes and the Renaissance*. Edited by M. D. McGaha. Easton, Pa.: Juan de la Cuesta, 1980. 194–236.

Pérez Priego, Miguel Ángel. "Estudio literario de los libros de viajes medievales." *Epos* 1 (1984): 217–39.

———. "Maravillas en los libros de viajes medievales." *Compás de letras* 7 (1995): 65–78.

Peyràs, Jean. "L'Île et le sacré dans l'Antiquité." In *L'Insularité: Thématique et représentations*. Edited by Jean-Claude Carpanin Marimoutou and Jean-Michel Racault. Paris: L'Harmattan, 1995.
Piehler, Paul. *The Visionary Landscape: A Study in Medieval Allegory*. Montreal: McGill-Queen's University Press, 1971.
Pierce, Frank. *Amadís de Gaula*. Boston: Twayne, 1976.
Pinet, Simone. "Babel historiada: Un episodio del *Libro de Alexandre*." In *Literatura y conocimiento medieval: Actas de las VIII Jornadas Medievales*. Edited by Lillian von der Walde, Concepción Company, and Aurelio González. Mexico City: Universidad Nacional Autónoma de México, Universidad Autónoma Metropolitana, El Colegio de México, 2003. 371–89.
———. "The Knight, the Kings, and the Tapestries: The *Amadís* Series." *Revista Canadiense de Estudios Hispánicos* 30.3 (2006): 537–54.
———. "Literature and Cartography in Spain: Etymologies and Conjectures." In *The History of Cartography*.Vol. 3, *Cartography in the European Renaissance*, part 1. Edited by David Woodward. Chicago: University of Chicago Press, 2007. 469–76.
———. "Los tapices de la *Historia de Amadís de Gaula*." In *Amadís de Gaula: 1508 (quinientos años de libros de caballerías)*. Madrid: Biblioteca Nacional de España/Sociedad Estatal de Conmemoraciones Culturales, 2008. 403–5.
———. "La traducción de lo visible: Un tapiz del *Amadís de Gaula*." In *Los bienes cuando no son comunicados no son bienes*. Edited by Axayácatl Campos García Rojas, Mariana Masera, and María Teresa Miaja. Mexico City: Universidad Nacional Autónoma de México–Universidad Autónoma Metropolitana–El Colegio de México, 2006. 107–17.
———. "Walk on the Wild Side." In *Courting the Alhambra: Cross-Disciplinary Approaches to the Hall of Justice*. Edited by Simone Pinet and Cynthia Robinson. Special issue, *Medieval Encounters* 14.2–3 (2008): 367–87.
———. "Where One Stands: Shipwreck, Perspective, and Chivalric Fiction." In *El dominio del caballero: Nuevas lecturas del género caballeresco áureo (Homenaje a Francisco López Estrada)*. Edited by Ana Carmen Bueno Serrano and Antonio Cortijo Ocaña. Special issue, *eHumanista* 16 (2010): 381–94.
Place, Edwin B. "*Amadís of Gaul*, Wales or What?" *Hispanic Review* 23 (1955): 99–107.
———, and Herbert Behm, trans. *Amadis of Gaul, Books I and II*. Lexington: University Press of Kentucky, 2003.
Platts, J. T. *A Dictionary of Urdu, Classical Hindi, and English*. Oxford: Oxford University Press, 1982.
Pleij, Herman. *Dreaming of Cockaigne: Medieval Fantasies of the Perfect Life*. Translated by Diane Webb. New York: Columbia University Press, 2001.

Popeanga, Eugenia. "Lectura e investigación de los libros de viajes medievales." *Revista de filología románica* 1 (1991): 9–26.

Primaleón. Edited by María Carmen Marín Pina. Alcalá de Henares: Centro de estudios cervantinos, 1998.

Quint, David. "The Boat of Renaisance Epic." In *Romance: Generic Transformation from Chrétien de Troyes to Cervantes.* Edited by Kevin Brownlee and Marina Scordilis Brownlee. Hanover: University Press of New England, 1985. 178–202.

Ramos, Rafael. "El *Amadís* de Juan de Dueñas: 'La ínsola del Ploro.'" In *Actas del III Congreso de la Asociación Hispánica de Literatura Medieval.* Edited by María Isabel Toro Pascua. Salamanca: Biblioteca Española del Siglo XV, Departamento de Literatura Española e Hispanoamericana, 1994. 843–52.

Redondo, Augustin. *Otra manera de leer e Quijote: Historia, tradiciones culturales y literatura.* Madrid: Castalia, 1997.

———. "El *Quijote* y la tradición carnavalesca." In *Miguel de Cervantes y la invención de la novela moderna.* Barcelona: Anthropos, 1989. 93–98.

———. "Tradición carnavalesca y creación literaria: Del personaje de Sancho Panza al episodio de la Ínsula Barataria en el *Quijote.*" *Bulletin Hispanique* 80 (1978): 39–70.

———, ed. *Le Corps comme métaphore dans l'Espagne des XVIe et XVIIe siècles.* Paris: Publications de la Sorbonne, 1992.

Resina, Joan Ramon. *La búsqueda del Grial.* Barcelona: Anthropos, 1988.

Rico, Francisco. "El nuevo mundo de Nebrija y Colón." In *Nebrija y la introducción del renacimiento en España: Actas de la III Academia Literaria Renacentista.* Salamanca: Universidad de Salamanca, 1996. 157–86.

———. *El pequeño mundo del hombre: Varia fortuna de una idea en las letras españolas.* Madrid: Editorial Castalia, 1970.

Riley, Edward C. "Don Quixote and the Imitation of Models." *Bulletin of Hispanic Studies* 31 (1954): 3–16.

Río Nogueras, Alberto del. "Libros de caballerías y fiesta nobiliaria." In *Amadís de Gaula: 1508 (quinientos años de libros de caballerías).* Madrid: Biblioteca Nacional de España/Sociedad estatal de conmemoraciones culturales, 2008. 383–402.

Riquer, Martín de. "Agora lo veredes, dixo Agrajes." In *Estudios sobre el Amadís de Gaula.* Barcelona: Sirmio, 1987. 8–35.

Rodríguez de Montalvo, Garci. *Amadís de Gaula.* Edited by Juan Manuel Cacho Blecua. 2 vols. Madrid: Cátedra, 1987–88.

Rodríguez Prampolini, Ida. *Amadises de América: La hazaña de Indias como empresa caballeresca.* Caracas: Centro de Estudios Latinoamericanos Rómulo Gallegos, 1977.

Rodríguez Velasco, Jesús. *Order and Chivalry, Knighthood and Citizenship in Late Medieval Castile.* Translated by Eunice Rodríguez Ferguson. Philadelphia: University of Pennsylvania Press, 2010.

———. "Para una periodización de las ideas sobre la caballería en Castilla (*ca. 1250–1500*)." In *Actas del VI Congreso Internacional de la Asociación Hispánica de Literatura Medieval*. Edited by José Manuel Lucía Megías. Alcalá de Henares: Servicio de Publicaciones/Universidad de Alcalá, 1997. 2:1335–46.

———. "Teoría de la fábula caballeresca." In *Libros de caballerías (de "Amadís" al "Quijote"): Poética, lectura, representación e identidad*. Edited by Eva Belén Carro Carbajal et al. Salamanca: Seminario de Estudios Medievales y Renacentistas, 2002. 343–58.

Romm, James S. *The Edges of the Earth in Ancient Thought*. Princeton: Princeton University Press, 1992.

Rothstein, Marian. "The Commemorative Images of *Amadís de Gaula*." In *The Pictured Word*. Edited by Martin Heusser et al. Amsterdam: Rodopi, 1998. 99–107.

Roubaud-Bénichou, Sylvia. *Le Roman de chevalerie en Espagne: Entre Arthur et Don Quichotte*. Paris: Champion, 2000.

Rubio García, Luis. "La Ínsula Barataria." In *Estudios literarios dedicados al profesor Mariano Baquer*. Murcia: Imprenta Sucesores de Nogués, 1974.

Rubio Pacho, Carlos. "Reflexiones sobre el desarrollo de la literatura artúrica castellana." *Studia hispanica medievalia* 3 (1995): 169–73.

Ruta, María Caterina. "La descripción de ambientes en la II parte del *Quijote*." In *Cervantes: Estudios en la víspera de su centenario*. Edited by K. Reichenberger. Kassel: Reichenberger, 1994. 343–54.

Salvador Miguel, Nicasio. "Descripción de islas en textos castellanos medievales." *Cuadernos del CEMYR* 3 (1995): 41–58.

Santana Paixão, Rosario. "Ficção e realidade nos prólogos dos primeiros libros de cavalarias peninsulares." In *Actas del VI Congreso Internacional de la Asociación Hispánica de Literatura Medieval*. Edited by José Manuel Lucía Megías. Alcalá de Henares: Servicio de Publicaciones, Universidad de Alcalá, 1997. 2:1419–25.

Sassoferrato, Bartolo. *De Insula*. Madrid: Centro de estudios constitucionales, 1979.

Saunders, Corinne. *The Forest of Medieval Romance: Avernus, Broceliande, Arden*. Cambridge: D. S. Brewer, 1993.

Scafi, Alessandro. *Mapping Paradise: A History of Heaven on Earth*. Chicago: University of Chicago Press, 2006.

Scobie, A. "The Battle of the Pygmies and the Cranes in Chinese, Arab, and North American Indian Sources." *Folklore* 86 (1975): 122–32.

Sears, Theresa Ann. "'Lighting Out': Place, Space, and the Question of the Modern in *Don Quixote*." *Cervantes: Bulletin of the Cervantes Society of America* 27.2 (2007): 105–23.

Selig, Karl-Ludwig. "*Don Quijote* and the Exploration of (Literary) Geography." *Revista Canadiense de Estudios Hispánicos* 6 (1982): 341–57.

Serés, Guillermo. *La traducción en Italia y España durante el siglo XV: La "Ilíada en romance" y su contexto cultural.* Salamanca: Ediciones Universidad de Salamanca, 1997.

Sieber, Harry. "The Romance of Chivalry in Spain: From Rodríguez de Montalvo to Cervantes." In *Romance: Generic Transformation from Chrétien de Troyes to Cervantes.* Edited by Kevin Brownlee and Marina Scordilis Brownlee. Hanover: University Press of New England for Dartmouth College, 1985. 202–19.

Simmel, Georg. "Das Abenteuer." *Phiosophische Kultur. Gesammelte Essays.* Leipzig: Alfred Kroner, 1919.

Suárez Pallasá, Aquilino. "La ínsula firme del Amadís de Gaula." *Studia Hispanica medievalia II.* Edited by E. Penna Rosa and Maria A. Rosarossa. Buenos Aires: Facultad de Filosofía y Letras, Univ. Católica Argentina, 1992. 89–107.

Szkilnik, Michelle. *L'Archipel du Graal: Étude de l'Estoire del saint Graal.* Geneva: Droz, 1991.

Toledano Molina, Juana. "El elemento maravilloso en las aventuras de Roboán y en la leyenda del caballero del cisne." *Angélica: Revista de literatura* no. 3 (1992): 113–22.

Tolias, George. "*Isolarii*, Fifteenth to Eighteenth Century." In *The History of Cartography.* Vol. 3, *Cartography in the European Renaissance*, part 1. Edited by David Woodward. Chicago: University of Chicago Press, 2007. 263–84.

Toorawa, S. M. "Wāq al-wâq: Fabulous, Fabular Indian Ocean (?) Island(s) . . ." *Emergences* 10.2 (2000): 387–402.

Tous Meliá, Juan. *El Plan de las Afortunadas Islas del Reyno de Canarias y la Isla de San Borondón.* Las Palmas de Gran Canaria: Museo Militar Regional de Canarias, 1996.

Trueblood, Alan S. "El silencio en el *Quijote*." *Nueva revista de filología hispánica* 12 (1958): 160–80; 13 (1959): 98–100.

Turner, Hilary. "Christopher Buondelmonti and the Isolario." *Terrae Incognitae* 19 (1997): 11–28.

Vallvé Bermejo, J. "Fuentes latinas de los geógrafos árabes." *Andalus* 32 (1967): 241–60.

van Duzer, Chet. *Floating Islands, a Global Bibliography.* Los Altos Hills, Calif.: Cantor Press, 2004.

Vergès, Françoise. "Merveilles de la prise de possession." In *L'Insularité: Thématique et représentations.* Edited by Jean-Claude Carpanin Marimoutou and Jean-Michel Racault. Paris: L'Harmattan, 1995. 213–21.

Viré, F. "Wāḳwāḳ, Waḳwāḳ, Wāḳ Wāḳ, Wāḳ al-Wāḳ, al- Wāḳwāḳ (a.)." *Encyclopaedia of Islam.* Edited by P. Bearman et al. 2nd ed. Leiden: Brill, 2009. Brill Online. http://www.brillonline.nl.

Wagner, Charles Philip. "The Sources of *El cavallero Cifar*." *Revue Hispanique* 10 (1903): 5–104.

Weber de Kurlat, F. "Estructura novelesca del *Amadís de Gaula.*" *Revista de literaturas modernas* 5 (1967): 29–54.

Weiss, Robert. "Un umanista antiquario: Cristoforo Buondelmonti." *Lettere Italiane* 16 (1964): 105–16.

Williams, Grace S. "The *Amadís* Question." PhD diss., Columbia University, 1909.

Woodward, David. "Medieval *Mappaemundi.*" In *The History of Cartography.* Vol. 1, *Cartography in Prehistoric, Ancient, and Medieval Europe and the Mediterranean.* Edited by J. B. Harley and David Woodward. Chicago: University of Chicago Press, 1987. 286–370.

Yates, Frances. *The Art of Memory.* Chicago: University of Chicago Press, 1966.

Žižek, Slavoj. *The Plague of Fantasies.* London: Verso, 1997.

Zumthor, Paul. *Essai de poétique médiévale.* Paris: Seuil, 1972.

———. *La Mesure du monde: Représentation de l'espace au Moyen Âge.* Paris: Seuil, 1993.

Index

Abydos, 65 (fig.)
adventure, 11, 13, 64, 70, 101, 143, 149, 161–162, 167n3; absolute, 95; chivalric, xxxii, 79; etymology of, xxxiii; geography of, 162; heroes and, 117; insular, 78, 159–160; knights and, 80; notion of, 3; romance and, 2; unpredictability of, 4, 5
"Adventure, The" (Gilman), 161
Aegean Sea, 109, 139
Aeneas, 16
Aeneid (Virgil), 16, 17, 68, 103, 175n90
Aesop, 157
al-Dimashqī, Shams al-Din, 42
al-Ḥimyarī, 42, 43, 44
al-Idrīsī, 35, 43, 44, 45
al-Kazwīnī, 43
al-Khwārizmī, 42
al-Zuhrī, 44
Albadançor, 96
Alberti, Leandro, 62
Alcina, 28
Alexander, 16, 38, 68, 110, 125
Alfonso X (the Wise), xxviii, xxix, 3, 6, 7, 9, 10, 26, 35, 43, 146, 148, 169n18; kingly literary culture and, 14; legal discussion of, 88; Orden de la Banda and, 89
Alfonso XI, 14, 89

Amadís, 78, 82, 83, 85, 86, 92, 94, 95, 111, 113, 115 (fig.), 129 (fig.), 150, 156; adventures of, 101, 102; as Beltenbros, 144; Gandalín and, 98; *Ínsula Firme* and, 90, 91, 97, 149; as Knight of the Green Sword, 100; legend of, 197n39; Lisuarte and, 91, 136; penance and, 199n51; Urganda and, 102
Amadís de Gaula, xxv, xxviii, xxx, xxxiii, xxxiv, xxxv, 3, 5, 22, 27, 28, 77, 79, 82, 85, 86, 89, 90, 94, 95, 96, 100, 102, 106, 107, 110, 111, 113, 114, 131, 136, 137, 141, 142, 143, 153; archipelago of, 88; Arthurian models of, 80; audience of, 75–76; chivalry and, 78; famous episodes of, 120; folio from, 136 (fig.), 137 (fig.), 138 (fig.); geography and, 155; imagination and, 132; *Ínsula Firme* and, 84, 150; islands of, 78, 81, 147–148, 160, 161; space and, 79, 112, 132; success for, 125; title page of, 115 (fig.), 121 (fig.); *variatio* in, 134
Amadís de Gaule, 142; engraving from, 118 (fig.), 119 (fig.); folio from, 116 (fig.), 122 (fig.), 123 (fig.), 124 (fig.), 126 (fig.), 127 (fig.)
Amadís de Grecia, 139, 194n11
Amadisian archipelago, 73, 78, 81, 106–107, 125, 143, 155

223

Amazons, 42, 68, 70
Ammianus Mercellinus, 164n25
Amplificatio, xxxiv, 152, 153
Andanças e viajes de Pero Tafur, 25
Andanças e viajes por diversas partes del mundo avidos (Tafur), 25
Andandona, 97–98, 100
Antillia, 37, 39
Antipodes, Apollo and, 146
antiquity, xxiii, 1, 12, 68
Apolidón, 85, 86, 87, 91, 92, 130 (fig.), 189n34, 196n32
Apolidón's Tower, 93
Apollo, 53, 68, 145, 146
Arabian Nights, 178n40
Arcadia, 10, 68, 160
Arcaláus el Encantador, 82, 83, 92, 125
Arch of Loyal Lovers, 87, 92, 93, 94, 122 (fig.), 129 (fig.), 190n52, 196n32
archipelago, 61, 70, 106; chivalric, 159; metaphor of, 73 (fig.); scientific/rational, 135
Ardián Canileo, 96, 100
Arioli, Angelo, 41–42, 178n40, 179n54
Ariosto, 111, 143, 152, 194n12
Aristotle, xx, 15, 16, 38, 44, 47, 146, 165n29
Arthur, 28, 107, 137
Astete, Gaspar de, 156
Athens, 56 (fig.)
Atlante Veneto (Coronelli), 73
Atlantis, 39, 105, 137
atlases, 134; *isolario* and, 45–47, 52–53, 60–64
Auerbach, Erich, 2, 4, 167n3, 168n11, 169n13
Augustus, 64, 68
Avalle-Arce, Juan Bautista, 77, 80, 145, 188n31, 189n33, 190n52, 196n32

Avalon, 67, 182n97
Ayerbe-Chaux, Reynaldo, 27, 175n91, 176n93
Āzādānī Iṣfahānī, 44
Azores, 24, 38, 39

Babel, xix, 97
Babylon, 135, 171n40
Bacchus, 53
Badiou, Alain, xxx, xxxv, 135, 159, 160, 161, 165n30, 166n46, 167n48, 167n52; generic extension and, xxxiii; reasoning and, xxxi; situation and, xxxii
Balán, 96
ballads, xxix, 114
Barataria, xxxiii, 141–154, 155, 161, 198n42, 201n72
Barberino, Andrea da, 110, 111
Barsinán (lord of Sansueña), 96
Basagante, 96
Bastidas, Rodrigo de, 189n33
Beatus of Liébana, 24, 37–38
Beaujeau, Renaut de, 28
Beauvais, Vincent de, 17
Bede, 135
Belianís de Grecia, 138, 139
Benedeit, 42
Benengeli, Cide Hamete, 145, 153, 194n14
Bentham, Jeremy, 166n41
Benveniste, Emile, 164n18, 178n36
Berceo, Gonzalo de, 8, 9, 26
Bernal, Beatriz, 140, 162, 194n11
Bernard of Breidenbach, 25
Bernardus Silvestris, 16
Bible, 23, 35, 99
Blackmore, Josiah, 165n31
Blaeu, atlas of, 73
Boccacio, 46

INDEX 225

Bognolo, Anna, 22
Book of Animals (Aristotle), 44
books of chivalry, xi, xxviii, xxix, xxxiv, xxxv, 8, 17, 19, 23, 24, 25, 27, 28, 42, 61, 63, 67, 68, 70, 78, 85, 91, 97, 113, 114, 133, 135, 137, 142, 161, 162; archipelago of, 84; first, 75, 76; historiography and, 80; insularity in, xvii, xxxi; interlacing/narration and, 111; interweaving in, 145; literary explorations of, 159; modernity of, xxix–xxx; philosophy and, 160; relationships among, 117; reworkings of, 141; romance and, 66; structure of, xii, 22, 79, 107; success of, 90; toponymy and, 86; traits of, 89; *variatio* in, 134
Bordone, Benedetto, 60, 61, 62, 71, 82, 180n68
Borges, Jorge Luis, 1, 162
Boron, Robert de, 186n7
Bosch, Hieronymus, 7, 17
Boschini, 62
Bosteels, Bruno, 165n26, 173n66
Bouloux, Nathalie, 37, 176n16
Bourdieu, Pierre, 190n49
Brangemor, kingdom of, 28
Braudel, Fernand, 23, 29, 64, 74, 184n113
Bravor, 96
Brazil, 37, 39, 104, 139
Breve diccionario etimológico de la lengua castellana (Corominas), 148
Brocéliande, 18
Brut (Wace), 186n7
Buondelmonti, Christophoro, xxxiv, 46–47, 53, 54, 55 (fig.), 58, 60, 62, 70, 71, 110, 113, 114, 134, 136; descriptions by, 47; Greek archipelago and, 52; *isolario* and, 61, 133; travels of, 109
Burke, James, 26, 175n87, 175n88

Caballero de la Triste Figura, 144
Caballero, Fermin, 147
Cabral, Álvarez, 139
Cachey, Theodore J., 60, 62, 109, 111, 181n74
Cacho Blecua, Juan Manuel, 78, 79, 80, 98, 125, 187n19, 187n21, 188n31, 195n21
Campbell, Mary Baine, 7, 36, 103, 177n27
Campo de Montiel, 18
Canary Islands, 24, 39, 103, 111, 192n74
Cantigas de Santa María (Alfonso), 9, 10, 26
Cantimpré, Thomas de, 7
Captive's Tale, 142
Cartadaque of the Defended Mountain, 96
cartography, xi, xiii, xxvi, xxviii, 5, 11, 14, 17, 31–32, 40, 41, 42, 60, 66, 70, 133, 139, 145; ancient/modern, 33; author-traveler and, 112; chivalry and, 109, 111, 113; development of, 30, 63; fiction and, 67; geography and, 110; Greek, 38–39; history and, 32, 61; insular, xvii, 30; Islamic, 38–39, 179n47; literature and, xii, xvii, 67, 109, 155, 162, 163n2; marvels and, 38; medieval, xxxiv; narration and, 30, 34; remote regions and, 31; romance and, xvii; toponymy in, 70; vocabularies on, 41
Casares, Adolfo Bioy, 162
Catalan atlas, 104
Cephalonia, 51 (fig.)

Certeau, Michel de, xvi, xviii, xix, 165n31, 173n66; analysis by, xv; causal links and, 163n8; on metaphors, xiv; practiced/lived space and, xxvii; space/place and, 163n10
Cervantes, Miguel de, xviii, xxxii, xxxiii, 71, 75, 98, 140, 142, 144, 147, 148, 150, 153, 162; *Amadís* and, 161; chivalric insularity and, 141; fiction and, 156; Insula Barataria and, xxxv; insular episode and, 152; *maravilla* and, 160; *mimesis* and, 199n50; power and, 149; space/limitation and, 198n43
Chaide, Pedro Malón de, 156
Chalchidius, 16
Chansons de geste, 1, 110
Charles V, 111
chivalric fiction, xxix, 5, 10, 22, 107, 110, 143, 156; cartography and, 109; culture and, 3; deforestation and, 18–19; ethical/political project of, 114
chivalry, 5, 14, 87, 106, 110, 114, 117, 158, 161; cartography and, 111, 113; changes for, 78; configuration of, 85; imitations of, 132; institution of, 89; marvelous and, 25; nobility and, 85; oral narratives of, 89; origin of, 88; romance and, 139; society and, 90; space and, 25; symbolic representations of, 89
Chrétien de Troyes, xxxii, 4, 19, 27, 94, 135, 148, 168n11, 186n7
Christianity, xx, xxv, 10, 14, 68, 98, 100, 101; Fortuna and, 175n88; leaving, xxiii; spatialization of, 165n29
Cicero, 32, 47
Çifar, 3, 27, 67, 90, 174n84, 175n87

Cildadán, King, 97, 102
Circe's island, 44, 68
Clemencín, Diego, 147, 196n36
cliffs, 57 (fig.), 58 (fig.), 138 (fig.)
Cligès (Chrétien de Troyes), 94, 135
Clutton, Elizabeth, 46
Columban, 19
Columbus, Christopher, 9, 10, 61, 139, 162, 177n27, 194n88, 196n38, 197n38
Columns of Hercules, xxiii, 44
Commentary on the Apocalypse of Saint John (Beatus), 37–38
community, xiii, 2, 79; individual and, 27; outside and, xiv, xvi
Conley, Tom, 61, 62, 66, 179n55, 180n68; on atlases, 63–64; *isolario* and, 63
Constantinople, 35, 46, 53, 71, 72 (fig.), 76, 79, 80, 85, 100, 101, 110, 180n60, 194n11; fall of, 135–136
Conto de Amaro, 182n97
Corfu, 52, 54 (fig.)
Corominas, Joan, 148, 200n67
Coronelli, Vicenzo, 62, 73, 81
Cortázar, Julio, 162
Cortés, Hernán, 162
Cosa, Juan de la: map of, 37
cosmography, 41, 61, 64, 158
courtiers, 116 (fig.)
Crates of Mallos, 32
Cresques Abraham, 104, 105
Cristalián de España, 194n11
Critias, 67, 105
Cuadragante, 96
culture, 12; absence of, 15; chivalric fiction and, 3; Islamic, 69; literary, 14; print, xii, 62, 75
Cuneo, Michele da, 193n88

Curtius, E. R., 10, 17
Cyclades, 29, 47, 50 (fig.)

Da Gama, Vasco, 139
Daedalus, labyrinth of, 48 (fig.)
D'Ailly, Pierre, 17, 105
Dalché, Gautier, 110, 111, 193n6
Dalli Sonetti, Bartolomeo, 60, 61, 71, 166n40
Dandasido, 96
Dante, 148, 175n90
Dasí, Emilio José Sales, 189n33
Daston, Lorraine, 7, 8, 9
De Bruyne, Edgar, 100
De imagine mundi, 104
De insulis (Silvestri), 46
"De montibus, silvis, fontibus" (Boccacio), 46
De natura rerum (Cantimpre), 7
De Republica (Cicero), 32
Del Encina, Juan, 86
Demosthenes, 47
Des monstres et prodiges (Paré), 7
Descriptio mappae mundi (Hugh of Saint Victor), 74
desert, 14, 68; forest and, 15; sea and, 42–43; spirituality/purity of, 15
Devil's Island, 100, 101
Devisement du monde (Polo), xxv
Diálogo de la lengua (Valdés), 156
Díaz, Juan, 117, 131, 193n86, 194n11
Díaz del Castillo, Bernal, 140, 195n19
Diccionario de Autoridades, 8, 148
Diccionario de la Real Academia Española, xxvii, 148
Diez Borque, José María, 114
Diomedes, 135
Dionysius, 33, 46
disparates, xxxi, 157, 160
Dodds, Jerrilyn, 10

Domesday Book, 13
Don Juan Manuel, 88
Don Quixote, 91, 141, 145, 150, 160, 194n12, 199n56; chivalric practice and, 143; effect, 190n49; generosity of, 151; penance and, 199n51; personality of, 146; poetic madness of, 199n53; Sancho and, 142, 144
Don Quixote (Cervantes), xviii, xxxv, 71, 75, 106, 141, 142, 149, 158, 161, 194n14, 197–198n42; *Amadís* island and, 147–148; language and, 152; *maravilla* and, 160; reading practices in, 202n8; space/poetics in, 202n7
Donzel del Mar, 83
Doria, Prince, 24
Du Val, Pierre, 105
Dubost, Francis, 102, 166n35, 182n98, 183n100
Duby, Georges, 99
Dulcert, 39, 103
Dumézil, George, 35
Dumont, Etienne, 166n41
Dunlop, J. C., 185n7

Ebstorf map, 35–36, 104
Echevarría, Roberto González, 142
Eclogues (Virgil), 16
Eden, 10, 14, 87, 103
Edson, Evelyn, 35, 40, 177n22
Egerton map, 44
Egidius Romanus, 89
El Nuevo Mundo descubierto por Cristóbal Colón (Lope de Vega), xxxi, 157
Elucidarium (Beauvais), 17
Embajada a Tamorlán (González de Clavijo), 23
Embracing Sea of Ocean, 43

228   INDEX

encyclopedias, 10, 36, 52, 69, 134; travelogue and, 64
Endriago, 77, 96, 98–99, 100; battle with, 124 (fig.)
Enéas, 135
epic, 24, 89, 91, 110, 163n3; romance and, 1, 12, 13, 111, 167n2
Epictetus, 146
Erasmus, 146
Eratosthenes, 32
Escala de Mahoma, translation of, xxix
Esplandián, 28, 111, 121
Essai de poétique médiévale (Zumthor), xxxiii
Estoire, 3, 19, 20, 21, 77, 172n64, 173n65, 173n66
Estoire de Saint Graal, 19
Estoria del Cavallero del Çisne, xxviii, xxix
Etymologies (Isidore), xxi, xxvi–xxvii, 7, 17, 25, 33, 34
etymology, 18, 45, 147, 159

Fábulas Milesias, 157
Famongomadán, 96
Felix (Llull), 7, 8
Ferdinand and Isabella, 75
Fernandes, Valentim, 71
fiction, 11, 40, 45, 78, 157, 161, 188n26; alternative possibilities for, 22; archipelago of, 140; cartography and, 67; chivalric, xxix, 3, 5, 10, 18–19, 22, 107, 109, 110, 114, 143, 156; geography and, xvii, 66, 109; historicity and, 26; historiography and, 64; islands and, xiii, xiv–xv, 66, 133, 155; narrative, 8, 76; reality and, 158; space and, xxviii, 30, 162; theory of, xxx, 82, 107, 159; truth and, xxviii, xxx, xxxi, xxxiv

Fish Island, 42
Flores y Blancaflor (Beauvais), 17, 135
Florestán, 83, 102, 188n31
florestas, 77, 78, 94, 142
Fogelquist, James D., 79, 89, 187n19
forest, 18, 19, 29, 78, 127; cultivated, 13; desert and, 15; engulfed, 74; islands and, 21; as place for knowledge, 15; royal privilege and, 14; seascapes and, 20; as space of isolation, 18; spirituality/purity of, 15
Fortunate Islands, 33, 39, 90, 103, 104, 105, 111
Fra Mauro 1459 mappamundi, 35
François I, 76, 120, 195n23
Fuchs, Barbara, xxviii, xxix, 2, 89, 167n43, 167n45, 168n5
Fuentes, Alonso de, 156

Gadancuriel, 96
Galahad, 20
Galaor, 82, 83, 84, 97, 102, 125, 150, 188n30
Ganadalín, 115 (fig.)
Gandalaz, 96, 97
Garcia, Rubio, 148
Garden of Earthly Delights (Bosch), 17
Garden of Loyal Lovers, 93
Garlande, Jean de, 135
Gasquilán, King, 97
Gaul, 80, 97, 185n7
Gaunilon de Marmoutiers, 102–103
Gaylord, Mary, 140, 141, 194n14, 198n42, 198n43
General estoria (Alfonso X), 35
Genesis, xx, 10, 14, 93
genres, xxvi, 120, 135, 199n51
Geoffrey of Monmouth, 3, 186n7
Geographies (Strabo), 32

geography, xii, 27, 31, 35, 52, 95, 152, 158, 163n1, 175n14, 177n25; Arabic, 43; cartography and, 110; concern with, xiii, 41; fantastic, 77; fiction and, xvii, 66, 109; fragmentation of, 35; framing past and, 40; history and, xi, xxiv; humanist, xi; insular, 41; literature and, xi; romance and, 79; as spirituality, 22; writing and, 109
Gerusalemme liberata (Tasso), 111
Gervasius of Tilbury, 9
Gilman, Stephen, 140, 161, 162, 194n19, 202n11
Goldberg, Harriet, 99, 100
Gómez Redondo, Fernando, xxviii, xxix, 3, 190n43
González, Cristina, 27
González de Clavijo, Ruy, 23
Gorgias, 47
Gospel According to Mark, The (Borges), 1
Gracia, Paloma, 99, 175n90, 196n32
Gran conquista de Ultramar, xxviii, 76
Grand Insulaire et pilotage (Thévet), 61, 70
Greek islands, 47, 52, 60, 64
Green Island, 39
Grimanesa, 85, 91, 92, 189n34
Gromadaça, 96
Guarino Mezquino, 110, 111
Guevara, Antonio de, 146
Guido de Pisa, world map of, 177n18
Guillaume de Conches, 16

Harney, Michael, 87, 88, 90, 91, 190n49, 191n57
Henry the Navigator, 24
Herberay des Essarts, Nicolas D', 76, 120, 127, 138, 186n7

Heredia, Juan Fernández de, 26, 35
Hereford map, 35, 74
Hermes, 68
hermit, 137 (fig.)
Herodotus, 32, 33, 165n29
heroism, xix, 64, 114, 117
Hesiod, 86, 87
Higden, map of, 37, 177n18
Higounet, Charles, 18
Hippocrates, 20, 172n62, 173n65
Historia Regum Britanniae (Geoffrey of Monmouth), 186n7
Historia verdadera de la conquista de la Nueva España (Díaz del Castillo), 140
Historias trágico-marítimas, xxiii, 165n31
Histories (Herodotus), 32
historiography, 1, 3, 5, 64, 80, 89; romance and, 6, 169n18
history, 31; cartography and, 32; geography and, xi , xxiv; literature and, xi
Holy Land, xxii, 22, 23, 135
Homer, xiii, 17, 44, 53, 165n29
homo viator, concept of, xxii
Honorius of Autun, 35
hortus conclusus, 14, 92, 95, 127, 142, 171n40, 191n53, 191n54
Hugh of Saint Victor, 74
hyle, 15–16

Ibn al-Wardī, 41, 44
Ibn Wasif Sah, 42
Il Guerrin Meschino (Barberino), 110
Ile Tournoyante (Nascien), 21, 78, 172n62, 173n65
Iliad (Homer), 44
images, 31, 44, 68, 117
imaginary, 18, 39; insular, 25, 43, 178

INDEX

imagination, 37, 132, 133
imago mundi, 35, 52, 105, 182n95
Inca Garcilaso de la Vega, 162
ínsula, xxvi–xxvii, xxviii, 41, 77, 81, 85, 146, 147, 148–149, 149–150, 152, 153; etymology of, 22; interpretation of, 125; Sancho and, 154; as temple, xxvii
Ínsula Barataria, xxxii, xxxv, 106, 141, 142, 144, 146, 147, 148, 150, 151, 153, 162
Ínsula de la Torre Bermeja, 81, 134
Ínsula de Mongaça, 80, 81, 96, 134
Ínsula de Santa María, 81, 112
Ínsula del Diablo, 80, 81, 84, 95–101, 107, 112, 113, 161
Ínsula del Infante, 81
Ínsula del Sepulcro, 138
Ínsula Despoblada, 138–139
Ínsula Firme, 28, 80, 81, 84–95, 105, 107, 112, 113, 125, 128, 132, 134, 136, 137, 142, 148, 161; Amadís and, 90, 91, 97, 149, 150; ethical utopia of, 131; garden in, 86; realm of, 91, 93; tapestry of, 131
Ínsula Fuerte, 81
Ínsula Gabasta, 81
Ínsula Gigantea, 138
Ínsula Gravisanda, 81, 83, 188n30
Ínsula Leónida, 81
Ínsula Liconia, 81
Ínsula Malandrania, 150
Ínsula No Fallada, 28, 81, 84, 101–107, 117, 131, 150, 159, 161
Ínsula No Hollada, 139
Ínsula Nublada, 139
Ínsula Profunda, 81
Ínsula Sagitara, 81
Ínsula Salvajina, 138
Ínsula Solisticia, 139
Ínsula Triste, 81, 191n61
insular turn, xxxiv, 25, 26, 135, 159
insular wonder, 22–28
insularity, xxxi, xxxiv, 45, 70, 83, 107, 155, 186n9, 201n75; concept of, 69–70, 133; discourse on, xvi; metaphorical use of, xxxv, 161; perceived/transformed/refigured, xvi; production of, xvii, xxxiv, 25; representation, 114
Ínsulas de las Landas, 81
Ínsulas de Romania, 80, 81, 135
Ínsulas Dotadas, 26, 27, 67, 174n84
Ínsulas Luengas, 81
interweaving, 79, 80, 111, 153
Isidore of Seville, xxi, 7, 17, 33, 34, 105, 164n16, 166n38; maps by, 24; on space, xviii
Isla Peligrosa, 131, 138, 193n86
Island of Candia, 48 (fig.)
Island of Gold, 28
Island of Happiness, 28
Island of Hell, 95
Island of Little Ones, 44
Island of Malakan, 44
Island of Masfahan, 43
Island of Paradise, 103, 104
Island of Reason, 44
Island of Saint Brendan, 39, 103, 182n98
Island of the Boiling Lake, 81
Island of the Devil, 84
Island of the Heroes, 87
Island of the Red Tower, 96
Island of the Seven Cities, 39
Island of the Waq-Waq, 44
Island of Women, 42
islands, xi, 34, 57 (fig.), 62, 70, 74, 127, 132, 148–149; adventure and, 78; depiction of, 37–38, 38–39;

entrance to, 86; fiction and, xiii, 66, 155; forests and, 21; genres centering on, xii; geographical, xxvii; legendary, 37; literary, 26, 149; lost, 67; mapping, 40; metaphor of, 73 (fig.); political situations and, 73; presentation of, 125; real/imaginary, 39; ships and, 20; stories of, 53; theory of, 30; topography of, 125; travel and, 30
Islario de todas las islas del mundo (Santa Cruz), 84
Isle of Man, 24, 104
isles, theses on, 64, 66–71, 73–74
Isocrates, 146
isolarii, xxxiv, 26, 45, 46, 47, 60, 62, 70, 74, 82, 113, 133, 134, 155, 159; end of, 63; model for, 61
Isolario dell'Atlante Veneto (Coronelli), 62
isolario, xi, xii, xvii, xxxiv, 70, 73, 82, 109, 112, 113, 133, 135, 137, 139, 140, 162, 180; atlases and, 45–47, 52–53, 60–64; books of chivalry and, 155; fragmentation of, 66–67; literary explorations of, 159; topical, 71
Isolario (Pigafetta), 62
isolation, 18, 22, 24, 27, 69, 95, 133, 141, 142, 149, 153, 166n40
Isole appartenenti alla Italia (Alberti), 62

Jacob, Christian, 40, 63, 131, 133, 178n36; on archipelagos, 38; on atlas, 61; cartography and, 67; on maps, 31; Miller Atlas and, 178n30
Jameson, Fredric, 4
Jardin amoureux (d'Ailly), 17

Jean de Meun, 16
Joaõ II, 106
John the Baptist, 14
Joly, Monique, 145
Jordano de Ursinis, Cardinal, 113
Joseph of Arimathea, 19, 20

Kalila e Dimna, xxix, 148
king, 116 (fig.)
Kingdom of the Islands, 27–28
Kitāb al-yawārih (Baghdadi), 14
Kitāb-i Baḥriyye (Re'īs), 71
Kitāb nuzhat al-mushtāq fi ikhtirāq al-āfāq, 44–45
knighthood, 4, 89, 91, 97
knights, 8, 11, 12, 82, 86, 87, 89, 91, 93, 98, 100, 107, 110, 126 (fig.), 131, 143, 149, 154, 158; adventure and, 80; model of, 201n72; squires and, 146; virtue of, 94
Köhler, Erich, 2, 10

La Araucana (Ercilla), 193n8
La Celestina (Rojas), 12
La Cosmographie universelle (Thévet), 62, 63
La Fazienda de Ultramar, 22–23
La Mesure du monde (Zumthor), xxvii
La mort le Artu, 19
Laberinto de Fortuna (Mena), 25, 174n84
Lacan, Jacques, xxviii, xxx
Lancelot, 28, 168n12, 172n59, 190n52
Lancelot, 19, 76, 77, 168n8, 172n65, 173n65
landscapes, 11–17, 21, 128; Arthurian, 28; changing, 19; symbolic, 16; uniform, 13

language: cartography and, 178n36; isolation of, 141–154; maps and, 39; self-denying, 159; translation and, 120
Languines, King, 83
"L'Archipelago del Mexico" (Coronelli), 73 (fig.)
L'Arcipelago (Boschini), 62
Las sergas de Esplandián, 75
Las siete partidas (Alphonse), 6
Lastra Paz, Silvia, 79, 187n14
Lazarillo de Tormes, 91
Le Goff, Jacques, xviii, 7, 8, 10, 11–12, 38, 170n29
Lefebvre, Henri, xiv, xix, 11, 29, 170n38; literary criticism and, xv; study by, xxvii; theory of space of, xvi, 163–164n11
Lefkada, 55 (fig.)
legends, 52–53, 70, 109, 113
Legrand, Émile, 47, 180
Lemarchand, Marie-José, 103
Léry, Jean de, xxiii
L'Escoufle (Renart), 12
Lestringant, F., 39, 61, 70, 139, 177n27, 181n83; mapping islands and, 40; panoptism and, 69
L'Etre et l'événement (Badiou), xxx
Li beaux inconnu (Beaujeau), 28
Liber de monstrosis hominibus Orientis, 68
Liber insularum archipelagi (Buondelmonti), 46, 47, 52, 60, 61, 71, 109, 113, 134, 155, 180n67
Liber monstruorum de diversis generibus, 7
Liber sancti Jacobi, 170n39
libro de a bordo, 103
Libro de Alexandre, 125, 135, 148
Libro de Apolonio, 19

Libro de Buen Amor, 125
libro de faltriquera, 23
Libro de Josep de Abarimatía, 3, 19, 21
Libro de la montería (Alphonse XI), 14
Libro de las animalias que caçan, 14
Libro de las maravillas (Polo), 23
Libro del Anticristo, 99
Libro del caballero Çifar, 13, 25, 26, 75, 146
Libro del conoscimiento de todos los reinos, xxiv, 23, 104, 170n39, 174n84
Libro del infante don Pedro de Portugal, 23
Libro di Benedetto Bordone nel qual si ragiona de tutte l'isole del mondo (Bordone), 60
L'Île mysterieuse (Verne), xii
Lilliput, 44
Lima, Miguel Sánchez de, 156
limitation, xviii–xix, 69, 166n40, 198n43
Lindoraque, 96
Linehan, Peter, 10
L'Isole piu famose del mondo (Porcacchi), 62
Lisuarte, King, 91, 102, 125, 136
Lisuarte de Grecia (Diaz), 84, 85, 131, 138, 194n11
literature, 11, 25, 42; architecture and, 163n8; cartography and, xii, xvii, 67, 109, 155, 162, 163n2; chivalric, 185n1; geography and, xi; history and, xi
Livre d'Artus, 19
Livy, 47
Llibre de meravelles (Llull), 7, 8
Llull, Ramon, 7, 8
Locus amoenus, 14, 16–17, 86, 93, 95, 127, 132, 140, 142, 191n53, 198n42

INDEX

Lope de Vega, Félix, xxxi, 157
López de Ayala, Pero, 89
López Estrada, Francisco, 186n9, 200n68
López Pinciano, Alonso, xxxi, 156, 157, 158, 201n5, 202n7
Lost Island, 28, 102, 104, 105, 174n86
Loyola, Ignacio de, 76
Lyotard, Jean-François, 109

Machiavelli, Niccolo, 149
Macrobius, Ambrosius Theodosius, 32
Madarque (giant of Sad Island), 96, 97, 98
Madásima, 96
Maier, John R., 84, 86, 87, 88, 91, 187n13
Malkiel, Lida de, 76
Mandanfabul, 96
Mandeville, John, xxiv, 23, 37, 45
Manifest Perdition (Blackmore), 165n31
Map of America, 105
Mappe de Les Isles Canaries (Du Val), 105
maps, 11, 47, 128, 154, 155; encyclopedic, 37; fictive, 66; inclusion of, 52; Isidorian, 24; language and, 39; legends and, 109; mappaemundi, 33, 35, 37, 40, 46, 61; mappamundi, 24, 36, 37–38, 62, 69, 104, 105; marvel and, 162; materiality of, 35–36; medieval, 37, 40; schematic, 34; as symbol of sacrifice/salvation, 34; T/O, 34; texts and, 46, 66; zonal, 34
Maria de Molina, Queen, 75
Marin, Louis, 88, 90
Marín Pina, María Carmen, 194n11
Martín, Adrienne, 199n53
Martín, Oscar, 164n14
Martines, Joan, 39

marvelous, 12, 22, 30, 42, 43, 69, 82, 83, 92, 134, 138, 139, 160; changing, 132; as fiction, 41; inventory of, 81; land policy and, 10; reflection on, 6; relocation of, 25; romance and, 5, 97; space and, 25; transformation of, 9; vocabulary of, 170n29
marvels, xxvi, 5–11, 22, 41, 43, 160, 162; cartography and, 38; chivalric, 25, 158; objectivity and, 38
Matière de Bretagne, 27, 174n87, 196n32
Mediterranean Sea, 33, 43, 66, 177n18
Méla, Charles, 169n16
Meliadus (Rusticiano), xxv
Mena, Juan de, 25
Menéndez Pelayo, Marcelino, 156, 190n52
Meneses, Alonso de, 23
Menocal, María Rosa, 14
Merleau-Ponty, Maurice, 163n10
Merlin, 3, 19, 28, 76, 77
metaphors, xxxiii, 2, 22, 38, 61, 71, 73, 141, 157, 158, 161, 176n14; meaning transposition and, xv; referents and, 147; spatiality and, xiv; metonymy, x, 3, 39
Mexía, Pero, 156
Middle Ages, xix–xx, 12, 15, 23, 36, 43, 104, 142
Miguel, Salvador, 26, 174n84
Milagros de Nuestra Señora (Gonzalo de Berceo), 9, 26
Milione (Polo), xxiv, xxv
Miller Atlas, 38, 39
mimesis, 67, 199n50, 199n51
mirabilia, xxv, 9, 26, 36, 42, 68, 70, 170n39
Montaigne, Michel de, 63

Montalvo, Garci Rodríguez de, 70, 75, 76, 80, 89, 94, 105, 107, 113, 114, 131, 134, 138, 143; *Amadís* and, 112; chivalric program of, 106; intervention by, 77, 84; linguistic awareness of, 196n33
Montano, Arias, 156
Morais, Francisco de, 117, 131
More, Thomas, xii, 91, 200n68
motifs, 5, 10, 17, 22, 24, 25, 26, 42, 67, 68, 69–70, 77, 80, 95, 97, 98, 99, 100, 104, 127, 136, 147, 153, 171n40, 172n64; Arthurian, 191n64; chivalric, 141, 142, 143; forest as, 16; heraldic, 114; hunting, 14; lake, 175n90; literary, 140; narrative use of, 11; nautical, 19, 20; recasting, 11
Münster, Sebastian, 9
Mykonos, 50 (fig.), 53
mythology, 29, 31, 32, 53, 69, 113

narration, xiv, xv, 62; cartography and, 30, 34
narratives, xi, xiv, 21, 78; Arthurian, 79; itinerary of, 155; medieval, 40; techniques, 78, 80
Nascien, 20, 21, 172n62
Natural History (Pliny), 38
nature, 6, 12, 135
Nava, Karla Amozorrutia, 110
Navigatio Sanctii Brendanni Abbati, 42, 103
Negroponte, 56 (fig.)
Nobleza, kingdom of, 27
Not Found Island, 84, 102, 105, 106
Novae Franciae, 42, 105

ocean, 43; boundaries/boundlessness of, 32
Octavia, 68

Odysseus, 149
Odyssey (Homer), xiii, 17, 24, 46, 68
oikoumenē, xxi, 31–32, 37
Oikoumenēs Periegesis, 46
Olschki, Leo, 24, 78, 106, 174n80
On Poetry (Swift), 29
Ordaz, Diego de, 195n19
Oriana, 83, 92, 93, 100, 129 (fig.), 132, 189n34
Orlando Furioso (Ariosto), 28, 111, 112, 114, 152, 156
Orosius, 33, 35, 165n29
Orozco, Sebastian de Cobarruvias, xvii, xviii, 139
Orsini, Cardinal, 46, 47
Ortelius, Abraham, xi, 63, 105
Other, xxi, 67, 91, 95, 96
Otia Imperialia (Gervasius of Tilbury), 9
Ovid, 47, 175n88
Oviedo, Gonzálo Fernández de, 156, 194n11

Páez de Ribera, 194n11
Palmerín d'Inglaterra, 120, 131, 138
Pantagruel, 28, 139
Paradise, 24, 26, 35, 39, 68, 69, 94, 104, 127 (fig.), 171n40, 182n98
Paré, Ambroise, 7
Park, Katharine, 7, 8, 9
Partidas (Alfonso), 88, 148
Paulus Festus, xxvii
Peles, King, 28
Pélops, 68
Peña de Galtares, 81, 83–84
Peña de la Doncella Ecantadora, 81
Peña Pobre, 80, 81, 107, 134, 148
Perceval, 28, 168n12
Pérez Priego, Miguel Ángel, 25
Perion, King, 95

Petrarch, 109, 194n11
Peut-on penser la politique? (Badiou), xxx, 167n52
Philip the Second, 64
Philosophia antigua poetica (Pinciano), 156
Physics (Aristotle), 47
Pigafetta, Antonio, 60, 62
Piglia, Ricardo, 162
Pillars of Hercules, xxiii
Piraeus, 64
place, xv, 163n10, 185n7, 188n24; images of, 114, 117, 120, 125, 127–128, 131–141; isolated, 45; space and, 114, 142, 163n10; static, xxi
Place, E. B., 76
Plague of Fantasies, The (Žižek), xxx
Plato, 15, 16, 67
Pliny, 37, 38, 43, 44, 47, 103, 105, 176n16
Plutarch, 32, 47, 146
Poem of the Cid, 13
poetics, xiii, xvi, xxvii, xxviii, 22, 26, 135, 140, 144, 153, 156, 158, 162, 201n7; politics and, xxxiv; romance and, 201n1; space and, 141, 197–198n42, 202n7
Policisne de Boecia, 139
Politics (Aristotle), xx
Politics of Aesthetics, The (Rancière), 155
Polo, Marco, xxii, xxiv, xxv, 23, 24, 37, 45, 158
Pomponius Mela, 103, 176n16
Porcacchi, Tommaso, 62, 71, 73
Portolan charts, 36, 37, 39, 52, 192n74
Post-Vulgate, 3, 19, 76
Postmodern Condition, The (Lyotard), 109

Prester John, 103–104, 158
Primera Crónica General de España (Alfonso), 187n20
Prince, The (Machiavelli), 149
Princeton University Art Museum, tapestries from, 127, 128, 128 (fig.), 129 (fig.), 130 (fig.)
Production of Space, The (Lefebvre), xv
Prometheus, 53
Ptolemy, 32, 53, 111, 158, 165n29, 176n16, 193n6; scholarship/cultural reception of, 176n17
Purchas, Samuel, xi

Queen, farewell by, 136 (fig.)
Queste del Saint Graal, 3, 19

Rabelais, 61, 63
Rancière, Jacques, 155
reality, 2, 66, 166n41, 169n16; chivalric, 78; economic/political, 74; fiction and, 158
reasoning, xxxi, xxxii
Redondo, Augustin, 142
Re'īs, Pīrī, 71
Renaissance, xi, 1, 23, 63, 110, 139, 183n106
Renaissance atlas, 39
Renart, Jean, 12
Repertorio de caminos (Meneses), 23
Resina, Joan Ramon, 4, 5
Rhodes, 47, 68, 180n60, 194n11
Riḥla, xxiv
Riḥla (Ibn Baṭṭūṭa), xxv
Rivero, Chiong, 200n70
Rodríguez Velasco, Jesús D., x, 88
Roger II, King, 45; map for, 35
Rojas, Fernando de (Celestina), 12, 17, 170n38

Roman d'Alexandre, 182n97
roman d'antiquité, 1, 16, 19
Roman de la Rose, 94
Roman de Troie, 169n23
romance, xxix, 10, 19, 30, 38, 40–41, 77, 92, 125, 142, 155; adventure and, 2; Arthurian, 1, 2, 3, 16, 22, 75, 76, 94, 97, 172n57; cartography and, xvii; Catalan, 90; chivalric, xxvi, xxxii, xxxiv, 4, 5, 11, 17, 90, 109, 110, 139, 148, 156, 169n13; descriptions in, 11; development of, 8–9, 12, 66, 79; economy of, 91; epic and, 1, 12, 13, 111, 167n2; geography and, 79; grotesque nature of, 120; historiography and, 6, 169n18; landscape of, 21; marvelous and, 5, 9; radical effect on, 3; rise of, 2; sea and, 19; spatial ideology of, 11, 12, 13; structure of, 11–12, 17; types/styles of, 1
Romance (Fuchs), xxviii
Rome, xxii, 85, 136
Romm, James S., 38, 164n18, 169n21, 176n14, 177n25
Rothstein, Marian, 117, 133, 195n26
Ruiz, Juan, 8
Russell, Bertrand, xxvii
Rusticiano de Pisa, xxv

Saavedra, Eduardo, 147
Sad Island, 96, 97
Saint Anselm, 102, 174n86
Saint Anthony, 14, 68
Saint Augustine, 101, 102, 106, 171n40
Saint Brendan's Island, 104, 105, 177n27, 192n74
Saint John, 49, 171n41, 194n11
Salomon, 20, 21, 172n62, 172n65
Salvador Miguel, Nicasio, 25

Sancho, xxxiii, xxxiv, 91, 98, 142, 146, 152, 160, 199n55; Barataria and, 149; chivalric practice and, 143; governorship of, 153, 199n60; island of, 147, 150; location of, 161; popular sayings/proverbs and, 147; quixotification of, 144; Ricote and, 154
Sancho IV, xxviii
Santa Cruz, Alonso de, 61, 62, 63, 84
Santa Teresa de Jesús, 76
Santana Paixão, Rosario, 112, 194n10
Santiago de Compostela, xxii, 110
Saronic islands, 56 (fig.)
Saunders, Corinne J., 13, 15
sea: desert and, 42–43; shaping/defining, 30
Sears, Theresa Ann, 141
seascapes, 17–22, 119 (fig.), 132
Segre, Cesare, 2, 168n5
Semejança del mundo, 36
Seneca, 146
Sergas de Esplandián (Montalvo), 80, 107, 121, 137, 138, 189n33, 194n11, 196n32
Servius, 16, 17
ships, 116 (fig.)
Sieber, Harry, 79, 90
Sierra Morena, 142, 143, 144, 153
silva, 15, 16, 18
Silvestri, Domenico, 46
Simmel, George, 161–162
Skopelos, 58 (fig.)
Somnium Scipionis (Cicero), 32
Song of Songs, 93
Sovereign Map, The (Jacob), 40
space, xv, xviii, 21, 43, 91, 112, 159; building, 11; cartographic, 70; chivalric and, 25; deserted, 14; dialectical, 29; discourse on, xvii; of

INDEX 237

everyday existence, xxi; experience of, 45, 135; fiction and, xxviii, 30, 162; function of, 79; historical, 41, 67; images from, 66; insular, xvii, xxxiv, 39, 162; marginal, 67; marvelous and, 25, 41–42; meaning and, xvi; as metaphor, 158; neutral/pure, xxii; organization of, 131; of penitence/sanctity, 81; place and, xv, 114, 142, 163n10; poetics and, 198n42, 202n7; practiced/lived, xxvii; production of, xv, xvi, 29, 43, 66, 74; relationship with, 45; representation of, 132; romance and, 11; rural, 22; social, xx–xxi; spirituality of, 14; theory of, xvi, 163–164n11; time and, xviii, xxviii, xxiv, 80; travel and, xxii; unknown, 11; of world, 30
spatiality, xv, xxiii, 6, 11, 17, 27, 64, 158, 161, 165n29, 165n30; isotopic, 163n10; limits on, 164n16; metaphors and, xiv; motifs for, 69–70; political implications of, xxxiii
Spiering, François, 127, 128, 130
spirituality, 2, 15, 35, 36
Stevenson, Robert Louis, xii
Story of Amadís de Gaula (tapestry), 128 (fig.)
Strabo, 18, 30, 38, 176n16; on cartographers, 31–32
subjectivity, 31, 66, 109
Sulaymān, 41, 42
Summo Bono (Ulrich of Strassburg), 98–99
Swift, Jonathan, 29, 44
symbolism, 16, 20, 175n93
Szkilnik, Michelle, 19, 20, 21, 172n59, 172n65, 173n65

Tablas Alfonsíes (Alfonso X), 148
Tafur, Pero, 25, 26, 174n84
tapestries, 125, 127, 128, 128 (fig.), 129 (fig.), 130 (fig.), 131, 132, 133, 135
Tasso, Torquato, 111, 140, 185n7
Tenochtitlan, 140
Tesoro de la lengua castellana o española (Covarrubias), xvii
texts, xiv, 62, 68, 166n40; chivalric, 27, 90; illustrations and, 109; image and, 117; maps and, 46, 66
Theatrum orbis terrarum (Ortelius), 63, 105
Thevet, André, xxiii, 61, 62, 70
Ticknor, George, 185n7
Timaeus (Plato), 15, 67, 105
time, 41, 160; space and, xviii, xxiv, xxviii
Tirant lo Blanc, 186n8, 196n32
Tolias, George, 46, 61, 73, 179n58
topography, 18, 125, 144, 177n27
toponymy, 86, 110, 112, 139
topos, xiv, xxxv, 9, 11, 13, 14, 16, 37, 42, 70, 95, 97, 113, 135
Toscanella, Orazio, 114
Tower of Babel, 12, 170n40, 191n62
Tragicomedia de Calisto y Melibea (Rojas), 12
Traselli, Carmelo, 184n113
travel, xxiii, 52, 62, 63, 64, 109, 110; imagination and, 37; islands and, 30, 134; literature, 25, 42; Renaissance, 23; space and, xxii
travelers, xxii, 46, 52, 53, 113, 131
travelogues, 10, 41, 95; encyclopedia and, 64; fiction and, xxiv
Treasure Island (Stevenson), xii
Treaty of Alcáçovas (1479), 103
Tristan, 16, 76, 77, 114, 186n7
Trotsky, Leon, 164n25

Troy, 59 (fig.)
truth, xxxiii, 112, 156, 157, 166n41;
    fiction and, xxviii, xxx, xxxiv;
    political, 159; value, 5
Turner, Hilary L., 52, 71
Turning Castle, 92, 196n32
Turning Island, 28

Ulrich of Strassburg, dictum of, 98–99
Urganda la Desconocida, 82, 84, 107,
    137, 193n86, 196n35; Amadís and,
    102; Ínsula No Fallada and, 151; ship
    of, 123 (fig.); space for, 105
utopia, 10, 69, 87, 90, 91, 131
Utopia (More), xii
Utopus, King, 91, 147

Valdés, Alfonso de, 146
Valdés, Juan de, 156, 158
Van Mander the Elder, Karel, 125, 127,
    128, 129, 130
Venice, 60, 61, 71, 74
Vera Storia (Lucian), 194n14
Verne, Jules, xii
Viaje a Tierra Santa (Bernardus of
    Breidenbach), 25
Viajes (Mandeville), 23
Virgil, 16, 47, 54, 86, 175n88
Virilio, Paul, 165n30

Vita Merlini, 67
Vivas, Juan, 3
Vivas, Luis, 156
Von Sinner, Ludovicus, 180n61
Voyage de Saint Brandan, 42, 103, 104,
    182n98
Voyage to the Holy Land (Bernard of
    Breidenbach), 25
Vulgate cycle, 19, 76, 186–187n7

Wace, 148, 186n7
walled city, 118 (fig.)
Weber de Kurlat, F., 187n19
"What Is a Map?" (Jacob), 40
Williams, Grace S., 76, 186n7,
    190n52
Wonder and Science (Campbell), 7
Wonder and the Order of Nature (Park
    and Daston), 7
woodcuts, 120, 132, 133, 135, 166n40
Works and Days (Hesoid), 86
writing, 11, 38; geography and, 109

Yvain (Chrétien), 4, 19, 27, 168n11

Zeus, 68
Žižek, Slavoj, xxx
Zumthor, Paul, xvii, xix, xxvi, xxvii,
    xxxiii, 18, 40, 164n18

SIMONE PINET is associate professor of Spanish and medieval studies at Cornell University. She is the author of *El baladro del sabio Merlín: Notas para la caracterización del personaje en España* and coeditor of *Courting the Alhambra: Cross-disciplinary Approaches to the Hall of Justice Ceilings*.

www.ingramcontent.com/pod-product-compliance
Lightning Source LLC
Chambersburg PA
CBHW031804220426
43662CB00007B/519